What tl

"John Bunyard successfully trail-blazes the unlikely but inevitable path from where we got lost to where we want to be. In doing so, he leaps from ancient ideals to disruptive technologies like a champion gymnast".

Dr Harry Witchel, psycho-biologist and TV expert

"He has got an incredibly important message - a powerful and revolutionary idea. He deserves to have his name in bright lights for developing and explaining it".

Alan Mitchell, marketing journalist and author of *Right Side Up*

"This book is important and sets out to change existing practice on the basis of advocating the use of sound scientific principles and current knowledge in the field of cognitive neuroscience... a great read".

Professor Francis McGlone, cognitive neuroscientist

"His thinking deserves a much, much wider audience. It is one of the genuinely fresh and important perspectives amid a crowd of business writers simply pouring old wine into new bottles".

Adam Morgan, consultant and author of *Eating the Big Fish*

"He hit on something big and it's great to see him taking it all the way. With the demise of brands/traditional branding methods, marketers will be clamoring for this".

Caroline Hunt, MD of Energetic Communications, New York

"If I had to choose to endorse only one person, ever, it would be John Bunyard. If your competitors engage his thinking, you're honestly done for!"

David Foster MBA, business consultant

JOHN BUNYARD

The Honest Persuaders

lulu.com

Published by Lulu Enterprises, Inc 2010

Copyright © John Bunyard 2010

ISBN 978-1-4461-9443-0

John Bunyard has asserted his right under the Copyright, Designs and Patents Act 1988 to be identified as the author of this work.

This book is sold subject to the condition that it shall not, by way of trade or otherwise, be lent, resold, hired out, or otherwise circulated without the author's prior consent in any form of binding or cover other than that in which it is published and without a similar condition, including this condition, being imposed on the subsequent purchaser.

No part of this publication may be reproduced, stored in or introduced into a retrieval system or transmitted without the prior permission of the author. Requests for permission should be directed to thomas@thenewcomen.com or posted to Permissions, The Newcomen Group, New Broad Street House, 35 New Broad Street, London EC2M 1NH.

*Dedicated to the memory
of Thomas Newcomen*

'If you're working on things
that everyone accepts,
you're not working on anything'.

Dr. Allan Snyder, quoted in The Times

Contents

Prologue   p13

1. Reason to Believe   p19

No hidden persuaders 19
Advertising's rational assumption 21
An idea that sold 24
A dubious cultural legacy 26
The power of professional faith 28
Ubiquitous hokum 31

2. Brand faith   p35

Paradigm shift 35
Noble intentions 37
The new position 39
The resurrection of the brand 42
A matter of accountability 44
Deaf to evidence 45
The dead brand 49

3. The Power to Prime   p53

Enhanced experience 53
A conceptual leap 57
The acid test 59
Moving on 62
The weight of experience 65

4. Fast to the Future   p69
An inauspicious start 69
A long, hard haul 71
FAST in practice 74
The conclusive proof 77
The longer FAST effect 81

5. The Lesson of Experience   p85
The Experience experience 85
Brand theatre 87
The new experiential orthodoxy 89
Experiential follies 93
Managing the experience 95
The Heuristic take 97
Heuristic profiling 100
Any change? 102

6. A Little Learning   p105
21st century, 1930's research 105
Trouble with words 107
A different perspective 110
Brain drain 111
The true measure 115
Moving on again 117
Upstream thinking 119
Digging deeper 121
A neural network 124

7. The Truth Drug   p127

Subjective reality 127
Psychology's dismal history 128
The rigid mind 130
An evolutionary compromise 132
Quick-and-easy decision-making 134
Proof of the pudding 137
Congruence: the brain's mode of choice 139
A matter of personal chemistry 140

8. Practice Made Perfect   p145

The case for caution 145
Putting life into Water 146
Honda: The Power of Heuristics 150
Heuristics in mid-air 155
How and how not to sell 156
New approaches 157
The perfect security blanket 158

Epilogue   p162

Plus ça change 162
The beauty of change 171

References p177

Index p185

Copyright & Trademarks p195

Acknowledgements p196

About the author p197

Prologue

Ralph Waldo Emerson is usually credited with the maxim that a man who invents a better mousetrap will have customers beating a path to his door. Emerson plainly never worked in business. The mousetrap vendor will need some form of publicity to create awareness. He will also benefit from selling skills to secure the best price. But that's only the beginning. If the real world is any guide, there'll soon be equally good rodent-entrapment devices on sale all over the woods. He'll be advised to use market research to identify the practical and emotional needs and wants of his potential customers, so that he can highlight the ways in which his particular mousetrap satisfies them. If that fails to do the trick, he'll be encouraged to resort to brand creation, and envelop his product in an engaging blanket of imagery designed to generate standout and loyalty. Once his competitors do the same, he'll find himself embroiled in a battle to find ever more imaginative ways of expressing the concept that buying his mousetrap is a gateway to a new age of pest-free living. Before too long, the days when he simply aspired to sell a better mousetrap will be a cloudy memory.

Most entrepreneurs are actually more interested in the mousetrap than all the paraphernalia that surrounds it in any contemporary customer-oriented business. Why? Because the vision of earning fame and fortune out of mousetraps is what gets them out of bed in the morning. By contrast, the paraphernalia are seldom more than a necessary evil. I say 'evil' in part because they are a distraction of time, money, and resource from the laudable goal of creating bigger and better mousetraps. What's worse is that, once you start thinking beyond the physical reality of the mousetrap, you stray into the realms of claptrap. And the lure of marketing paraphernalia can become magnetic to rank-and-file employees of a less entrepreneurial bent. We're now so accustomed to the elevated claims and counter-claims of 'brands' that they are an integral feature of our cultural landscape. It is taken as understood that getting away with talking in a language slightly (or, better, considerably) divorced from reality is a remarkable talent. The more distinguished brand magicians are even awarded honours. What is less widely understood, however, is the unconscious effects of such a practice on the very people one hopes to influence. It is one thing to query how it makes them truly feel about your mousetrap. Quite another is how it makes them feel about *you.*

Let me be clear: this is not a book about business ethics. It is a book about business efficacy. My argument is simple. Pulling the wool over customers' eyes is superficially cunning, but in truth damages not only the customer *but also the vendor.* This assertion may draw a pained laugh in the world that has witnessed the antics of the disgraced city types who cried all the way to the offshore bank. But the argument here does not really concern the resourceful 'big swinging dicks'. All businesses bent on survival are inclined to become interested not in what is right but in what might sell. And the attitude to selling anywhere on the planet tends to be 'whatever it takes'. All but the most insensitive feel a need to give their hard-nosed intentions the sugar coat provided by marketing spin. The unintended consequence of this ubiquitous chicanery is that businesses find themselves faced with unprecedented public cynicism. What the public perceives when it considers enterprise today is a cabal of corporations aspiring to separate it from its cash with a maximum of guile. And even the hardest-nosed businessperson will have to acknowledge that a grudging customer is not the best disposed to buy.

Encouragingly, it is turning out that the necessary evil may actually be an *unnecessary* evil. A new wave of investigation into the human brain and mind is revealing extraordinary insights concerning the ways in which enterprises can change how they are regarded - ways that happen to be good for both customer *and* business. At the core of it is science's unfolding understanding of what really makes humans tick. Though a natural predator, *homo sapiens* has evolved to be a social species. The reason we get on with others is that there is a net survival benefit in doing so, whatever sacrifices this may entail. We tend to form extensive networks of mutually trusting individuals. But our brains don't admit people to that circle of trustees on a considered basis. We unconsciously scrutinise them to ascertain how well they match up to the expectation they've set. If they pass muster, a controlled release of the neurotransmitter dopamine gives us a good feeling that encourages repeat exposure to them. Conversely, those who see a benefit in letting us down are marked with a dopamine deficit that urges us to tread warily with them in future - especially if they try to engage our conscious brain with specious arguments. Accurate expectation-matching happens *unconsciously*, and makes us behave in ways that actually contradict what we consciously believe to be the case. When any individual (or entity) is accorded this special trusted status, the good feeling we obtain makes us want to reciprocate. That is how mutually beneficial societies are formed, and so too markets and economies.

Now, this may come as news to many businesspeople; yet it's already old hat to anyone with an interest in neuroscience. The critical point about it is this: a business that swims with the neural tide by setting expectations that it then lives up to will make itself a lot of friends who - and this is the important part - will unconsciously wish to pay it back for its plain and simple honesty. To appreciate the import of those words, you need to contrast them with a world of neo-classical economics that believes business to be all about representing the best value for the consumer's buck; or old-school advertisers who believe that, in a world of product and service equivalence, the world belongs to the best spinner; or the new breed of business gurus that argue for unforgettable business experiences. Not only does each of these viewpoints have the burden of empirical evidence to contend with; now the winds of scientific knowledge are set firmly against them. For the first time, we are getting genuine insights into what drives humans when they are in the process of deciding whether and what to buy. The opportunity for speculation is diminishing fast, thanks to new neuroscientific tools and an appetite for scientific experimentation that are making a mockery of what used to pass for business-school best practice.

It's the custom for business books to wax positive about life, the universe and everything. Though the message of this book is ultimately optimistic, it will pull no punches, and with good reason. The period of unprecedented turmoil that world has just gone through still threatens to be just the first squall in a long storm. Its ramifications have already extended into every last corner of the commercial world, testing to the utmost the evolutionary fitness of countless institutions and practices. Many, like the already enfeebled dinosaurs who found a meteorite strike the last straw, have passed into history. But every extinction presents a new ecological niche. We are witnessing an explosion of new ideas to replace the redundant old ones. Many of these are merely the product of fertile imaginations. Most will not survive the test of time. How, then, can any business leader who hopes to stay in the race know which to embrace, and which to spurn? One of the virtues of pursuing the scientifically demonstrable truth is that it does shed harsh light on much of what is sold, and even sold as science. Consequently, I aim to express a frank opinion on some of what's now out there, if nothing else to demonstrate that the new leaf supposed to have been turned over by business often turns out to be just the old one reprinted.

On the bright side, exploiting the scientific method to arrive at more dependable business truths is not as daunting as you might suspect. Science is nothing more or less than a relatively foolproof means of getting to the heart of the matter by one simple process: forming a hypothesis on the basis of known facts, and designing a hard test of that hypothesis. Using the scientific method, businesses are in a position to build a picture of the way their customers truly behave, one step at a time. What this means is that businesses are no longer dependent on simplistically asking the opinion of customers, as has for so long been the case. And, happily, we are not at square one. There is already twenty-five years' worth of academic experiment and market-place evidence to suggest a crucial truth: that rejecting the practices that come naturally to old-school marketers, in favour of one that comes instinctively to evolved human beings, is very good for both business acquisition and repeat business.

I recognise that, for some, there is a potential stumbling-block: as soon as you see the word 'science', it's easy to imagine that there is challenging reading ahead. Rest assured, then, that your author is no hard-core neuroscientist, but has learnt all you will read here in the course of a career in business that demanded nothing more than an inquiring mind. Distilling thirty years of discovery into less than a couple of hundred pages could make for heavy weather; so I have chosen to relate these ideas as a narrative, recounting the journey I have been on since starting my working life as a graduate trainee to my current role as co-founder and director of an international group of scientists and business professionals dedicated to putting such thinking into action.

To understand my argument more thoroughly, all you need to do now is to read on. If your time is short, or you are the impatient type, you may prefer to leap straight to chapter 7, 'The Truth Drug', and read through to the end of the book to get the state-of-the-art thinking; my guess is that you'll then want to rewind to chapter 1, 'Reason to Believe', to find out what happened to one or two cherished beliefs along the way. Alternatively you can take the methodical approach of starting at the beginning, which may keep you in suspense but will make sure you can see the case building logically, as it did over time in my own head. Either way, I trust you'll get a real flavour of the ideas that still dominate today's marketing landscape, and the voyage of discovery I have been on that has taken me to the forefront of what we are now learning about the decision-taking brain possessed by every one of your customers.

If I'm to be your guide on this journey, you'll need to feel you're in good hands; so let me briefly tell you a little about myself. I was born a natural scientist, I think, having been fascinated in astronomy from my earliest remembered days, an interest that developed over time via a casual interest in particle physics and genetics into neuroscience. My academic misfortune, in retrospect, was that I was born with an enlarged Broca's region: not an affliction, but a particular capacity for acquiring linguistic skills. In consequence, I was actively channelled through my school years into studying modern languages at Oxford. So, if I am honest, I am in truth a scientist *manqué*. However, the wonderful silver lining was a classical education that gave me a thorough grounding in the history of western thought - something that has taught me to treasure the scientific method, a tool that has served me well during a long career in business.

I hope you the reader will accept that much as sufficient qualification to act as your guide. This book is intended to be in the great tradition of empiricism: the philosophy that actual experiences are worth more than any amount of speculation, and that people who have those experiences are duty-bound to record them for the benefit of both contemporaries and posterity. It's a tradition most of us are familiar with through such works as Samuel Pepys's diaries recording the tribulations of the Plague, the Great Fire of London, and the bloody Dutch Wars. Such personal experiences form part of the databank by which we verify our existing predictions, and if possible form new ones; so they can be invaluable in sparing us the need to have all those experiences for ourselves. What is critically important, however, is that the narrator of the experience should be trustworthy. Faulty expectations derived from others' false accounts can be dangerous, and it is no surprise that we react viscerally to being misled.

I'm happy to promise without fear of disappointing expectations that, if you'll bear with me for the length of a long-haul flight, you'll read a story that will in one way or another change your beliefs about how business works. Being human, you may think afterwards that it feels like common sense; and so you should, if it accurately reflects reality. Alternatively, you may find it hard to assimilate alongside your existing system of beliefs, but nonetheless will benefit from knowing what the new thinking has got to. Or you might think - as business people have said to me on more occasions than I now can recall - something along the lines of, 'I've always somehow felt this, but no one ever actually explained it before'. Irrespective of which camp you're in, I will happily make a wager: that, if your brain could be scanned with the appropriate technology, we would see synaptic activity where previously there was none. Whatever else, I hope that, because I shall tell the story with as much scientific accuracy as my all-too-human brain can manage, it will make at least an unconscious difference to the way *you* do business: a difference that will be reflected in real-world indicators, whether your business's or your own.

1
Reason to Believe

No hidden persuaders

At precisely 9am on Monday, September 19th, 1977, I walked into the offices of SSC&B Lintas: London for the first time as an employee. What struck me first about this top-ten ad agency was the sheer size of the building compared with the number of people inside it. What struck me second was the attractiveness of the people working there. The ones that weren't particularly attractive turned out to be particularly clever. The ones that were very attractive were by no means stupid. And the ones that were both attractive and clever were devastating. I soon learned that the reason for the empty floors was the terrible recession we were still passing through, which had accounted for the jobs of more than half the personnel. The reason for the remaining staff resembling the glamorous cast of *Mad Men* would take longer to sink in.

I was given an early clue by my first boss, a charming, bronzed and well-seasoned individual with the voice of a subaltern in the army of the Raj, who was too nice to deserve being identified here other than as Stephen. Just as I was counting my blessings that I was being paid to work in such a splendid place, he said to me, 'Of course, you've missed out on the best times. You should have been here in the 'sixties'. He then described in graphic detail how a typical working day might have consisted of an hour or two's desk work, then away to a client meeting to cover off any business on a leave-it-to-me basis in the first half hour and fill the rest of the afternoon amiably in Quaglino's or Le Caprice. It was a quiet day that didn't end with a 'party' somewhere in Chelsea. I daresay the memory of it had become embellished with age, but it still chafed to consider how much less hard we, the new graduate intake, might have had to work had we only been born a decade earlier. Which is not to say that the job didn't have its social component: a liquid lunch was an almost daily occurrence at that time, not to mention endless awards dinners, sports fixtures, charity balls and the like; and the art lay in getting the work done amidst the never-ending task of keeping a smile on the client's face.

Though socialising is seldom something to complain about, it was not enough on its own to justify embarking on a career in this tough business. What particularly interested me about advertising was the idea that, by virtue of sheer cleverness, it was possible to change the behaviour of millions. As a schoolboy I had had my interested whetted by Vance Packard's top-selling *The Hidden Persuaders*[1], which presented a convincing and rather sinister picture of the cunning new ways in which advertisers were able to manipulate us into doing things we do not want to do. At around the same time I read a scary paperback called *Techniques of Persuasion*[2] by JAC Brown, written in an era of mind-boggling paranoia (1963) when ideas like brainwashing, hypnosis and propaganda were taken far more seriously than today. As much as anything, I distinctly remember thinking it would be fun to find out exactly how they did it in practice, and whether the purposes to which these ingenious techniques were put would prove quite as underhand as they sounded. If they were, surely they'd have been outlawed?

As things turned out, I needn't have bothered giving it any thought at all. When, for example, I asked about subliminal advertising shortly after arriving, all I got was blank looks; and there was just as little interest in the research tools of Ernest Dichter and his Institute for Behavioural Studies, or the many cunning design techniques Packard had described whereby consumers could be hypnotically drawn to buy a particular product. It wasn't that anyone had strong feelings against it all. Rather, they appeared not even to give it a moment's thought. Packard's persuaders were not just hidden: they weren't even there. At first I was perplexed about this and, the naïve novice, thought perhaps I had something new to bring to the table. But could they all really have missed such a seminal work as Packard's? The answer, of course, was no; they hadn't missed it, they'd dismissed it. 'A load of post-Freudian gobbledygook', was the way one friendly researcher eventually described it to me - the nearest I ever got to an argued critique. I eventually realised the actual reason why we admen paid this theory of subliminal motivation no attention: *we didn't need it.* The agency had a perfectly good model of persuasion of its own that everybody we account managers dealt with - the creative department, the media that disseminated our output, the marketers who were our clients, the journalists who loved to laud our earthly works - could all earn a good living from.

Interestingly, we graduate trainees were never given a formal in-doctrination into the nature of that model. It was as though we were supposed to take it on board osmotically. This was surprising, seeing that Lintas (Lever INTernational Advertising Services) had been created in 1899 as a division of Unilever, the world's biggest packaged-goods manufacturer and a fortress of classic old-school marketing. Lintas was still part-owned by Unilever, and its client base was richly laced with Unilever products. If any ad agency was likely to propagate explicitly a standard theory of advertising and marketing, it was Lintas. In retrospect, it's very clear why there was no active proselytising: the model was taken as read. All its assumptions and all its implications were believed to be so obviously correct that they were barely worth mentioning. The last line in any dispute about it, had there been any, would surely have run, 'It's just common sense, isn't it?' There would have been as much point in arguing about it as in disputing intelligent design with a Southern Baptist. And that model was by no means a Unilever preserve. It was pretty well universal. To judge by the output of most marketing-services companies, it is still taken as gospel today in many large corporations and remains influential in others, despite the extraordinary changes that have swept over the communications world since the advent of the digital revolution. So what exactly is it, this pervasive ideology that has commanded the collective imagination of generations of marketers?

Advertising's rational assumption

To understand that best, we have follow the French maxim of taking a step backwards in order to leap further. Though advertising is generally regarded as a branch of marketing, it is actually very much the older discipline. While the first marketing textbooks appeared in the 1960s, one Henry Sampson was able to compile a 616-page *History of Advertising*[3] as long ago as 1874. Nor was Victorian advertising a modest affair. The frontispiece of that tome is a dramatic full-colour foldout portraying the scene at a contemporary railway station, a scene packed with so many in-your-face commercial messages as to belie the myth that advertising overload is a phenomenon of the electronic age. So established was advertising by the time marketing theory emerged that the latter can legitimately be construed as a later endeavour to co ordinate advertising and the various other activities undertaken by manufacturers in support of their products. The fact that, even today, advertising continues to swallow up the lion's share of marketing spend, and advertising agencies until recently exerted comprehensive influence over marketers, provides *de facto* evidence.

By Mr Sampson's era, advertising had certainly had plenty of time to gestate. Excavators at Pompeii were startled to find advertising scrawled on walls all over town; the fact that much of it was sexual in nature suggests that not much has changed in that respect, either. In all probability, the need to announce goods for sale has existed for as long as commerce itself. The name 'advertising' in fact derives from the Latin *'animadvertere'*, meaning 'to bring to someone's attention'. This primary sense of advertising as a means of announcing the existence of products, developments or events is reflected in its name in many languages: in French, Spanish and Italian, for example, the name is the equivalent of 'publicity'. This function of announcing makes a lot of sense in itself as far as human behaviour is concerned. Rather obviously, it's not likely that anyone will seek out a product they've never heard of. More subtly, it is a fact that you are likely to prefer a product with which you happen to be familiar over another of which you are ignorant. If this sounds irrational, it isn't necessarily. What's at play is what's known as the *recognition heuristic.* Professor Gerd Gigerenzer of the Max Planck Institute for Human Development has demonstrated experimentally[4] that we generally reckon things to be bigger when we've already heard of them, compared with ones we haven't; and, more often than not, we're just about right. Where there's a true correlation between quality and fame, this small advantage may make all the difference.

This principle was exploited by the very first advertising agency, established by Charles Barker in London shortly after the Battle of Waterloo, which specialised in buying the front page of *The Times* and selling it off in countless small parcels of space to businesses and individuals wishing to publicise themselves or their wares. Discerning that many customers lacked the time or skill to pen their own message, Barker later offered a service whereby, for an extra charge, he would do so himself. No doubt it would at length have occurred to him (and others) that there was a competitive edge to be had, not to mention money to be made, from increasing the size and complexity of such messages. Over time, it came to seem sensible to do more than just announce a product's or service's existence, and say something about the nature of the product at the same time. Pears Soap thus became the stuff of a youthful complexion; Sunlight Soap the essence of purity. Under competitive pressure, the communicators' sophistication naturally grew with the passing of time, and took on a more competitive edge. Eventually, however, a message on the lines of 'ours is better than all the others' became the lowest common denominator; the big idea that prevailed at last was that the advertiser must offer a compelling benefit. What was implicit in this was the notion that nothing persuades like a good argument, and the Victorians were nothing if not inventive in the claims they made for their sometimes dubious merchandise.

It is hard in retrospect to see any greater logic to this than what appeared in advertisers' judgment to be common sense. There is little to be learned from even the best authorities in pre-War years, which tend to read like rather assertive manuals for junk-mail copywriters: handy tips for grabbing attention and presenting a compelling argument. One of the few suppositions that began to approach a communications model was the idea that people make their way towards a particular make of product as though climbing a mountain, and can be accelerated through the various stages along the way by advertising. The Attention-Comprehension-Understanding model proposed in 1903 by Northwestern University's Walter Dill Scott[5] suggests that advertising can usher us by degrees from a state of ignorance to a position where we know a bit about the product - the obvious inference being that, even if this was about as much as advertising could manage, it was all that was required of it to make the sale.

The better-known AIDA model (Awareness-Interest-Desire-Action) was a 'fifties derivative that, presumably in response to demands for better return on investment, more ambitiously aspired to stimulate a desire to act. It seems elegant and sensible when taught as part of a marketing degree course, but only a few minutes of study and contemplation need be applied to see the stitching come undone. For one thing, Leon Festinger's 1957 'theory of cognitive dissonance'[6] argued convincingly that behaviour doesn't follow attitudes; on the contrary, we adjust our attitudes in order to justify our behaviour. (He's since been proved right even by neuroscientists using fMRI brain-scanning[7]). For another, common sense alone suggests that we frequently take an interest in things in consequence of desiring them, and not the other way around. Though the majority of market research (MR) still concentrates today on quantifying levels of 'loyalty' and the likelihood of adoption or defection, it is apparent even at the level of everyday experience that whim, impulse, caprice, instinct and spontaneity frequently make the transition from indifference to loyalty more akin to instant conversion on the Road to Damascus than a journey through a spectrum – experience that again is borne out by data[8]. When was the last time you said, 'Darling, I've a confession to make. I've become hopelessly aware of you, and I suspect I'm about to become interested'?

AIDA was nonetheless immensely successful in the sense of evolutionary fitness, no doubt because of its tremendous value (which I admit to having resorted to myself) in convincing clients of the unrelenting need to keep up the advertising pressure or risk seeing customers disappear back up the pipeline. It was not the only tool to be put to such use. In 1943, Abraham Maslow had invented his famous 'hierarchy of needs'[9] that placed a value framework on our requirement for food, fame and frolics. As founder of the humanistic school of psychology – the one that gave the world the sort of hand-holding group confessionals that still provide a good living for countless self-actualising therapists both in and outside of New York - Maslow had good reason for applying his ingenuity in this way. The unfortunate thing (as I recall all of us graduates commenting when we had it explained to us at a Communications, Advertising and Marketing evening class) is that it's entirely speculative, and some of it laughable - such as its assertion that we would normally turn down sex in favour of a meal. Why it found its way into marketing textbooks should however be obvious. If the sorts of benefits offered by advertising correspond to psychological *needs* - identified by a man who's practically a *scientist* - then the client has to see that he's in good hands.

An idea that sold

This was the context into which was launched the concept of the *unique selling proposition*, expounded by Rosser Reeves of American ad agency Ted Bates in 1961[10]. The well-chosen name for the concept says it all. The assumptions it made were that (i) one needs to have something specific to say about a product or service ('proposition'); that (ii) it needs to be cogent enough to persuade somebody to buy that product or service ('selling'); and that (iii) there is no point in making the same claim as others ('unique'). Put simply, the reasoning sustained the belief that human beings are fundamentally rational, and must therefore respond co-operatively to argumentation. The beauty of this idea was that it was immensely understandable, memorable, and more than anything *plausible.* The zeitgeist was right, for it coincided with the cognitive revolution then unfolding in psychology that for the first time in half a century focused attention on the rational capabilities of the human mind. More than that, it was easy to explain to vendors of goods and services who did not necessarily know a lot about the human mind, but could certainly recognise a good spiel when they heard one.

By the time I came across it, the u.s.p. had evolved slightly insofar as any advertising brief not only demanded a proposition in the form of a benefit or *promise*, but also one or two *reasons why* anyone should believe it. Underpinning this development was another deeply rationalistic belief: that any claim supported by 'proof' is more persuasive than one without. This requirement naturally stretched both the intellect of the brief-writer and, sometimes, the attention of the viewer, prompting Monty Python's spoof 'Crelm toothpaste' ad whose promise of superior dental protection was vouchsafed by the claim that it contained a miracle ingredient called *frauduline*. To be fair, the notion of customer good sense had a long and hitherto respectable academic heritage. The story had begun with Jeremy Bentham's 18th-century theory of utilitarianism[11], which gave rise to one of the cornerstones of neoclassical economic thought, 'utility'. The basic argument - that, because we humans each want the best for ourselves, we rationally consider competing options and calculate the optimum value to ourselves - sounds again like homespun good sense. The theory implies that, in order to achieve this, people will happily request, ingest and digest information to aid them in arriving at purchasing behaviour representing their best economic self-interest, or *utility*. The argument has evolved over time into today's Rational Choice Theory (RCT), which embraces many different fields in which decisions must be taken between competing options in order to arrive at the one which delivers the best utility in the sense of satisfying needs.

The underpinning psychological assumption is that the human brain works something like an organic calculating machine: information enters the brain, which processes it, stores it in memory, and uses it in some basically logical way in the person's best interests. Such is the mental functioning of *homo economicus*, a species to be found in many an economics degree course but unknown to anthropology. Now, it's hard to imagine that the pioneers of RCT weren't familiar with the overt irrationality of much human behaviour; it may be that we have to regard the theory as normative (i.e. a recipe for an ideal world) rather than a genuine description. In practice, however, the model simplified the equations by taking out the unpredictable human element at the expense, as more recent theoreticians would have it, of its ability to predict. Defence of the model is nonetheless tenacious, and Dr Gary Becker of the University of Chicago, reckoned the guru of RCT, even won a Nobel prize for a body of work running back to 1957 that amounts to an impressively coherent account of 'rational' behaviour in spheres from crime and punishment to the family.

Given this heavyweight academic pedigree, it is perhaps less surprising that the u.s.p. became so ubiquitous. By the time I came into advertising, it was taken as indisputable, whether one was talking to the French office or the Japanese. From a cultural point of view, this ought to seem rather odd, particularly given the outspoken resistance to American ideas in many nations. But it was not academic arguments alone that carried the day. One could argue that its success ultimately derives from the Bretton Woods conference in 1944, when the USA torpedoed Keynes's plan for getting the world's other major economic powers back into play quickly after the War. The Marshall Plan that followed in 1948 effectively proved a means of loaning money to war-torn nations so that they could afford American manufactures. The consequence was that, while its trading rivals struggled to their feet throughout the 1950s, America enjoyed its salad days, shooting to the pre-eminent position it has enjoyed for half a century. As American corporations came to inherit the earth, their philosophy informed its future business credo. The business textbooks for the new global order were all written by Americans, and it is unsurprising that, coming from a nation that prided itself on having been born of a rationalist revolution, the consumer was invented in the rationalists' own image. But for that historical accident, marketing theory might now be very different.

The rest of the world went along with it for want of anything better. After all: whatever its limitations, the model served marketers, admen and media owners well in providing a common language that had a ring of confidence. Nor were they alone. The concept of general rationality has proved enduringly popular with those who benefit from faith in such a culture, from politicians anxious to legitimise their position on the basis that the electorate has applied itself rationally to mandating its optimal representative, to public bodies claiming that the populace needs to be kept informed so that it can make the right choices. And, needless to say, it has also provided a useful academic framework for generations of vendors who see no harm in raising a generic product's price by sexing up its perceived value to the user. But it is the advertising industry that brought the thinking most visibly into people's homes.

A dubious cultural legacy

The u.s.p. has subsequently given rise to myriads of ads, from the birth of commercial television onwards, that follow the classic copywriting formula: *Brand X solves Problem Y because it contains Ingredient Z (which rival Brand N doesn't).* Though it will sound crude (and possibly idiotic) to the modern reader, this was the fundament of tens of thousands of advertising careers, and still provides the cornerstone for many a packaged-goods business. Most worthy of mention among these is Unilever's arch rival Procter & Gamble (P&G) which, with its countless Crest and Tide and Daz and Dreft and Bold and Ariel commercials, has indelibly moulded popular culture across the world ever since and is generally considered the 'university of marketing'. Its single-minded philosophy demanded that the most crass and crude advertising executions be drummed into our consciousness with infuriating regularity, on the basis that housewives would thus remember and be likely to act on them. The big question, however, is whether this uncompromising rationale was what underlay P&G's success. The belief at Lintas was that the company simply had an outstanding Research & Development department - so good, in fact, that the mere publicity afforded by the company's lavish media expenditure more than compensated for its lowest-common-denominator messaging. That fact has not stopped countless other companies less well endowed product-wise from seeking to emulate the P&G communications model.

Irritatingly formulaic arguments were not the only consequence of this love affair with stark reason. Housewives were considered by far the primary consumers of advertising on account of being the ones who did most of the shopping while hubby was at work. Consequently, great store was set on establishing vehicles for communicating to housewives a well-honed promise and its supporting reasons-why in such a way that they would best be remembered the day after. This concept of next-day recall came to be the acid test for many advertisers on the under-standing that, if the message could not be played back in the morning, it was not stored in memory and could not be acted upon at the supermarket. More than one MR company did exceptional business catering for this want. Meanwhile, advertising agencies made a point of making sure that, if they alighted on a vehicle that performed well against this criterion, they stuck with it.

Thus were born such omnipresent devices as the Voice of God, when a disembodied male voice would interrogate some hapless woman on the subject of why she risked upsetting her spouse by using the wrong washing powder; or the Doorstep Swap, featuring an aggressive door-to-door salesman offering two of the regular powder for one of the advertised make; or the Two Women in a Kitchen (known derogatively in the trade as a 2CK) in which one housewife breathlessly solves some desperate household problem for the other by introducing her to a highly advertised product that the friend happens never to have heard of. Of course, it was all extraordinarily patronising by today's standards, singularly lacking in imagination, yet so enduringly good at passing the recall test that still today all three techniques can be seen in use around the world. How much good it did for sales is another matter. The problem, as I discovered for myself, is that consumers are irritatingly hopeless at remembering for any length of time which make has told them what, and will generally assume by default that any claim has come from the market leader. We might recall seeing Brand X advertised on the TV before the news last night, and even the claim that was made, but that is not at all the same as making an enduring neural connection between the two.

Another product of the culture of u.s.p. was the device called the 'slogan', from the Gaelic for a war-cry. The thinking that created this strange convention is fairly obvious: if your product usefully satisfies youngster's appetite in mid-afternoon without making him turn his nose up at suppertime, then say so, memorably, as a parting shot. For added memorability, consider setting it to a jingle. These principles are fine at first sight: recall of the u.s.p. is indeed aided by such a device, and we do remember song better than the spoken word. Take for example the immortal '1001 cleans a big, big carpet for less than half a crown', sung by a male choir, which Britons of a certain age can still remember as though it were yesterday. Over time, however, the original purpose of the war-cry was lost. Increasingly, the slogan (or strap-line or end-line or tag-line as it also came to be known) morphed into being not a literal recapitulation of the u.s.p. but, first, merely a means for tying up the action of the commercial into a rounded whole ('That's the wonder of Woolworth'); and later a vestigial appendage signifying precisely nothing ('Believe in better'). Redundancy aside, it's doubtful how much value slogans have per se. I recall trying to supply some light relief at a Unilever sales conference by inviting delegates to match famous slogans to their makes. To my horror, this deliberately easy task tripped everyone up, the average score being under four out of ten. It did not surprise me years later to hear anecdotally of a test in which slogans were randomly rotated among ads, and nobody noticed.

The power of professional faith
Of course, all such peculiarities that have now become part of the culture only exist by courtesy of an original faith (for such it is) in the power of rational persuasion. This demands some thinking about. Indeed, a time-traveler arriving here today would find it hard to imagine where such a faith, unquestioningly parroted by countless marketing managers every day of the week, might have come from, so contrary is it to everyday experience. If you were to ask most humans which things in their life are objectively unique, they would struggle to think of anything; even spouses can rarely lay claim to such a status. And as for reasons, most behaviour surely dwells (unless one falls prey to the spirit of post-rationalisation) in the realms of 'I just felt like it'. In fact, it can easily be demonstrated by experiment that *irrationality* plays a major role in decision taking.

By the time I began my career, the hegemony of neo-classical economics was already being challenged in the academic domain, notably by two psychologists named Daniel Kahneman and Amos Tversky. Their empirically grounded Prospect Theory[12] provided a solid foundation for the new rival discipline of 'behavioural economics'. It was also to give rise to a wealth of telling experimentation. In the much investigated 'Ultimatum Game'[13], one subject is given a sum of real money to share with a second, and must decide how much to offer; the snag is that he gets to keep his own share only if the second subject accepts the amount offered. It turns out that people would rather take nothing than accept an offer they consider unfair, which is illogical in any utilitarian sense; in consequence, we tend to offer more than we logically should. In another experiment[14], two groups were given respectively a coffee mug and a chocolate bar and invited to exchange gifts. Neo-classical economic theory would predict that, since the two gifts were both worth $6, you would expect a lot of offers to trade. Extraordinarily, nine in ten of *both* groups decided to hold onto their gift, suggesting a dynamic (known as the 'status quo effect') that is anything but utility-seeking. In a third and particularly illuminating test[15], subjects asked to give a reason for their choice of product actually changed their choice to align with the reason, and ended up less satisfied than ones who'd chosen intuitively!

The case against rationality is supported by the work of the social psychologist John Bargh of Yale. His particular argument is that free will is a psychological illusion, expressed in the concept of 'automaticity'[16]. This may sound a little exotic, but the evidence is real enough. In one classic experiment, he was able to prime subjects to walk more slowly just by showing them a passage containing 'elderly' words, graphically demonstrating the principle that the power of unconscious suggestion can actually alter physical performance[17]. Subsequent experiments have shown that even subliminal priming can have such effects. For example, he has demonstrated that just holding a hot rather than a cold drink can fundamentally alter the way we regard others[18]. Bargh's work tallies with studies of split-brain patients that have revealed the existence of actions taken for reasons opaque to the conscious mind[19]; and brain-scanning has revealed activity in the cerebral cortex of normal subjects signifying an intention well before a conscious decision to act, detected through both EEG[20] and fMRI[21] brain-scanning.

Needless to say, rationalists continue to dispute the matter hotly on both technical and theoretical grounds. As so often happens in life, however, it is the evidence of the real world that most stridently contradicts even the most elegantly argued theory of what ought to be, and the ingenious output of Chicago School economists shouldn't blind us to simple human truths. The UK Consumer Association's *Which?* magazine, that offers price-related comparisons of the performance of competing makes within a category, was born out of a belief in the old theory. It is indeed a model that seems to function reasonably in cases where most risk is involved - for example, in the purchase of certain high-ticket durables. Yet, though durables are referred to incessantly by business pundits as an exemplar of their thinking, such cases are not the rule but the exception. Precious little else in the commercial arena comes close even in principle. And even they, though getting the benefit of more customer thought than most products and services, are still liable to non-rational considerations. In practice, we tend to 'satisfice' ourselves[22]: take decisions on the basis of the barest information, such that we'll usually buy a durable after visiting only one store, just as we are able typically to select fifty items from a 50,000-line superstore in fifty minutes. In *The Paradox of Choice*[23], Professor Barry Schwartz even demonstrated that consumers presented with more choice actually become less likely to buy. Indeed, cutting choice experimentally by three-quarters *increased* the conversion level by a factor of ten. Making one's mind up is a fag. If the reverse were true, then *Which?* magazine would surely be as indispensable in every household as a television.

Many economists first lost faith in the concept of 'efficient markets' not during the crash of 2008 but as long ago as the 1973-4 oil crisis, when highly erratic behaviour by ostensibly level-headed experts put paid to rosy optimism. It may just be that the laws of economics that made sense within nation economies no longer function in the vastly more complex world markets of the post-War era. Economist Paul Ormerod's book *Butterfly Economics*[24] demonstrated graphically how chaotic principles predominate in financial markets as much as they do in weather systems. Even at the individual level, the concept of cause and effect seems to apply as little in the bear-pit as it does in the supermarket aisle. But it seems as though no one ever told marketers who continue to scratch away at the same old seam, and the 'that's why' tendency (as in 'Ordinary cleaners can leave unsightly marks. That's why we've created new Bloggo...') still seems as popular as ever on daytime television.

Ubiquitous hokum

What exacerbates the problem is that u.s.p.-based marketing speaks in a tongue that, though not often patently false, seldom sees any virtue in literal authenticity. It refuses the possibility of advertising that says, 'This soft drink quenches your thirst pretty much like all the others on the market, and it comes in a yellow can', unless as tongue-in-cheek humour. Indeed, virtually all contemporary marketers would scoff at the thought: if reality offers neither uniqueness nor persuasive force nor benefit, then reality must be expendable - or at least bendable. The model is instead obliged to devise messages that are only incidentally true ('You'll have a real laugh with this beer') and as often as not become pure hyperbole ('Our staff are your closest friends'). This is not to say that marketers are naturally mendacious. The inescapable truth is that they are paid to do a job, and if products and services the world over are much of a muchness, they feel they have no alternative but to be creative with the truth. The whole point about a u.s.p. is that, whether deliberately or not, it ordinarily will automatically imply distancing a product from its experiential reality. It may be less deceitful than political spin, but it serves precisely the same purpose.

There is an easy way to verify this for oneself: by sitting in front of the TV for an evening and thinking about what every ad is claiming to be the truth, and then imagining the reality of consuming the product by comparison. It is a sobering experience. So overwhelming is the sheer volume of hyperbolic marketing that, over three generations, it has inspired a culture of disbelief. This fact of life is no disincentive to most marketing managers, who are paid to do a job and cannot afford to be put off by the very kind of cynicism which they themselves may evince in their private lives. You might however think that, if a culture of exaggeration does not deter them, the prospect of personal failure should. It struck me in my Lintas days - at a time when my job seemed to concern itself more than anything with alighting on an expression of the 'truth' that the advertising authorities would let us get away with - that businesses would do well to mark the experience of Anne of Cleves, one of the unfortunate wives of Henry VIII. Whilst she was still single, her courtiers had her painted - by Holbein, no less - for the purpose of beguiling her prospective husband. Her attractive likeness was enough to persuade him to marry her; but the truculent king's response on actually meeting her ('I like her not!') says it all about their short-lived relationship. If the purpose of marketing is (or should be) to engineer not just a meeting but a marriage, setting up unrealistic expectations ought to be taboo.

The trouble is, hyperbole comes naturally to most humans in a selling situation. We take it as common sense that we must impress with superlatives if we want others to be convinced. There is probably a fundamental reason for believing so: trust may be the basis of lasting relationships, but there are sufficient occasions in a lifetime to profit by fibbing to strangers as to confer an evolutionary advantage on the fibber. Such basic human drives were naturally carried over by entrepreneurs to the first corporations. It has long been the practice to call companies Acme, Summit, Zenith and the like, even if the businesses themselves might more accurately be described as Nadir, Lowlands or Chasm. The custom obviously served travelling salesmen well, if they weren't expecting to come back this way again; but in an age where one can seldom make a profit on the basis of a single sale, setting customers up to be disappointed is unsophisticated, to put it kindly. Few businesspeople in my experience baulk at this objection when it's presented to them; so how is it that they don't routinely challenge the usual practice? Why do they still automatically assume that, where spin is concerned, There Is No Alternative?

I would argue that it is the very search for a cogent u.s.p. that obliges advertisers to deal in a currency of part-truths. If people are assumed to take decisions on the basis of the 'information' available to them; if the business-owner's livelihood depends on presenting prospects with the best possible competitive 'information' about the product; and if most products have little to say by way of a benefit that in any sense genuinely differentiates them from their competitor set - then there can be only one outcome. An example was provided a while ago by P&G itself, which owns a perfectly good shampoo called Pantene. The marketing team claimed in advertising that the product makes hair 'up to ten times stronger' (promise) because it 'replaces key amino acids' (reason why). After complaints that this represented a misleading use of scientific terminology, the Advertising Standards Authority heard from an expert that the product did not actually contain the two amino acids most likely to be lost; nor could the 'ten times stronger' claim be substantiated. In its defence, the company reportedly argued that the public does not treat advertising claims literally - which begs the question what sense there is in the exercise. More to the point, one wonders what kind of marketing philosophy puts as reputable an organisation as P&G in the position where it has to put its credibility on the line. Nor is this by any means a uniquely P&G problem. Early in 2009, even Coca Cola was chastised by the Australian authorities for a 'totally unacceptable' campaign that had dismissed criticism of its dietetic, dental and caffeine demerits as 'myths'.

The orthodox model does rather oblige marketers to live in a dimension one step removed from the real world. It's not just about fast-food companies that film their product to look misleadingly large in TV adverts, or toiletries companies that retouch pictures of ageing fashion icons who show off their wares. In the news pages of the marketing press there are countless stories of the not-quite-real: of Vimto wishing to 'educate' mothers; of Quaker terminating its Oatso Simple deal with marathon runner Paula Radcliffe because she neglected its promise to 'go the distance'; of the Pot Noodle marketing manager refuting complaints about a 'horn' joke in its advertising on the basis that it reflects a 'simple brand truth'. The hokum can become institutional. A pundit defends retailers massaging their figures because it's what you'd expect; an advertising campaign wins awards galore but leaves the business 19% down year-on-year; a door-to-door campaign is worth a write-up because it worked 130% better than the previous one - whatever that means. You cannot blame reporters for recounting verbatim what they are told by the industry from whom they earn a living, but the cosy relationship does nothing to challenge the air of unreality.

Even when I joined the industry, the theoretical contradictions of the old model were perfectly apparent to many, as we shall see; yet, though now much diminished in power, its tenacity has seen it through to the present day as the dominant force in advertising communications. At that time, it was a strait-jacket. I experienced its conservative power for myself on the first occasion that I was given the chance to take authorship of the brief for a TV commercial, those being the days when account managers were still allowed to do that sort of thing single-handed. The client was the large American bed-maker Sealy Inc, and the product their Posturepedic mattresses. They had recently launched in the UK, and were justly proud of the product's quality, the health benefits of its superior construction, and the sheer quantity of these beds they had sold: more than any rival in the world.

Realising that this was a perfect chance to show what I could do, I spent a lot of time agonising over the brief, determined to achieve better than the easy and obvious. I decided in the end that our first step must be to make Britons comfortable with the daunting product name by imbuing it with some personality. We must do this single-mindedly, I thought, and not let complicating arguments muddy the waters. I fell at the first hurdle. My board director Tony Douglas - silver-grey while still young enough to be a bit of a heartthrob in the agency - was having none of it. Although he 'heard what I was saying', I was 'missing a trick'. Needless to say, the script ended up talking about the corporate identity, the key product feature (reason why), and the health benefit (promise). The client was delighted, Tony went off to run one of London's biggest agencies, and I stayed behind, at least for a bit longer. I console myself with the hope that perhaps I was just ahead of my time.

2
Brand Faith

Paradigm shift

We are inclined to imagine that, when the conventional wisdom alters across whole cultures, communities or industries, it is because many people within them have changed their minds at more or less the same time, rather as though a new way of seeing things had spread like a virus. Of course that can happen, as when a fad or fashion propagates itself memetically, or general opinion turns in response to some striking event or other. Such changes as these tend not, however, to be of the enduring kind. The reason is simple: we are remarkably conservative in our beliefs (even if, ironically, those beliefs are 'radical'), and our brains spend much of their time seeking confirmation and spurning change. As a result of this instinctual doggedness, we tend to take our beliefs with us to the grave. The ideas which change for good (if not always for better) are normally *generational* changes: ideas that come to the fore when an ageing group is replaced by a junior one that has spent its life wondering what on earth its predecessor was up to.

By the time I started out in advertising, the formal u.s.p. model had already been knocking around for nigh on twenty years, and the practice thereof rather longer. All of us who were fresh to the industry at that time had grown up with it, exposed daily to huge volumes of its broadcast progeny. Naturally we had strong feelings about what worked and what didn't, and they did not always match the conventional wisdom of our older advertising generation. My first experience of this clash of cultures had occurred when, still a student, I was interviewed by one of Lintas's major rivals, Grey Advertising - a big American-owned P&G agency. Asked to define what made for a successful ad, I'd replied, 'One that makes me laugh'. The wonderfully assertive interviewer more or less told me that I hadn't a clue; the answer he was looking for was an unforgettable u.s.p. Needless to say, he didn't offer me a job. If it hadn't been for the strength of his convictions, I might never have gone to Lintas, and my whole life would have taken another course. I've reason to be grateful to him.

Change had already been in the air by the time I turned up in London. Rock music was giving way to punk, industrial strife had brought the economy to its knees, and Britain was on the way to having its first female and neo-liberal prime minister. The first portent of change I actually saw in advertising is still vivid in my memory. I was walking along the corridor two or three years into my career when I noticed a nattily dressed fellow we'll call Jeffrey in an empty office, apparently measuring up. There was nothing especially unusual about this, except that Jeffrey was a member of the media department, which planned and booked advertising airtime, and belonged on quite another floor. 'What's *he* doing in there?' I asked one of the secretaries. 'He's moving in', she answered. 'It's the new Account Planning department'. Now, I happened to have learned from the trade press that one or two of the bigger agencies offered this 'account planning'. I also had a vague impression that it was about turbo-charging the brief-writing process with more cerebral strategic insight. What I couldn't understand was why Jeffrey - a very well-spoken chap with a disarmingly faltering manner who, though a canny operator, never came across to me as an intellectual - should have anything to do with it.

As usual, the key to enlightenment was Stephen. 'I expect he's filling in', he told me, 'until we recruit someone permanent'. So why not wait until we'd found one? I wondered. 'Oh, you can't hang about', was the reply. 'Never let clients think your competitors have got something you haven't'. I should say I found the whole thing bewildering. Before long, the researchers whose job had been to commission surveys had been converted into strategists who, a little to my chagrin, took away formal responsibility for what I considered the most enjoyable part of the account man's job: writing the briefs that commissioned whatever work you wanted out of the creative department. The entire dynamic of the creative process changed, as the tidy one-to-one relationship between account man and creative team became a three-way affair. Though novices to it, however, we were soon talking about account planning as though we'd always had it, and had probably even had a hand in inventing it. Nevertheless, it's doubtful that we lived up to the hype in any practical sense, even when a man we'll call Rick, a real account planner, came to show us how it ought to be done. Though I never felt this new confection sat terribly comfortably athwart our old-school culture, it did at least achieve the trick of reassuring clients that we were abreast of the latest trends - which after all is what it was there for.

Noble intentions

Account planning had in reality been invented by London agency Boase Massimi Pollitt (BMP) about a decade earlier. It was a specific reaction against the thoughtless account management-led style of brief-writing that probably worked fine in a 'sixties bistro but, let's face it, was frustrating to creatives and no inducement to a good-looking agency showreel. Its big idea was that the conceptual thinking that went into the creative brief should be based on the consumer's true beliefs, attitudes and perceptions, rather than determined by the logical dexterity of a client-oriented account manager. Such thinking would necessarily be the brainchild of someone recruited for his or her intellect, rather than people-handling skills; and a psychology degree would also come in handy. This explained the qualms I'd had about Jeffrey: unfairly or not, I'd assumed that what he'd known beforehand about psychology could have been written on the back of a postage stamp.

BMP certainly did very well out of it, and not just because it gave them something new to talk about when it came to pitching for new business. It was as though the creative work they produced had been set free of the shackles forged by Rosser Reeves. No doubt this was partly down to their brilliant creative director John Webster - a true *wunderkind* - and the talented team he built around him that was responsible for a string of famous award-winning campaigns. The beauty of this new genre was that any u.s.p. involved was invariably disguised behind a sumptuous cloak of charm, style, wit, or humour. The man at Grey must have hated it. Yet, the advertising industry being the most perfect magpie, there were eventually agencies all over London doing what Lintas had done and seeking to emulate BMP. The turning point for account planning had come when the sharp-minded Stephen King (yes, really) of J. Walter Thompson (JWT) - then still American-owned and the greatest agency in the world - took up the cudgels and gave the new discipline international credibility. It was however Chicago agency Chiat Day that imported account planning with conspicuous success into the USA, and its role in the modern agency was secured.

Whatever my initial feelings as an account man about losing our monopoly on the strategic thinking, I ended up relishing the advent of account planning for the way that it introduced a lot more intelligence into a part of the process in which, quite frankly, the industry had been getting away with murder. What I soon learned was that, by cultivating the account planner like a best friend, it was perfectly possible for an account man to make a major input to the strategy, and the conceptual debate to be had along the way was at least as invigorating as the relatively mechanical matter of making TV commercials. But, for me, this was not to happen at Lintas; because, after trying unsuccessfully on two occasions to get a job at BMP, I was headhunted by Ayer Barker, the UK love-child of Charles Barker (of Waterloo fame) and NW Ayer - a US agency founded some years even before JWT. Apart from offering me a mouth-watering set of accounts to work on, Ayer had a proper account-planning department staffed by real planners under the tutelage of Charles Channon, one of the founding fathers of the discipline at JWT, possessor of a rare intelligence, and a grievous loss when he died prematurely all too soon thereafter. There's no doubt however that Ayer felt very much like second choice. The irony was that, by the time I came to be on friendly terms with the chairman of BMP years later, I already had my own business.

What was also ironic was that I owed my appetite for proper planning to the aforementioned Rick, who at Lintas had spent much of his time trying to beat the principles into us with a thick stick. I remember him as a wiry man with a speed of movement that delivered his gnarled face in front of you with unnerving suddenness. When I think of him now, I cannot imagine him smiling. He'd seemed to me to feel that account planning was neglected at Lintas because we were stupid, or malevolent, or both, and it was particularly we account men who were to blame. Consequently he'd exacted a terrible retribution. On a regular basis we'd return from one of our demanding lunches to find a ream of paper deposited on each of our desks - this being the days before email - that he'd ordained to be required reading on the subjects of account planning, advertising strategy, consumer insight and the like. The man must have been personally responsible for felling a forest the size of Bolivia, and the memory of ploughing through all that stuff on the way home is still with me. (I once incurred his wrath by showing him an agency flow-chart from which I'd accidentally omitted his department; though I'd like to claim it was an innocent blunder, I suspect there were more elemental subconscious forces at play). Nevertheless, I should thank this hard taskmaster for opening my eyes to another way of doing things.

What I learned when I went to Ayer is that account planning was all about using research - primarily 'focus groups' and individual 'depth interviews' - to find out what was really going on inside the consumer's head, and to use that knowledge to create more emotionally oriented advertising strategies. Considerable use was (and still is) made of surveys to quantify frequency and amount of purchase in particular markets; attitudes towards and usage of different makes; awareness and understanding of the advertising for those products; and more. But it is qualitative research that has always been account planning's most conspicuous feature. I learned that a lot of planners had acquired a knowledge of psychology with a distinctly Freudian bent. This accounted for the prevalence of lines of inquiry that had much to do with this curious entity known as the subconscious, that dark entity lurking within us whose secrets could be prised out of it with 'projective' techniques that involved getting people to imagine they were talking about something else, as if on the analyst's couch. At the time it struck me as novel, if not altogether scientific.

The real pleasure of account planning at Ayer was that it provided the opportunity to bring more open-minded debate to the matter of advertising strategy. Whether it substantively changed the core thinking underlying the subject, however, is another question. Though it's often said that account planning introduced emotion to the communication mix, I think that's patently untrue. Think, for example, of P&G's Fairy Liquid, which for years had banged away at the proposition that the product leaves mother's hands feeling as soft as her face. No doubt it had started as a hard-nosed u.s.p. concocted by a bunch of Madison Avenue suits, and I always suspected that the omnipresent infant was introduced as a device to *imply* that the skin in question feels as soft as a child's, maybe because the advertising authorities would deem such a claim to be unsustainable. Yet the mother-daughter combination in practice proved a powerful emotional hook, and P&G executives for many years were astute enough not to throw it away just because the emotion was an unintended consequence. And that was P&G. All the time I was at Lintas, Unilever prided itself on being that much more in tune with people's inner lives, an approach that allowed Persil to remain the number-one make of detergent in the UK even on a smaller share of advertising voice.

The new position

In truth, account planning in the twentieth century never was so radical that it spurned the concept of a proposition that was unique and would sell. It was really only the expression that became less brutal. Evidence of this can be found in the concept of 'positioning', a term popularised in a 1980 book by 'gurus' Al Ries and Jack Trout[1]. The basic idea is that the planner draws a grid whose axes represent in his or her judgment the different dimensions of choice in the particular market. For example, he might decide that the spectrum of positioning opportunities in a toothpaste market ranges from 'traditional' to 'fashionable' on one axis, and 'scientific' to 'no frills' on the other (though these dimensions are often quite arbitrary and he might prefer, say, 'minty' to 'medicated'). Then he decides where all the various competitors sit. He may find that two or three occupy the scientific/traditional quadrant, another couple are firmly in the fashionable/no frills quarter, and the market leader has the traditional/no frills sector to itself. If the make he is responsible for happens to sit perilously close to a competitor, he needs to find somewhere vacant that offers the chance to make it more 'differentiated', whilst still offering an ostensibly desirable benefit - perhaps by making a bold (or foolhardy?) leap into the fashionably scientific sector. This he defines as its positioning, which dictates its proposition and therefore its communications; and, more to the point, what price it will command.

Now, I should add that, many years later, I would get to know a person who had earlier worked for Trout & Ries and informed me that the former originally intended positioning in the late 'sixties only as a diagnostic tool, rather than the prescriptive one I've outlined above. However, it was the bigger-talking book that was to catch the industry's imagination. What you've just read accurately portrays the way my colleagues and I routinely approached strategic challenges, and nobody ever questioned our competence. Just as long as the message (i) was differentiated from competitors' messages, (ii) offered some kind of benefit to the potential user, (iii) did not overly cheapen the product, and (iv) was not downright illegal, indecent or dishonest, it would serve perfectly for the advertising strategy. It is fair to say that any positioning arrived at by this method would be deemed a thing of intellectual beauty irrespective of how accurately it matched up to the real-life experience of using the product or service in question. The match was sometimes good enough that it worked a treat: Lucozade was famously converted from an aid to convalescence to a sports energy drink. As so often, however, the odd success has served to justify any amount of hit-and-miss.

In agency life at that time, positioning was gospel. It was the account planner's job to come up with the proposition, the creative team's to bring it plausibly to life in film or print, the media department's to put it about, and mine to make sure that neither client nor advertising regulator obliged us to change a word of it. If this sounds a trifle sardonic (as is intended), I confess that I went along with it wholeheartedly at the time. To me, without the benefit of hindsight, it appeared a great leap forwards. One example: together with a brace of clever planners and some creative genius from Trevor Beattie - now co-founder of a recent UK Agency of the Year - I exploited the whole armoury of account planning to take the Bertie Bassett character, who had become reduced to a mere logo, and turn him in the course of five years into a national icon. As a result, the Liquorice Allsorts range reversed a thirty-year decline and, five years later, was arguably unlucky to be beaten in the Institute of Practitioners in Advertising's (IPA's) Advertising Effectiveness Awards by a BMP campaign for, would you believe, door-to-door milk deliveries. You don't get that far on the kinds of budgets we were given (this being in the days before big-spending Cadbury Schweppes and then Kraft Foods acquired the business) without some nifty thinking along the way. And just to prove that it was no fluke, we went on to reapply the formula to Bassett's Jelly Babies, turning a set of featureless lumps of gelatine into a family of characters loved now by two generations of toddlers.

Now, there's a scene in Douglas Adams's *The Hitchhiker's Guide to the Galaxy* where the alien Slartibartfast mentions with pride that he once won an award for designing the crinkly Norwegian coast. Admen always sound slightly ridiculous in the same way when they recount their meagre achievements. (Even Sir Salman Rushdie, who left his job as an Ayer Barker copywriter around the time I joined, has to live with the fact that his legacy to commercial culture was 'Naughty but nice'; he's fortunate also to have a Booker Prize to point to). When I mention such an 'achievement', I don't do so with foolish pride, for reasons that will become clear in due course. I do so to make the point that I took the model very seriously, and worked at it assiduously with talented individuals close to the top of their profession to produce both work and results that were considered excellent by industry standards. And yet, with the benefit of hindsight, it could have been done infinitely better. I believe today that there was a fundamental flaw in our thinking: a flaw as egregious as Reeves's cult of the rational. To explain it, I need to address for the first time the 'B' word - the Brand.

The resurrection of the brand

Before account planning came along, branding had retained much of its original sense as a device for marking out one's property. Branding seldom amounted to much more than the logo tacked on the end, and one of the account manager's perennial jobs was to arbitrate between the client who always wanted it a bit bigger and the art director who wanted it smaller or, preferably, not there at all. Enlightened thinkers used to talk about the importance of making the proposition so synonymous with the make that one could guess the branding without the logo – which was fine for big-spending juggernauts like P&G, Mars or Kellogg, but hard for the relative small fry who depended on creative ingenuity to compensate for their lack of media weight. In my experience, if great creative ideas are a rarity, great *well-branded* creative ideas are the province of only the most gifted creative talents; or the luckiest.

What changed with account planning - not overnight, but over time, in a vast tumescence that continues even today - was the advent of the all-encompassing concept of the *Brand*. Lazy writers always suggest scale by talking of the number of references thrown up by a Google search, but this is one case that merits a look. Type in 'Brand' and you will be astonished, not only by the mere number but also by the plethora of interpretations, variants, critiques, rationales, and developments. Now type in 'God' and prepare to be truly amazed. The comparison is not idle: much marketing and indeed business literature today has as its start-point a quasi-religious belief in the Power of the Brand that just did not exist a generation ago. (I recently attended a MR webinar that began with the words, 'What all of us will agree on is that *the Brand is everything*'). It is above all account planning that effected that change, in urging marketers to present their products not as manufactures with their provenance indicated, but as *personalities* with which prospective customers can form relationships of the same ilk as those we form with other human beings. The ramifications of this development on a global scale have been enormous.

My suspicion is that the original impetus for this development was the plain belief that, because we perceive humans more readily and more emotively than inanimate objects, there must be commercial value in anthropomorphising products and services: a neat modern example of the so-called 'pathetic fallacy'. Of course, it is hard to judge how consciously most admen over the last three decades have followed that precept; one can only speculate. Most likely, some pioneer or other set a knowing example that others emulated without appreciating why. What we can observe in the real world, however, is that brands are routinely described as having the qualities of human beings, and professional analysis routinely assumes the consumer's relationships with brands to be correspondingly complex. Thus we hear much discussion of brand personas, brand identities, brand personalities, brand values, brand preferences, brand bonding, brand relationships, and that ultimate goal, brand loyalty.

It is the stuff of modern-day advertising - nay, marketing - to agonise over the nature of the first seven of these in order to secure the eighth. But there's a problem. As any objective observer of focus groups would have to testify, consumers themselves seldom speak spontaneously of brands in this way. They have to be led there by a research moderator, using occasionally risible questions such as, 'If this detergent were an actor, which particular actor would it be?' The look on most subjects' faces suggests that the only time they would ever even contemplate answering such a question is in a focus group, though they are happy to play along rather than lose the attendance fee. The moderator is also being paid to do a job, and in practice is obliged to subjugate any personal doubts to compliance with accepted industry norms. It is no surprise if, told what's expected of them, a researcher ends up faithfully reporting back not the objective truth but something rather more helpful to the client. What is recounted at research debriefs then finds its way almost ineluctably into brand marketing, and in particular into the advertising.

Once back in the marketplace, however, consumers reward the brand builder's ingenuity with all the fidelity of a porn-flick starlet. This startling fact first became evident to me while studying sequential lists of individuals' purchases: shoppers appear perfectly happy to spread their affections around as the fancy takes them. Purchasing is not actually random, even in the relatively risk-free environment of supermarkets. In most categories we tend to have a small repertoire from which we select. But where repeat purchasing occurs, the best one can say is that purchasers tend to be victims of brand *habit* (for which read inertia) rather than any particular loyalty[2]. This is no great secret: in the course of attending hundreds of research debriefs from groups to audits - as is the lot of any career marketer or adman - one sees and hears more than enough of the way consumers relate to brands in the real world to have reason to doubt their real-world value. The result is that demonstrating the commercial value of conventional brand-building is so difficult that, notwithstanding the occasional success story, its inputs (advertising in particular) have increasingly been pitched as a cost of doing business, rather than a device for growing it.

A matter of accountability

If the Brand is a matter of faith, a heretic is entitled to ask how much commercial value it has brought any corporation that shells out a king's ransom in creating one of these mythic beasts. The event that specifically focused my own attention on this question was the 1987 stock market crash, which severely dented confidence in the run-up to a new year. After several years of gloriously creative advertising marked by massive production budgets, extravagant salaries, awards ceremonies galore, and a worrying amount of hubris, I suddenly found myself having to demonstrate the commercial value of the money our clients had invested in us. It mattered enormously, as the next year's fees depended upon it; so I threw myself into it. Although I might already have had some quiet doubts, I was shocked at how bad the numbers appeared. It all kicked off when one of my account managers reported to me that her own analysis on one brand looked good: we had spent £1.5 million, but sales value had risen by almost that amount, so the client got her money back. Of course, the argument washed only if the brand enjoyed 100% margins. (Sadly, this account manager was no more innumerate than some senior admen I've met). The picture she drew was worryingly typical. It was hard to make a commercial case for anything but launches or relaunches. We had to argue that, by charging up the brand with 'values', we'd sustained a price premium; or that sales would have fallen if we'd not advertised.

Though confidence soon returned, I was left wondering why the model we trusted wasn't more conspicuously effective at influencing customer behaviour. My first port of call was the aforementioned Advertising Effectiveness Awards, already held up as the industry touchstone, which might reveal where we were going wrong. What became obvious was that the thick biennial volume in which they were published, *Advertising Works*[3], couldn't help us. The tally of entrants appeared to represent under one percent of all campaigns; of these, just a handful won awards; and even these winners revealed no consistent picture of commercial reward. A review of the first few volumes that I later commissioned privately only served to confirm my concerns about payback. Years afterwards, I would point this out to the IPA's director general at a conference at the London Business School, prompting a bout of verbal fisticuffs that culminated in him shouting, 'What's your problem?!' Though the organisers thought it fine entertainment, the explanation I was given later - that the Awards are only intended to showcase examples of best practice - didn't persuade me that much enlightenment was to be found in them.

By then, Professor Michael Schudson of the University of California, San Diego had published a pungent critique[4] that began, *'Advertising is much less powerful than advertisers and critics of advertising claim, and advertising agencies are stabbing in the dark much more than they are practising precision microsurgery on the public consciousness'* - a stark contrast with the credulity of his fellow journalist and social critic, Vance Packard, a quarter-century earlier. It seemed to me a riddle that shoppers did not seem to respond in large numbers to our immensely sophisticated brand blandishments in anything like the way we presumed to imagine. Talking to friends at other agencies made it clear that our track record was nothing unusual; but there seemed to be precious little concern about it. I took a dissenting view. I didn't like to feel we were selling a defective product. But this wasn't a matter of being sanctimonious. I reasoned that, if we were getting this account planning stuff wrong, there might be real competitive advantage in analysing the matter more scientifically - and devising a better solution.

Deaf to evidence

The difficulty I encountered, it almost goes without saying, is that few boardroom colleagues appeared to see it that way, at least publicly. We were paid to make money for the agency within the current fiscal year, not to rock the boat. If there was a problem with what we were selling, then it was account management's job to sell it better. And that was the view of the ones who agreed there was an issue. Those others who thought the product we offered was fine (or, more usually, 'great') considered it lunacy even to consider that the brand-building model had a problem. It didn't help that, by this time, the agency had a new boss who had imported a number of directors after his own *outré* brand-loving image, whose big new-business idea was to tell prospective clients that we were good at both reason *and* emotion. Ultimately it was their passionate conservatism that made me determined to plough my own furrow. Before very long, I came to have such a contrarian view that

I kept having to remind myself of the brand mantra every time I was about to open my mouth.

The frank conclusion I'd arrived at after much cogitation was that the 'power of the Brand' was less a useful construct for understanding how consumers are driven to buy than a cunning device for justifying continuous expenditure on marketing. For a time, I wondered whether it was anything but pure fabrication. Once upon a time, in a world of uncertain health & safety standards and trades descriptions, a brand had been a warranty that one would not be poisoned or cheated. Since then, in a new age where legislation and refined production processes ordinarily guaranteed safety and consistent quality respectively, it had evolved into...a what? Was it really a lattice of cultural and emotional associations that constituted a surrogate identity? Or just a ragbag of marketing memories that people carry around like refuse in a tramp's supermarket trolley? Whichever way I looked at brands, there seemed less to them than met the eye. Of course there were always exceptions: some people might feel happier to fly British Airways than Ryanair even if it was dearer; the average teenager would rather wear Levi's jeans than St Michael, irrespective of how they compared functionally; you were probably happy to pay more for a Fiat than a Seat, despite suspecting they'd the same engineering. But such oft-cited examples would cost a huge amount of time and investment to achieve, and were becoming increasingly atypical in a world that was already growing weary of the volume of marketing thrown at it.

Naturally such sentiments were guaranteed to prompt not just boardroom colleagues but any marketing mainstreamer to throw up his or her hands in horror. What is this guy *on?* Doesn't he know that products perform better branded than blind in tests? Isn't he aware how much more supermarkets can charge for a brand than for their own label? Hasn't he read Stephen King? Or Al Ries? Or *Advertising Works?* It's understandable: knocking brands is bad for the business. I learned it was better to work quietly underground than become the dead hero. I'm convinced there were others who had the same concerns; but I found it all but impossible to locate them. You can be forgiven therefore for thinking that the whole industry can't have been wrong, and that I was mistaken. If so, I have to fast-forward to the present day and refer you to the chief research officer of the Advertising Research Foundation. The bombshell he delivered early in 2009 was that consumers are mostly, as he put it, 'not engaged' with the brands they buy[5]. I would argue that it was evident a very long time ago; the industry just couldn't bear to hear it, and still can't.

What we do hear in the media today is the argument that something *changed*. It's often asserted by journalists and marketing pundits alike that people are more media-savvy (i.e. less gullible) than earlier generations, though without much justification being provided: even half a century ago, 86% of American women in a Gallup poll expressed the view that advertising was dishonest[6], and a national survey undertaken in the US in the mid-1980's reported that 60% of consumers concurred that 'advertising insults my intelligence', whilst over 70% professed that they 'don't believe a company's ad when it claims test results show its product to be better than competitive products'[7]. What undeniably has changed, by courtesy of media proliferation, is the number of stimuli we are exposed to, of which marketing forms a small but substantial part. Indeed, we are certainly exposed en masse to more stimuli now than at any time in our history. This inevitably makes it harder for any particular brand to stand out (the standard argument for yet more marketing!) and demonstrably adds to public weariness with marketing intrusiveness.

But I think now, as I already did in the late 1980s, that the argument runs deeper. You need to ask whether the concept of brands as personalities we relate to ever made a lot of sense. Though 'eighties practitioners made much of the difference in response to branded and unbranded products, we were already familiar at that time, well before Gigerenzer, with the simple human truth that *any* form of identity (even Brand X) influences us more positively than a blank cover - as witnessed for example by countless tests in which users were happy to pay more for the same product with a name attached than without. How well this justifies the leap to asserting that business is all about great brands is quite another matter. The truth, I suspect, is that the people who have much the strongest relationship with brands are the ones who invent them.

It always struck me, whenever I had the chance to meet real consumers face-to-face and hear them talk about brands, that they were indifferent to most brands and even a little hostile to the corporations that made them. Despite natural inertia, they did not seem resistant to checking out new ones. They'd forgotten, without anguish, well-established old brands whose owners had decided to move to new territory. In later years one would see them accept Opal Fruits morphing into Starburst and Ulay into Olay (or is it Olaz?) For every protest you heard about the removal of a Heinz Salad Cream from the market, there would be countless brands like Brobat, Kennomeat and Skol - household names only a generation ago, built with millions of advertising pounds - that disappeared without a murmur. How long did anyone mourn Norwich Union, Abbey National and the Midland Bank, all household names to which tens of millions had entrusted their hard-earned cash? And then there's Egg, raved about as a pinnacle of the brand-creator's art, but never a money-spinner and perhaps soon to ejected at a loss from Citigroup's frying pan.

This is not to say, of course, that there's *no such thing* as a great brand. Think of Apple, for example: the consequence in large part of Steve Jobs's instinctive ability to design products that set themselves apart from the herd. What you see at work there is the principle of *affordance*, or product functionality that's designed to correspond with human intuition. The benefit is that, if you take to the concept, you know that you can consistently find it with the Apple name attached, and the brand name takes on real meaning for you: a liked and trusted face in a crowd of near strangers. Consequently, you'll be more forgiving when, as is inevitable, things go wrong. Contrast this with the norm, which is to say a plethora of me-too products and services with nothing much to distinguish them but a different logo. The supposition of every marketing primer, think-piece and paper is that, no matter how small you are, you too can be a little bit like Apple, provided you get your marketing right. It's as preposterous a notion as suggesting that, if you just wear the right trainers, you can truly be a little bit like Michael Jordan. Of course, we can always imagine that we don't need the hard work, the ambition and the plain talent that it takes to be special in the real world, as long as we talk a good game; but, with no substance to underwrite it, who are we fooling but ourselves?

To answer this fully, you have to put yourself in the shoes of the person you become at some point in almost every day of your life: the customer. Reflect on it when you're walking around Tesco or Dixons or the Motor Show. How many of the brands on display can you honestly say you have a relationship with? Indeed, how many actually mean anything to you at all, beyond the name itself? If your answer is something other than 'a handful', there's only one thing to say: you're not typical. What you buy, you will most likely select because you've had it before and it didn't let you down. In other words, it's your previous *behaviour* that establishes whatever relationship you may have. You try something; it lets you down; you don't buy it again. Or you try something, it works for you, and you stick with it to save you the trouble of making another mistake. You can reasonably call brand 'loyalty' a default position or a weak force that's nice for a business to have when it happens to work in your favour; but, in all but the exceptional cases like Apple, it's seldom more powerful or resilient than that.

The dead brand

All the enticements of marketers will pale beside this fundamental law. And yet, when you do look around a store or showroom, almost everything on display will have got there only after passing through the clutches of a marketer. So what exactly do marketers think they're trying to achieve? The answer is painfully simple. Once upon a time, the superior mousetrap might have got customers to beat a path to the maker's door. But what happens when every manufacturer can offer more or less the same mousetrap? Marketers have the answer: you *invent* difference. You wrap tinsel around the product with which you attempt, as if by magic, to differentiate it from its competitors and give customers a surrogate reason to prefer it. This is what most marketers imagine the brand to be. The obvious point to make about it is that it is artificial. It is from the same school as the fake religiosity that art dealers attach to piles of bricks in the hope of making a mint out of them.

Yet, even at the intellectual level, the concept of a brand barely stacks up. What *is* a brand? Let's say it's a commercial product or service that has a set of distinguishing emotional associations attached to it. But what if we mention Madonna, John Lennon, and Buddy Holly? Same thing, in the sense that they are 'for sale'. How about Conservative and Liberal, Democrat and Republican? Not strictly commercial products or services; but perhaps they too may be considered brands. Then what of England, Mexico, or Ruanda? How about the Atkins Diet, genetic modification, or reflexology? Or even cloud, home, hockey, self-interest, or aquamarine? All are phenomena with a set of distinguishing emotional associations attached. The fact is that almost nothing - even single words - comes without its affective baggage train. For all the years of investment, does Persil really mean any more to you than Paris, the Grand National, Friends, Hallowe'en, or the Rose and Crown? If the distinguishing feature of brands is merely that they are 'for sale', we might as well revert to calling a spade a spade - or a product a product.

It's the fashion today to insist that there's nothing wrong with such artifice if you can get away with it; but that 'if' is a worryingly big one.

Naturally you *can* occasionally get away with it, sometimes very profitably. The instances that are always cited are those Siamese twins of the commercial world, fashion and luxury goods, whose purchasers experience that primeval need to flaunt their opulence even if to the rest of us they simply look pound-foolish. Of course there are cases where all of us have bought one brand rather than another, even a brand of sticking plaster, just because of some vague sense that it felt more right than the alternative. But these are exceptions. The quantity of marketing-inspired baggage we carry around worthlessly in our heads dwarfs the amount that ever has any worthwhile effect. For all the journalistic hype, brand-creation is like sex: too much talked about, seldom well done, and best avoided with strangers.

Confronted with such a contention, brand consultants tend to protest, 'What about the great brands that have been built on great brand values? What about Ford, which became great bringing us decent cars ordinary people could afford? What about McDonalds, promising predictably simple food in tidy locations? What about Coca Cola, with its unique sugary taste and outstanding refreshment?' Yes, you might well reply: what about them? The fact is, these were not brand values. They were product features that went with a proprietary name attached. They worked because they were real, and worked in the real world. The job for marketing was to make them known. It's only when such companies have wandered away from them that they've run into trouble. And that's the big point here. Real people can normally detect the reality gap between claim and performance a mile off. When a brand has an offering that actually delivers on the hype, you get real loyalty to proprietary products. Offer them nonsense and they will give your product one shot... if you're lucky.

Such were the views I nurtured at Ayer. I was not entirely alone, I'm glad to say: the one good thing the new boss did was to hire from JWT a new senior planner who had witnessed the account planning movement from its apex, observed hundreds of focus groups and turned their output into strategies, scrutinised with a gimlet eye the new model's fatal flaws, and come to not dissimilar conclusions. That man, Roger Titford, a fervent football fan with Bob Dylan hair and a resistance to sartorial style that sat well with his academician's memory and intellect, used to join me regularly in the pub next to the office to compare notes and plot a way forward. I'm glad to say that, twenty-odd years later, we're able to recall those years together like a nostalgically shared wartime experience. The reason for that feeling was that we were still working in a brand manufactory, yet it was looking very much as though the Brand was *dead*.

Now, when Nietzsche wrote that God is dead, he can't have been unaware of the effect his words would have on the pious citizenry of the Second Reich. But he was under no illusion that what held logically for a nineteenth-century German philosopher would instantly become true for all his peer group. Harking back to Plato, he went on to write that, such are man's spiritual needs, the concept of God would live on like a shadow on a cave wall for centuries to come. If I said the Brand is dead, I meant much the same thing. The brand as a concept lived on, as it does today, but only like a ghoul. Though everywhere about us, it had already outgrown its practical use for customers; indeed, it was worse than useless, interfering with a realistic conception of their relationship with the things they buy. Of this I was convinced; but I underestimated how long the people that make money from the myth would continue to prop it up and jiggle its limbs around.

Another decade would pass before the outstanding marketing academic Professor Andrew Ehrenberg of South Bank University in London published a devastating paper in which he demonstrated empirically that, as he concluded, *'there is little evidence that brands as such are seen by their users as possessing differentiating added values'*[8]. It would be borne out later by evidence that, given a free choice on the world's biggest marketplace, the internet, human beings do not resort to brands like beacons on the stormy sea; anything but. One recent study revealed that only 13.6% of respondents - less than one in seven - would turn to a brand website to find the solution to a need. Much preferred were dependable comparison sites where the desired *product* can be obtained most propitiously. And if you imagine the study was biased, it was in fact conducted by a research house part-owned by WPP[9], owner of several of the world's biggest ad agency groups.

Without such evidence, Roger and I ended up standing aside from the mainstream culture of the agency, looked at askance because we didn't really fit in, but immovable because we were holding down important business just by refusing to regard the clients as milch cows. If it sounds a bit worthy, I can only reply that it worked. The new boss's string of early successes turned out to be short-lived, and the international board eventually got fed up with his lack of delivery and, as they say, let him go. His coterie quickly followed, and the two of us were left in charge of the best part of the agency's client list. Yet, though we felt events had vindicated our distrust in brand dependency, we knew we were no closer to answering the big question: how do we make advertising worth doing? As it turned out, a chance encounter with a man called Gordon Brown was waiting just around the corner - an encounter whose consequences were to touch the lives of almost everyone in the country.

3
The Power to Prime

Enhanced experience

Imagine that I gave you two soft drinks: one in a can with a triangle on it, and one with a circle. Imagine that I then asked you to describe the two drinks and express a preference. Imagine that I could predict which you preferred with 80% certainty. Nothing so extraordinary about that, you might think, until you learned that the two products were *identical.* The landmark experiment that makes me so confident was conducted in the 1930s by Louis Cheskin[1], one of the pioneers of research into psychological aspects of brand choice. I knew about it as a schoolboy. I know I knew, because Packard reported it in *The Hidden Persuaders*. But I forgot about it, having presumably concluded that it was just a designer's magic trick and not a pointer to any greater underlying truth. As it happens, we now know that the brain has a strong preference for rounded edges over sharp angles, possessing an acquired ability to respond more quickly to pointed objects at the neural level, for rather obvious evolutionary reasons[2]. Less obvious however is the fact that exposure to different surface designs can elicit entirely different *qualia*: that is, differing sensory perceptions. This remarkable effect plainly deserved much more thinking about than I had given it.

It was almost by accident that Cheskin's finding found its way back onto my radar. In 1991, I received an unsolicited copy of a 76-page monograph called *How advertising affects the sales of packaged goods brands*[3]. The author was Gordon Brown, a man who shared a name with a then little known politician but little else. Gordon was co-founder of Millward Brown, an up-and-coming British rival to the huge American-owned research houses. It looked like the sort of soft-bound sales literature that you routinely file in the bin, and all that made me hold onto it was the name on the cover. I'd come across Gordon a year or two earlier when he'd presented to a seminar I'd attended. I was only there because it had been organised by one of our clients, Gillette, and woe would have betided anyone in the account team who'd missed it. Instead of the usual soft soap, however, we were treated to an intellectual *tour de force*, when for the first time in my experience a market researcher actually took stock of what he'd learned about how advertising does and doesn't work, and what questions we really needed to ask in order to create advertising that worked. It was no surprise to learn that Gordon was by education a scientist, and the refreshingly data-rich basis of his deductions led me to think that anything he wrote might have that rare virtue of offering something worth thinking about.

His monograph argued, on the basis of thousands of Millward Brown tracking studies, that advertising can assist brand sales in three ways. The first of these was so-called 'Immediate Challenge', or communicating convincing news that can broaden the set of products we might contemplate using. The second was 'Interest-Status', by means of which products from jeans to fragrances to automobiles may be invested with positive extraneous associations, capable of adding value in the public's mind compared with other, equivalent products. The third and, to me at least, most intriguing was what he termed 'Enhancement', by which he was referring to the psychological characteristic of *priming*: the establishment of a neural template of a phenomenon that colours our response to any subsequent exposure to the real thing. Now, enhancement is plainly a powerful tool. Intriguingly, it can create a propensity to act in ways that deliver ostensibly poor utility; for example, perceiving a fashion-label garment as worth much more than an identical item you might have bought for half the price in the High Street. Some of advertising's most vaunted successes use precisely this model. Yet the tool was little understood by marketing practitioners, and its real potential underexploited.

I am not sure what it was about this concept that registered with me. Perhaps it was some intuitive sense that it was important, or maybe just an echo of that Cheskin story that caused a neglected old neuron to fire. It wasn't that, however, which gave me the pretext to contact Gordon with a slightly impertinent request. Some of the commentary in the monograph - such as the controversial statement that advertising almost never pays for itself - was frankly embarrassing to the ad industry, and I got his attention by letting him know that I'd like to understand better what had prompted him, a supplier, to broadcast such ideas. I didn't happen to disagree, but I thought I might at least get some more clues out of him. To his credit, he did better than just reply. He came to our offices and spent some hours with Roger and me telling us a whole lot more of what he'd learned. What we didn't know at the time was that he was planning to sell up and retire before too long, so I guess the empiricist in him just wanted to leave a brutally honest record behind.

What I always found a pleasure about Gordon was his manner. With his bald pate and wispy white beard descending from his jaw line, he resembled in every inch the respectable Victorian gentleman; and his manner matched up to the appearance. He managed with aplomb the knack of dispensing his knowledge and wisdom without patronising; and, though I didn't always agree with his more sanguine views on advertising, I could always appreciate that there was an evidence-based logic to his views that contrasted starkly with the culture of wishful assertion and eclectic self-justification we'd grown used to. The big favour Gordon did me subsequently was to send me an academic paper called *Can advertising influence experience?*[4] by Professors John Deighton and Robert Schindler of the University of Chicago, written three years earlier. It was a revelation to me, a proper scientific treatise with a hypothesis, scientific design, results, statistical proof and conclusions that were meticulously thorough and hard to refute, but concerning a business subject close to my heart. Cerebrally, it was a delight.

All Deighton and Schindler had done in reality was what scientists do by rote: they'd designed a tidy experiment to test out a hypothesis. Students were asked to rate one of three Boston radio stations for the truth of the claim that it played original music. They then were played commercials that specifically made that claim. The advertising barely changed their belief in the claim, if it all. And, two weeks later, it also turned out that the advertising had not induced them to listen to the station any more than previously. However, they were then asked to rate the station for a third time against the claim, and this is where the researchers witnessed something extraordinary. The students who happened to have listened to the station for which they had heard advertising were now significantly *more* likely to believe the claim. Indeed, the more they had experienced the station, the more they had come to believe the claim. Conversely, those who had *not* listened to the station for which they had heard advertising still believed the claim just as seldom. The same was true of the ones who had listened to a station for which they had heard no advertising. It was as though the advertising had been a limp sail waiting for the wind of reality to blow life into it.

Like Cheskin's finding, this needed some explaining in terms of contemporary theory of advertising, which was supposed to create interest or add to perceived value but would not be expected to change the actual experience. Deighton had already argued in another paper four years earlier[5] that the old model was basically 'adversarial', the communicator attempting to persuade the customer against his or her will. Conversely, the two-step model he proposed on the basis of experimentation held that exposure to advertising may induce the consumer to entertain, albeit tentatively, a 'hypothesis' about the product. When evidence that bears on the hypothesis becomes available - in the form of product experience - the consumer 'tests' the hypothesis. This is often not a rational, conscious process, but a passing recognition of a fulfilment (or not) of an expectation that is unlikely to absorb a great deal of the consumer's attention. However, this type of low-level processing generally favours the *confirmation* of such expectations. This was a critically important notion which suggested that advertising unsupported by product trial was as useful as glue without the hardener. It went largely disregarded by the ad industry.

The concept of product trial as pivotal and advertising as an adjunct was not Deighton's idea alone. The marketing research supporting the 'Integrated Information Response Model' proposed by Professors Robert Smith of Indiana University and William Swinyard of Brigham Young University in 1982 revealed that product trial created stronger positive emotion - in other words, commitment sufficiently powerful as to secure high-value purchases - than did advertising. When I say 'higher', we're not talking a close-run matter. The difference was 43% for people who'd had an experience, and a miserable 8% for those exposed to advertising. Since advertising appeared much less likely to be trusted as an information source than the evidence of customers' own senses, IIRM's creators suggested for it a less ambitious role, namely to influence the way people experienced products they might be trialing instead of trying directly to create emotional change in those exposed to it. As they concluded, *'the focus of marketing efforts should be to make the circumstances surrounding product trial as likely and as favorable as possible. Contingent upon this direct experience, a strong evaluative base may be formed, affect (i.e. emotion) generated, and reasonably consistent behavior should follow'*[6]. This was in fact a revolutionary shift, placing the experience at the centre of the marketing universe and relegating advertising to a satellite. Again, the ad industry ignored it.

In the same year as Professor Deighton's landmark radio experiment, Professors Lawrence Marks from Kent State University and Michael Kamins from the University of Southern California developed the ideas of the IIRM by investigating the varying effects on product trial following exposure to advertising that contained more or less exaggerated claims[7]. Their findings suggested that highly exaggerated ads resulted in consumers' expectations not being met. This disappointment promoted a contrast effect: consumers then actually rated an advertised product lower than in the absence of advertising! When only slightly exaggerated ads were used in combination with product samples, however, *'such an approach appears to enhance people's expectations about ensuing product performance, but not to a level dramatically inconsistent with the sampling experience'*. The lesson was that typical advertising hyperbole is counterproductive, whereas a closer match between expectation and reality is rewarded. You can guess what the ad industry did about it.

A conceptual leap

These were the ideas that were swirling about in my head late in 1992. I cannot claim to have read this material, sat in a dark room to digest it, and then logically concluded what must come next. In those days before the advent of the internet, just coming across the source material was itself a slow process. Nor did the reports of Deighton and Schindler, Marks and Kamins, Smith and Swinyard possess for me a coherence such as I've expressed them above. They were curiosities that I struggled to fit with what I thought I knew. It would have been easy to ignore them as extraneous to my purposes; yet they seemed enormously convincing compared with the usual MR-based insights on which business decisions depended. What kept the door ajar was the fact that the industry's conventional wisdom left me queasy. Our textbooks had no place for product experience, except in respect of product trialing - through the sample-size giveaways to be found in magazines or on your doorstep - for which the logic was nothing more or less than 'Give them a taster; they might like it'. The notion that experience could have a central role in changing behaviour was at first a bridge too far.

At that stage, in any case, I had a lot else on my mind. During the last days of the previous regime, I and the uncommonly loyal people in my team had held on doggedly in the belief that, in the end, the righteous would prevail. What actually happened was that the head of Ayer's European network decided to import a new senior management team, presumably on the grounds that those of us that remained were tarred with the same brush as the last lot. The new gang of three certainly had a more sober outlook than their predecessors. What everybody soon concluded, however, was that they also had no big plan for growing the business. When new billings failed to come in, they decided to make themselves useful by involving themselves actively with my accounts, which annoyed one longstanding client so much that he took his business away. Roger departed to set up his own research consultancy, while I was left thinking hard about what to do next. By this time, you'll understand, my patience was running a little thin.

It was no doubt in that frame of mind that I found myself one November evening, when everyone sensible had gone home, staring out of the window. All I recollect of it now is that one of the new triumvirate had asked if I would dream up some insight or other that could be used as a new business tool. In truth I was gazing into the darkness wondering how I might acquit myself, and my mind drifted. I don't recall my thought process any more, but I do remember everything suddenly coming together in a flash, as if I'd known it all along and a veil just needed to be whipped away. When it hove into view, it was surprisingly complex for something that just sprang to mind. I suspect now that all that had happened was that my brain had suddenly knitted two or more connected sets of neurons together. It was like one of those stories you hear about solutions to complex problems that occur to people in dreams, as when James Watson imagined two intertwined snakes, prompting the idea of the DNA double helix. Though no Nobel Prize-winning concept, the idea that formed in my head had a pleasing roundness.

There were two parts to it. The first was the idea that Smith and Swinyard's formula of advertising-then-sampling needed to be not just a description but a *tool*: in other words, if we wanted to change minds on a commercial scale, we marketers needed to force the action of experiencing the product or service *systematically* in the immediate wake of exposure to advertising. The second, inspired by Marks and Kamins and building on Deighton and Schindler, made a mental leap to the idea that the advertising should not just set up a hypothesis that would tend to be confirmed by subsequent experience; it should deliberately establish an accurate expectation that the experience would *inevitably* confirm. What inspired this thought was a concern I'd had about the radio-station experiment: that, though the levels of belief about the advertising claim had moved significantly, the overall levels were still pretty *low*. Deighton's 1984 paper had mentioned an earlier theorist called Herb Krugman who'd argued that advertising tends to influence behaviour when viewers don't actually process it consciously[8]. I'd wondered whether the behavioural effect might be working at a level at which we are simply unaware of it. Maybe the content of the advertising was less important than the fact of it. Maybe the advertising just needed not to exaggerate; or even sell.

When I sat down to write this out schematically, I immediately came to the conclusion that we would need to be making a different type of advertising that would not claim or position but simply evoke the true experience of consuming the product we were selling. We'd then need to get people to check out that evocation for real while the memory was still fresh. I assumed this would require very intensive advertising to plant a strong mental impression for a short while, and very large-scale product sampling immediately thereafter - an activity about whose feasibility I had not so much as a clue. I also realised later that special research would be needed to establish the true nature of the product experience we'd want to evoke. It must have occurred to me that all of this would be a tall order in view of the natural conservatism of the ad industry - not least the challenge to the creative discipline - but I cheerfully assumed that, if it all made things even a little better, then no one could but applaud it.

The first thing I opted to do was share the idea with Roger, who was still working with me on a freelance basis. His reaction ('sounds interesting') was in Roger-speak a gleaming endorsement. The new bosses also proved enthusiastic, encouraging me to develop it as a pretext for talking to potential clients. The friendly media director was helpful in working out the sort of media campaign that would be called for if we were to achieve the requisite level of advertising coverage, and over what sort of period. In working out the numbers, it was obvious that we would require a very large number of product samples to be distributed in a very short period of time if sense were to be made of the media expenditure. We were by no means sure, as novices in that field, whether it could even be done. At that stage, however, executional issues were the least of my concerns. The idea was still just an idea, and possibly a crazy one at that. What I needed first was evidence that it held water; and, having now been exposed to the rigour of science, I was determined that only a pukka experiment would suffice.

The acid test

Over lunch in our favourite pub, Roger and I worked out, with less difficulty than we might have expected, a methodology whereby we could compare subjects' definite intention to purchase each of four packaged-goods brands. What we would contrast was four different cells consisting of subjects who had been exposed to advertising alone, to a product sample alone, to both, or to neither. Four products that could reasonably easily be trialed would be selected on the basis that we adjudged their advertising an accurate evocation of the experience of using that product. We decided the experiment should be called Project Janus, after the Roman god of doors who looked both ways; an apt metaphor, we thought, for the way that advertising enhances the experience and the experience makes sense of the advertising.

We shared the idea with Gordon Brown, who took to it straight away and kindly offered that, if we would provide the advertising and product stimulus, he would cover the cost of fieldwork himself among a sample of over a thousand women from a broad spread of age and socio-demographics. A second valuable contribution he made was Millward Brown's disguised stimulus: respondents would be asked to view a video recording of a soap opera into whose commercial breaks the ads had been inserted in rotated order, and afterwards given a small bundle of goodies, including the (also rotated) samples, as a thank you. They therefore assumed that they were taking part in TV programme research, and only afterwards learned under questioning the real purpose of the exercise. In this way, we were able to create a less artificial simulation of the process in action.

Finding the right products was no easy task. I had to sift through literally dozens of industry show-reels to find examples of ads that suggested more or less accurately what the actual experience was like. The exercise vividly brought home the fact that, whatever else it does, advertising seldom aims to reflect reality. The majority of ads simply presented a u.s.p. that, though not actually at odds with the true experience, was normally incidental to it, like selling a devious politician on the claim that he's a family man. The minority tendency, born of positioning and account planning, was essentially remedial. In other words, the thought process seemed to run, 'If there's a perceived problem with product performance, we'll have to change the perceptions'. Instead of the said politician mending his ways, he must be reminded to smile whenever in front of the cameras. Nearly all were by design essentially *specious*. We did nevertheless find three whose u.s.p. happened to coincide with the product experience; and we already had a fourth that we'd previously produced for one of our own clients against a brief deliberately designed to capture the experience.

All we then had to do was acquire very large quantities of the product. The brands had been chosen to represent a spread of categories, namely a food, a drink, a confection and a toiletry. These were, respectively, Fox's Crinkle Crunch biscuits, whose advertising featured their appetising crumbliness; Aqua Libra, evoking the sense of doing one's insides good; Needlers Sensations, which used a heavy-metal band who turned out to be softies as a metaphor for their chewy centre inside a hard shell; and Wisdom Reflex toothbrushes, whose moving bristles gave a sense of closeness to the tooth and gum-line. Once we had sent off the stimuli, all we could do was sit on our hands. For the first time I had the feeling that every scientist experiences when waiting for an experimental result to come through. It is a unique mixture of excitement and trepidation, like anticipating the outcome of an exam that will determine one's future. What added to the nervousness in this instance was the fact that, if the result was negative or even equivocal, there would be no retake.

Eventually, after what seemed an eternity, I got a message to say that the results would be coming through that afternoon. My heart was in my mouth as I was eventually handed a single sheet of shiny fax paper. What I learned then is something that I now know perfectly well: that, when you've done your homework sufficiently thoroughly to create a sound hypothesis, the empirical results are nothing to be afraid of. The worst they can do is tell you a rethink is needed, which at least means you're wiser than you were before. In this instance, no rethink was called for. The numbers were stunning. All four brands showed the same pattern, and when averaged provided an unequivocal vindication of the hypothesis. What they revealed was that an average of 12.6% of the control sample would definitely buy the four products without having been exposed to either advertising or product sample. This figure became 14.6% among those who had had a sample only, compared with 10.4% who had seen just the advertising. But the score among those who had both seen the advertising and had the sample was 20.3%. Not only was this significantly higher than the control (the 12.6%); it was obvious that the increment was far too high to be explicable as the additive effect of sampling and advertising, the latter of which in any case had shown no significantly different effect from doing nothing.

Gordon presented the findings with his colleague Andy Farr to the Market Research Society (MRS) annual conference in the spring of 1994 in a paper called *Persuasion or Enhancement?*[9] in which they generously acknowledged the provenance of the thinking. It was a moment of quiet triumph mitigated only by the fact that, in the paper, they expressed the results as a finding about advertising and sampling generally, rather than about experientially accurate advertising in particular. This had after all been a key feature of the original proposal, and the Millward Brown personnel who had co-operated closely with us in executing the fieldwork were well aware of the lengths we had gone to in order to find the right ads. The reason they gave in the paper was that the issue concerned advertising enhancement in general. One could however also have forgiven them for fearing that the ad agencies within Millward Brown's client base would be unsympathetic to a supplier telling them what made for good copy. This reservation detracts only a little from the excellent job they did in exposing an audience that contained many advertising researchers to challenging new evidence.

Moving on

By this time, however, I was no longer to be found at Ayer. The European network had been sold, and the new management team morphed into the new *former* management team. The incoming network owner opted to merge the London operation with a trendy creative hot-shop that before long turned out to have gone a bit tepid. The latest gang of three made their intentions clear by turfing me out of my General Manager's office into a room I shared, ironically enough, with an account planner. To be fair to them, they were decent people who were only wanting to make the most of their investment, and must have seen me as an anomaly in their new set-up. I was then in my late thirties and becoming a statistical quirk in a business whose median age is in the mid-20s. I had finally learned the hard way why ad agency personnel had to be young and attractive. It was, as Stephen could have told me, one of the ways whereby they compensated for struggling to show what clients got for their money. As a senior client (now a colleague) once said to me, 'I love lunching with the agency: it's the only time a gorgeous woman takes me seriously, and *she* pays!' Having seen and thus far survived the carnage that had purged so many of my contemporaries, I knew I'd have to get out of the warm bath some time.

The new chairman, who had been at the forefront of making Saatchi & Saatchi great before setting up not one but two highly visible agencies of his own, did take some avuncular interest in my project and even gave me one or two contacts on whom I should try it out. Encouraged, I suggested that the agency might like to embark on a joint enterprise whereby I could pursue it full time and be out of their hair as concerned the mainstream advertising business. They were not keen, however, presumably having enough on their plate with their new venture. Roger likewise seemed to find that the values we espoused were even more at odds with the new wave of creative flamboyance than in the old days. On top of all this, I'd by then married and fathered two children, who would doubtless prefer to grow up with a contented paterfamilias than a grouch. Everything pointed to a change.

It was around this time that I had lunch with Trevor Beattie, who had long since moved on to Omnicom-owned TBWA, an agency that was already recovering its earlier status as one of London's hottest properties - a process that was to propel Trevor towards celebrity status in British advertising. It was no surprise that he instinctively understood the principles of the new model, having created more than one award-winning campaign that brilliantly captured the essence of the product experience. To him, what I should do next was a simple matter. If ever you need a new home, he said, come and join us. When things came to a head at Ayer, I met Trevor's chairman, Alasdair Ritchie, and the following Monday found myself walking to TBWA's King's Cross office alongside the very railway tracks that would one day carry Harry Potter's Hogwarts Special.

Alasdair turned out to be an extraordinary man, a true country gent in a business for street warriors. A scion of the hunting, shooting 'n' fishing class, he had immaculate diction and perfect manners that belied an entrepreneurial style. (I had first met him years earlier when he came to the sales conference of one of my clients to talk about *My First Toothbrush*, an idea that he had actually persuaded them to manufacture and sell). After the frustrations and upheavals of recent times, it was a delight to be in the company of a person who shared one's passion and, more importantly, was straight as a die when it came to negotiation. It was also fun to be back in the professional company of Trevor. He may have been lampooned in the media from time to time for small crimes like self-publicity and bigger ones like perpetuating the myth of New Labour. But I remember him as the cheeky young talent who could take even the most cerebral brief, feed it back accurately before the words had left your mouth, and come back a month later with creative work that not only met the brief but did so with breathtaking panache. Were there a few more young Beatties in advertising, it would in my opinion be a madder but more rewarding endeavour.

What was less satisfying at first was that, because I joined in such a hurry, there was no real space, and I was given a windowless room that had to be emptied specially for me over the weekend. I worked out of that box for about a year until TBWA took over more floors in the wonderful building that was then their home. Unlike the glass and concrete monstrosities I'd worked in hitherto, this was a converted warehouse adjacent to Battlebridge Basin, a backwater of the Grand Union Canal. At length I was to enjoy a fantastic view of the waterfront out of my large window, the first time I'd had anything much to gaze at since having my corner room in the West End taken away. It brought home to me how conducive a pleasing environment is to productive thought and work; or, conversely, how deleterious a thoughtlessly constructed workplace can be. It was a feeling that would shape my thinking considerably more than a decade later.

The arrangement I struck with TBWA was very simple. They would bear all the set-up costs of creating a division to exploit the new thinking commercially, and in return wanted to share the profits with me on an equitable basis. There were some observers who thought I should simply set up on my own; I thought they were wrong. Going in with TBWA (where, incidentally, half a dozen former Ayer friends now coincidentally worked) gave me access to business-minded advice and support, first-rate creative talent, considerable market intelligence, and secretarial and admin back-up, all of which would have been time-consuming to get and expensive to maintain. They also had a sales promotion subsidiary whose MD was able to give me invaluable advice on how we might tackle the issue of large-scale product sampling. To anyone in a similar situation, I would always recommend consideration of such an arrangement as a way to get started that allows you to concentrate on your business instead of bureaucracy.

It was while I was residing in my cosy little box that Gordon Brown presented his paper and promptly retired. Millward Brown was sold to WPP, where it was to be joined by other massive MR agencies. Having already bought out both JWT and Ogilvy & Mather, WPP would later complete its account-planning-driven colonisation of Madison Avenue by acquiring Young & Rubicam and, to my great amusement, Grey Advertising. After Omnicom, it is today the world's second-largest marketing communications behemoth. I never saw Gordon again after that; he told me he was going off to sail around the world, presumably on the advice of his accountant. I still find it hard to grasp that this genial, kindly man had the toughness to build a wildly successful enterprise and then strike a deal with someone as gargantuan as £28 million-per-annum Sir Martin Sorrell. On the other hand, when Gordon introduced me to the then Mr Sorrell, a chartered accountant by training, I found him almost deferentially polite. Perhaps there is still a way for gentlemen to be outrageously successful in business after all.

The weight of experience

The Millward Brown chapter of this story does have a final twist. When we eventually started running market exercises of the kind prescribed by the new model, we came to have doubts about the dependability of the 'definite intention to purchase' measure. Although still highly regarded today in the ad industry (albeit in variant guises like 'brand preference'), it struck us that a stated intention to purchase is quite different from actual purchasing, even when the intention is definite. Indeed, we even found that claimed intention was sometimes directly at odds with the marketplace sales data we had, for reasons we have only recently divined. What is more, if the truth be told, it still rankled that the importance of experiential accuracy had been underplayed in the MRS paper. It was because of these reservations that I decided to undertake another round of such research. This further study would again be conducted by Millward Brown. This time, however, without Gordon to subsidise it, I set up a syndicated study, paid for by myself and a group of major brand-owners who were invited to enter their own advertising copy. Continuing the classical theme, it was called Project Mnemosyne after the Greek god of memory, for ironic reasons that you might be able to guess.

What we used this time was a heterogeneous mix of ads, from experientially accurate ones to others that were by design plainly hyperbolic. The key measure now was not purchase intention but the harder one of recent actual purchase. Again we awaited the results expectantly, though perhaps no longer with the same bated breath. As anticipated, we achieved a coherent aggregated picture. This time, however, it disguised the fact that there were obvious variations from the pattern of the earlier study. The reason was transparent. The combinations of advertising and sampling where the advertising was weakly experiential simply did not work. For example, a typically over-the-top toiletries ad from L'Oreal actually *depressed* purchases when linked to trial as compared with trial in the absence of seeing an ad, endorsing the findings of Marks and Kamins. Conversely, the most transparent exemplar of the new theory, a decaffeinated coffee ad from Kraft that accurately promised to taste exactly like ordinary coffee, became a seminal demonstration of the effect. Advertising raised recent purchase not one iota, but sampling lifted it from 7% to 11% and a combination of the two achieved all of 17% recent purchase. It is impossible to explain such a result, I would contend, if the effect were merely the additive effect of the two activities. Clearly something else was going on inside people's heads.

Aside from sharing them with the sponsors, we decided to keep these results to ourselves, for reasons that will become apparent in the next chapter. We were now satisfied, as were our Millward Brown counterparts, that we had the solid experimental evidence we needed. What it said was that, even if the advertising models based on benefit-related differentiation had some other value, in the matter of creating behavioural change they were drastically inferior to a model of accurately primed experience. Like anyone with a curious mind would do, I became increasingly anxious to understand better what exactly was going on at the psychological level. The patterns we had been witnessing were nigh on impossible to explain within any previous paradigm.

As we have seen, most of the suppositions of marketing and advertising theory were based on the assumption that consumers' choices are the result of rational decision-making, led by conscious high-level processing. But this new phenomenon seemed to chime much better with ideas proposed by researchers like Professor Robert Zajonc of the Stanford Brain Research Institute, who had suggested in 1980, rather radically at the time, that emotion has the capacity to influence behaviour in a manner that bypasses rational cognitive processes[10]. If prior expectation could have a significant effect on the nature of one's subsequent exposure to a product, then the precise nature of the expectation was potentially a critical factor, and we needed to understand it as well as we could. What we faced, however, was the reality that, once we took investigation away from the cognitive realm in which MR happily sat, we were dealing with emotional undercurrents beyond the realm of consciousness. It was bound to be an interesting journey, in all senses.

The issue was given timely new impetus in 1994 by the publication of *Descartes' Error*[11] by neuroscientist Professor Antonio Damasio, of which I was sent a copy by a kindly psychologist in the week of its publication. What Damasio did with the skill of a good story-teller was explain to a wide audience how the brain functions as a physiological unit to shape the behaviour that will steer us safely from conception to procreation. Since the brain plainly cannot cope with all the world throws at it by simply thinking everything through, it must contain some other efficient machinery for dealing with the 'blooming, buzzing confusion' of reality, as the great psychologist William James expressed it[12]. Damasio emphasised the 'somatic markers' we attach to memories so that, when they are activated by subsequent experiences, we are able to draw on them rapidly for guidance on what action to take. So, for example, when a man in a bow-tie tries to sell us something, we don't reason, 'It is possible, among a plethora of other possibilities, that this man is sporting a bow-tie in order to communicate to me a sense that he is a respectable member of the mercantile class who can be depended upon to deliver on his promises, whereas in reality it is quite conceivable that he could be a cunning villain who may wish to lull me into such a false sense of security, although it's also possible that...' Instead, something just says to us, 'Let's get out of here'. That something is a feeling, and it is the product of a somatic marker that's been put down by all our previous experiences of bow-tied salesmen.

What we are getting into here is *heuristics*, the several dozen unconscious rules of thumb humans have acquired to help us get by. Whether they are a good or a bad thing depends on whether you are a glass half-full or half-empty type. It's a matter of fierce dispute among neuroscientists, psychologists and economists who converge in the academic discipline known as Judgement and Decision Making (JDM). Some emphasise the fast, frugal brain we enjoy because of these heuristics, while others concern themselves with the biases we are consequently heir to. In reality, both camps are right. The brain gets through a remarkable amount of work sufficiently well to enable us to function in a complex, dangerous world; yet much of what we do is outside of our conscious control, and the choices we make, being processed only at the most primal level, can easily work against us. Ask the police who shot dead an innocent Brazilian on the London Underground for no other reason than that he looked suitably foreign.

Heuristics are named from the Greek word *heurisko* meaning 'discover', indicating the centrality of previous experience in forming future behaviour. Where we had got to by the time of Project Mnemosyne was an understanding that any business would take a giant step forward if it obsessed itself solely with enabling potential customers to experience it. What especially intrigued me, however, was the way that communications could be engineered to affect perceptions of that experience. Expectation and experience looked to me like two sides of the same coin. But Professor Deighton was not the first to put into words the idea that experience somehow completes a circle begun by expectation. Somewhat earlier, the idea had been captured like this: 'Nothing ever becomes real till it is experienced - even a proverb is no proverb to you till your life has illustrated it'. The words of a top academic, perhaps? Or one of those public-speaking gurus? No, it was the poet John Keats who wrote them[13]. Nor was it the only time he proved himself an adept marketing theorist. He also wrote that we hate poetry that has a 'palpable design' on us, prompting Professor John Sutherland to comment[14] that this *'is why we inherently hate advertising, because we know they're telling us lies or, if not telling us lies, they're trying to get us to do something not for our good but for their good'*. It took only a handful of experiments nearly a couple of centuries later to prove Keats right.

This whole process of discovery had followed my reading of the Deighton paper almost like the unfolding of a good detective story. What had impressed me about it all was the way that the scientific method not only addressed questions that MR couldn't even consider; it also provided evidence you couldn't argue with. The enormous advantage we had by the mid-'nineties was that, reassured by Project Mnemosyne, a rather tidy handful of heavyweight packaged-goods marketers were taking a real interest in what we were doing and giving us the chance to try things out in the real world. The giant leap we were able to take was in sheer scale. Where academics traditionally work with samples of at best a couple of hundred students, and Millward Brown had given us access to a thousand members of a market-research panel, we were to be able to test out ideas on literally millions of members of the public. To anyone who enjoys experimentation, it was like being given a laboratory-full of guinea pigs.

Before long, we were seeing things we knew nobody had seen before, and that posed yet more questions about the apparently unfathomable workings of the limbic system that is home to our emotions. We learned more and more about the gap between the well-attested knowledge of academic psychologists and the stubbornly defended beliefs of professional marketers. We also observed the lengths that some of the latter are prepared to go to in order to ring-fence their expertise. But I'm getting ahead of myself. Let's rewind to that little box of mine, and some of the unprecedented events that unfolded from the time when it became my daytime home.

4
Fast to the Future

An inauspicious start

'It's rubbish', came the voice down the phone line. 'A total disaster. I'm sorry, but you need to know'. The voice belonged to Nick, director of one of the marketing services agencies retained by Dairy Crest, owners of the Clover brand of margarine. At the time, he was standing in front of a manned display stand we had erected outside of a supermarket in East Anglia. It was one of many that between them were distributing half a million samples of the product spread on a morsel of bread, all to be accomplished within four days. In the three days preceding, over 70% of the population of the region had been exposed to a TV advertisement communicating the psychological core of the product experience: the banal truth that, even though you were probably sceptical of the idea, it actually did taste quite a lot like butter. Now they had a chance to discover it was no lie. The sums said that about one in five of the populace of East Anglia would undergo an enhanced experience, and if only a tenth of these went on to buy, the brand would leapfrog its nearest rival. It was our first foray into 'face-to-face' product sampling, it was being done with an intensity seldom if ever seen before, and Nick didn't like what he was seeing.

As recipient of the call, I was naturally horrified. The reports I'd been getting from our team were admittedly mixed. A gale was blowing in from the North Sea that had made manipulating the large graphic panels comprising the display stand somewhat hazardous. Constant rain to complement the darkness that descended in mid-afternoon every day was also keeping shoppers away. This was after all mid-February; hardly the ideal time for such activity, but the client had confirmed the job on Christmas Eve and wanted it to happen literally as soon as possible. But otherwise, I'd been told, things seemed to be going fine, and clearer weather was forecast. Nick was on the scene because we'd agreed with the client to visit between us all the supermarkets where we were sampling and assess the activity in a standard questionnaire. As the man responsible for much of the company's regular field-marketing activity, Nick had volunteered to send out a few of his own people to take a good look. Now I was getting the benefit of his expert opinion.

That we were undertaking this absurdly ambitious project at all was down to a man called Barnett Fletcher. The first thing I'd done on joining TBWA was met the business development director of the Omnicom group's big field-marketing agency. When I'd explained what I wanted to do in terms of numbers, speed and experientially oriented communications, he'd more or less scoffed and suggested I stick to what I knew about. (Despite his conservatism, I noticed a couple of years ago that his agency had taken to describing itself as a pioneer of 'experiential' marketing, presumably in the same way that the big banks pioneered the new fiscal prudence). Fortunately I spotted in *Marketing Week* an ad doing something advertising indisputably does well: announcing the existence of a solution to a problem. The solution was Barnett Fletcher Promotions (BFP), a company that liked to say yes. Barnett was certainly true to his word. As I was to discover, he is a bit of an adrenaline junkie, who used to drive motorbikes and race Ferraris at Brands Hatch for fun, and more recently was selling power-boat experiences in the Mediterranean. When I told him what I wanted, he said simply, 'No problem', as he always does. Fortunately he also had the good sense to surround himself with people with an almost autistic attention to detail and the honesty to tell you when something really is mission impossible.

What Barnett taught me is the value of congenital risk-takers to society. Without them, you don't even contemplate some scenarios on the grounds of good sense. What I was asking Barnett to do on paper was such a big ask that most wouldn't bother; it was too much trouble. Barnett, on the other hand, took the same stance as Kennedy vis-à-vis landing on the moon: we are going to do this, gentlemen, so now find a way. And they invariably did. The great thing about the operations run by Barnett's protégés was that they didn't just manage to look, sound and feel good, with attractive staff and well-made rigs; they also were executed impeccably in terms of logistics. I recall as if it were yesterday one briefing session for uniformed personnel running into hundreds that had all the precision of a military exercise. The Clover operation however was our first together, so I had reason to heed Nick's warning. The next morning, I got up early to drive out to Norwich and take a good look for myself. Whatever problems Nick had seen, I had to conclude that they had been put right, because everything seemed to be running smoothly. Nevertheless, I went home with a heavy heart. If the activity was running well, the product just didn't seem to be selling in the quantities I'd anticipated.

The reason became apparent when we reconvened a couple of weeks later to review the early results. It looked as though we were selling the *product* rather well, but not the *brand*. The key beneficiary of the activity had been the supermarkets' own-label look-alikes, which were on sale at a fraction of the price. This taught us early on a critical lesson: that there is little point in stimulating sales of anything if your business-model basics are flawed. Although the exercise performed sufficiently well that the marketing director invited us back to do some conspicuously more successful operations for another of their brands - a flavoured milk drink called Frijj - I have to admit that I had put this one down as a disappointment until, two years later, he told us about the longer-term analysis he'd performed.

It turned out that the East Anglia region had improved from one of Clover's worst-performing regions to the very best, and also proved more responsive to subsequent advertising than all other regions, for reasons that would become very apparent to us in years to come. He could only attribute the difference to the work we'd done. The news can't have pleased Nick. He probably hoped he'd seen the last of us when, at the review meeting, one of our team cheekily put up a chart showing the mark out of ten that he and his colleagues had awarded the activity: fully two points lower than everyone else's, even including the verdict of the unsentimental Dairy Crest salesmen. I'll never forget him trying to explain himself; he actually *stammered*.

A long, hard haul

You may be surprised to find the narrator of a supposed success story even mentioning a set-back, let alone starting with one. I have good reasons. First, I warned you up front that this was to be an honest account. Second, if you ever want to have a crack yourself at exploiting the thinking in this book, you'll need to know what pitfalls you are likely to be exposed to. And third, it's important to appreciate that creating the best mousetrap in the world is no guarantee of wealth and fame. Whatever you read in optimistic American business books, no one setting up a new enterprise should have any illusions about the barriers to success presented by good old, bad old human nature. Every entrepreneur - and, indeed, every successful person in any sphere - can tell you that there's a lot of private rough to go with the public smooth, and it's the rough that makes you strong. Let me tell you more about both.

What Nick had been choking over was an early example of what I'd designated as the 'Focused Advertising/Sampling Technique', or FAST marketing. Though yet another acronym in a world that's full of them, it was at least memorable, extensible to other 'Fast' tools, and available to trademark internationally. The Clover exercise was not actually the first instance of FAST marketing the world had seen. That honour went, after a fashion, to Trebor Bassett, my former advertising client. A marketing manager there had asked me to submit a proposal for conducting a 'FAST market' on one of his smaller brands, Bassett's Wine Gums. After a long interval without hearing back, I learned that he was going ahead with 'something similar' but with an 'improved' sampling methodology; consequently he saw no need to pay me any fees. When I politely questioned whether such behaviour was quite appropriate - the company's new owners Cadbury Schweppes being very hot on corporate probity - he offered a token amount for my input but decided the results would be too sensitive to reveal. Fortunately someone else involved thought his actions left something to be desired, and helpfully leaked the results to me. Although the methodology he'd used was critiqued by the operations director I later hired in language even more derogatory than Nick's, the principle had shone through. It was a palpable hit.

Such conduct set the tone for much of what my team was to see in subsequent years by way of jiggery-pokery. Our relationship with Dairy Crest would ultimately become a victim, when an incoming marketing chief canned all ongoing work including ours (we settled out of court) before leaving shortly afterwards; end of story. Diageo, with whom we were to achieve some splendid results, hired a new head of marketing from America who despised her predecessor and all his works and, to get us out of the door, had our results recalculated on the basis that all sales increments under 10% or after six weeks or both were invalid; end of story. And then there was the marketer who disliked being told that she'd be wasting her money launching a soft drink in the winter, and went ahead regardless with an event agency's zany interpretation of our thinking; I can only relate that she was soon dispensing her expertise in another arena.

But it wasn't always so much conspiracy as cock-up. There was the manufacturer of a new household product who pressed the button on a FAST market when he still only had 7% distribution; we had told him a minimum of 75% was mandatory. Or the marketing manager who, determined to make the most of a FAST marketing-versus-control test, ran a price promotion immediately before the activity, creating out-of-stocks and hopelessly muddying the waters. But the prize for knuckle-headed machismo goes to the man who, politely asked by a body that oversees door-to-door sample distributions for written confirmation that his product was as safe as he claimed, sent a letter demanding that they get on with it or he'd see them in court. Needless to say, they told him to get lost, and his action culminated in a huge insurance claim. You get the general picture.

That's enough brickbats for the moment; it's time for some bouquets. When I first started talking publicly about FAST marketing, it was the kind of radical new concept you might call sexy. Not long after I arrived at TBWA, Alasdair fixed for me to meet a marketing journalist whom he expected would be interested in it; and sure enough he was, to the extent of submitting a gleaming write-up to *Marketing* magazine headlined 'New route to ad effectiveness?'[1] The editor shared at least some of his enthusiasm, and placed it on an early right-hand page. It doesn't sound a lot, but there was my picture alongside those of Gordon Brown and a senior Kraft Foods marketer called Phil Smith who later found fame at Camelot, and I sensed thereafter that the idea had gained the sort of establishment legitimacy it might otherwise have lacked. But it was no more than a start. There's a big gap between sowing and reaping. The worst thing about the early days in my little box-room was not lack of interest but lack of commitment. Almost universally among the would-be clients who liked the idea, the parting shot would be, 'Come back when you've got some case studies I can show the board'. It's a story I've heard many times since from aspirant entrepreneurs, and though a good salesman will tell you that you have to find ways around it, I was darned if I could think of them. I tried everything I knew.

When you try, try and try again, and a business just won't fly, it's easy to incline towards despondency. I never did, not least because I was surrounded by people egging me on, both at home and in the office. I was told all the inspirational stories of how perseverance pays off: Colonel Sanders finally getting a buyer for his recipe at the 1,010th attempt; Churchill returning from the political wilderness to greatness after decades of being ostracised for his admonishments; Ross Perot's warning that failed entrepreneurs tend to give up when they're on the one-yard line and don't realise how close they are. I fully subscribe to the idea that persistence is critical. If you stay in the game long enough and your idea is as good as you believe (an important 'if', obviously, and the reason why you need proof - for yourself, as well as for others), then your time must eventually come, unless you are cruelly unlucky. But you have to make your own luck, and making sure others know about you seldom hurts.

FAST in practice

When FAST marketing finally did take off after fifteen months, there was no obvious reason for it; suddenly I got an order, and then two more in the following week, and that was when the floodgates opened. I'd already taken on a handful of staff by this time, and was able to bring in more pretty quickly. Even so, the workload took us by surprise, and I had a spell where I was working all hours, catching up on financials in bed at night, and literally getting my exercise by walking to the bank every day to deposit the cheques. It went on like that for some months, with not so much as a day off. It's easy to imagine when a young business is going well that overwork is a temporary matter; but, even if you are fit and healthy, the strain can take a toll on your ability to perform. I didn't realise what harm I was doing myself until the summer evening when I met an old friend for a drink. He told me that, as I'd come along the river bank towards him, he hadn't recognised me; I looked like I'd just run a marathon. Now, one thing that doesn't inspire confidence among clients or staff is a boss who's worn out. I took a holiday straight away and made sure in future to match the intake of work more realistically to my ability to service it properly within a normal working day.

This experience was to have an impact on our entire manner of doing business. We decided we would not be open to all offers, but accept work that we'd enjoy and rid ourselves as discreetly as we could of any client that made our job less rather than more fun. With the exception of one or two relationships that for assorted random reasons dragged on longer than any of us would have wanted, we adhered to the principle faithfully ever after. I realise it's not a choice every business can afford to make; yet, paradoxically, the fact of being selective with our clientele seemed only to prompt more interest. And I seriously believe it was because the team had a sense of doing what we wanted to do, rather than having to, that the quality of results was positive from the off. FAST markets were very work-intensive, from planning through execution to evaluation; but we thrived on the pressure because the day on which the results became public was always uniquely exciting, almost invariably the source of emotions from satisfaction to triumph, and particularly rewarding to share with a client you truly liked.

It was when we'd garnered half a dozen good case studies that Alasdair introduced me to Alan Mitchell, whom I still consider to be the most insightful marketing journalist I've encountered. I must have spent a couple of hours with him at our first meeting in 1995 and, if its purpose had been to share with him the story so far, I came away with a whole bunch of new ideas to consider and books to read. The reason was that, when he had asked me why I thought simply matching expectations changed behaviour on such a large scale, I'd speculated that perhaps it formed a bond of trust between manufacturer and potential customer. This had prompted him to refer me to Robert Axelrod's *The Evolution of Co-operation*[2] and similar works that were already exploring issues such as empathy and fairness, reciprocity, and the formation of networks of mutually supportive individuals. It was to prove as influential an encounter for my future thinking as any I can recall.

Alan gave FAST marketing a prominent and sympathetic write-up, first in *The Times*[3] and subsequently in the marketing press[4]. At first this seemed an unmitigated good, certainly in terms of getting the word about. Trevor came to my office to tell me that, while in 'Signor Zilli', the Soho restaurant that by then acted almost as staff canteen to the creative industries, he'd overheard two senior businessmen at the next table talking about us in glowing terms. It felt at the time like we'd really made it. In fact, it was a harbinger of bad tidings. It was about six months later that a client rang from Madrid to say that his ad agency had just been trying to sell him a 'bastardised version' of our thinking. You can't stop imitation, but they actually were calling it 'FAST marketing', in breach of our trademark. Almost immediately thereafter, a former colleague told me that the American head office of a famous soft-drinks company had circulated a memo asserting the model as the author's own creation. It taught us that the Thomas Edison spirit of artful emulation was alive and well and perched on our doorstep.

In consequence, the Fast Marketing company drew the curtains on the work we did, and thereafter became as secretive as any consultancy in London. In retrospect this was a pity, because I'm still left wondering how big the business might have become if we'd remained more public. I did still manage to share the basic thinking face to face with more than 6,000 business people from around the world during the 1990's, in consequence of which we built as prestigious a list of packaged goods clientele (including Arla Foods, Bass Brewers, Coca-Cola Schweppes, Diageo, and Elida Faberge just to start the alphabet) as one could hope to see. Over the course of a decade, we therefore had access to many of the most famous brands there are; and, just as interestingly, their marketers, their agencies, and the thinking that surrounds them. We also undertook the best part of a hundred in-market exercises - about one a month - all of them carefully monitored and regularly incorporating test variables that enabled us to add to our knowledge as we went along. It was a unique eye-opener.

Before I reveal what we learned, let me take pause at this point to recapitulate what we used to do. The FAST marketing technique used intensive TV advertising for three or four days to set a population-wide expectation. This was not any expectation, but one that would inevitably tally with what the viewer would shortly experience through accelerated product trial while the advertising memory was still recent. Over the following three or four days, a large proportion of the populace would then be offered the chance to have the experience for themselves, immediately preceded by a subtle restatement of what the experience would be like. What happened in consequence, we believed, was that the actual product experience found a ready berth in the brain's neural structure already planted there by advertising whose low-impact nature had enabled it to bypass conscious scrutiny. It was like attaching a discreet bracket to a wall, onto which an appliance will neatly fit.

This marrying up of expectation and experience appeared fundamental to changing behaviour, yet was the thing that the orthodox marketing model conspicuously failed to do. Indeed, the orthodoxy neglected not only the role of expectations but also, critically, the all-importance of the experience itself. The FAST marketing approach to TV copy development was entirely different. On the understanding that advertising is in fact, in Professor Ehrenberg's description, a 'weak force'[5], it was expected to play a subservient (albeit crucial) role in FAST marketing campaigns. What this demanded was advertising that would establish the mental template as unobtrusively as possible, so that customers would not grapple with it cognitively. Its job was solely to slip in under the prospective customer's mental radar and thus, by evoking the product experience, to enhance trial of the free product sample that would be engineered a very short time afterwards.

Unsurprisingly, the approach met resistance from all parties who made their money from the orthodox model. We had umpteen battles with ad agencies over the nature of the advertising to be run in FAST markets, sometimes because the account team could see no value in copy that offered no benefit or big brand idea, and sometimes when the agency demanded to be the sole arbiter on creative work, especially if the source of the brief was perceived as a rival for the client's estimation. Few media agencies were much different. This cloud did however have a silver lining. It gave us ample opportunity to propose marketplace tests of new model against old. Over time we built a formidable library of knowledge gained from testing FAST marketing against any number of controls, from brand advertising alone through other combinations of advertising and sampling to straightforward sales-hiking promotions. In the account that follows, I have had to withhold the identity of the specific brands for contractual reasons, but you will get an idea of the sorts of lessons we learned.

The conclusive proof

The basic picture of what we came to expect was exemplified by an established but under-performing chewing-gum brand owned by Unilever. Its marketing majored entirely on its dental benefit. Our research established however that the core of the experience was part sensory, part psychological: a burst of invigoration that cleared the head of accumulated world-weariness. A TV ad was specially made to suggest this feeling, and a small sample packet of the product distributed door-to-door across the nation. Sales immediately almost doubled in size. Interestingly, none of the increment was lost in the following period. Such an extraordinary retention of the effect gainsaid any possibility that the effect was simply promotional. Analysis of results by store group demonstrated unequivocally that growth was behaviour-driven and not due to distribution gains. What we had done was simply this: we had established a new buying habit.

This test, being national, did not contain a regional control. A more typical test featured a range extension of a famous frozen-food brand owned by McCain. The activity was first carried out on a regional basis, the sample product being cooked outside of supermarkets. The control was a comparable region with orthodox TV deployment. The advertising campaign raised sales by not very much, and then probably only in consequence of high stock levels orchestrated by the sales force. FAST marketing in contrast raised sales higher by a factor of about six, and maintained the increment in subsequent periods, which suggested strong levels of repeat purchase. In other words, the FAST marketing had again established a new behaviour. Brand attitudes were not measured but, on Festinger's principle that attitudes follow behaviour, one might comfortably predict that the activity also beat the conventional activity even on its home territory.

One of the perennial challenges facing us FAST marketers was that, because of the exigencies of decision-taking deadlines, results were often tracked only for a period of eight weeks or so, the minimum required for most packaged goods to establish levels of uplift and likely settle-down levels. Mercifully there existed a good cadre of clients eager to satisfy themselves as to the longer-term picture. One very good example of sustained measurement yielding valuable learning featured a national price promotion that virtually doubled sales of a Unilever toiletry brand for a period, before falling back but later recovering in the Christmas sales period. The addition of TV advertising at first pushed up sales by an additional 31% points, but the pattern thereafter was very similar. FAST marketing on the other hand added four times as much as advertising to the promotional effect. Moreover, sales were consistently maintained at a much higher level thereafter, a pronounced upswing at Christmas attesting to high levels of retention of the behavioural effect even in a notoriously fickle market.

An exceptionally professional piece of long-term tracking was applied in the case of a relatively exotic Kraft Foods beverage whose manager stayed in the job for an unusually long time and showed proper determination to yield a good piece of science. After a test had been conducted in one region, she ensured that all subsequent brand advertising in that region - including over two thousand TV ratings over the next thirty-six months - remained virtually identical to that in all other regions, enabling an accurate long-term comparison. The outcome revealed a strikingly steady retention of the initial increment: a differential of 17% that barely wavered. This seems as solid evidence as one could ask for that the effects of FAST marketing were not tactical but strategic, and consequently enduring.

Along the way we gained excellent empirical proof of the importance of accurate priming. Kellogg routinely undertook research to check out the quality of advertising copy before it went into production. Their ad agency's first response to our brief had patently been designed to grab attention in the orthodox manner; but, despite its strong attempt to be different, it didn't do well at giving a realistic sense of what the product was really like to use. Their second effort, written more closely to the product experience brief, performed far better at this in pre-testing; almost twice as well. What was truly extraordinary, however, was what happened when we got subjects to rate a sample of the product immediately after they'd been exposed to the test films. After viewing the second (more true-to-life) ad, almost *twice as many* people in a matched cell said they 'really liked' the taste of the product. They were also able to give more specific, experientially based reasons why they liked it. In other words, the very way the product was perceived - the so-called 'quale' - had been substantively changed solely by the fact that expectations were better borne out by reality.

Subsequently to this we encountered a real-world example of the same phenomenon. We designed a standard FAST market in one region in which intensive TV advertising for a Diageo product was followed by product sampling; but there was a difference. In one part of the region we ran a specially created 'experiential' ad, as true to the product experience as we could make it on a limited budget. In the rest, however, we used a split-transmission facility to broadcast a different ad that had been designed to position the brand in a classic 'interest-status' manner. Because the media exposure of both ads was identical, it was a perfect test of the difference made by the only variable, the advertising content. The performance of the two ads was gauged with conventional MR. As expected, the orthodox brand-building copy won hands down on key measures like brand awareness, ad awareness, and proven ad recall. It was also considered more interesting and better-shot. Intriguingly, the experiential copy's only area of relative strength was its appetising communication of what the product was like to consume. The conventional view, however, would be that it did not get past first base.

The hard sales data told a different story. In the areas where the brand-building ad was seen, the brand's sales performance rose by 12.9% against a control region over the 16 weeks following the activity. In comparison, the areas where the experiential copy had run gained 22.3% over the same period. Other data showed that this differential continued into subsequent weeks, making a massive commercial difference to the outcome. Now, how could that happen? How could an ostensibly mediocre ad not just match a 'superior' piece of brand advertising in the marketplace, but substantially outperform it? One cannot tell exactly, because orthodox research tools are not able to ask the right questions. On the strength of Marks & Kamins, however, we could confidently speculate that the unthreatening, non-selling and undifferentiated copy had managed to do something the more obvious brand advertising failed to do: it had slipped in beneath the cognitive defences that normally screen out information that conflicts with existing beliefs, become lodged at back of mind or even on an unconscious level, and inevitably been borne out by reality. The ensuing 'eureka effect' provided a sufficiently powerful affective shock to provoke an enduring change of behaviour.

A very mature Nestlé food product yielded an even more emphatic example of the same phenomenon. We were called in because the brand team was spending a small fortune annually on advertising just to maintain its current market share. What we discovered from our research was that the core of the experience had next to nothing to do with the personality-endorsed nutrition claim of the advertising. Instead, it was all about the product's plain rawness. I well recall the old-school research manager getting very agitated about the idea of evoking this prosaic reality in the advertising, but he was overruled by his boss. We did however have to construct an immaculately controlled test, in which two TV regions received *pro rata* an identical amount of television exposure and product sampling. The sole difference was the TV copy: the conventional nutrition story in one region, and an evocation of the plain rawness in the other. After three months, sales were up in the conventional control by 5% - itself a creditable result, to be fair. But in the FAST marketing region they had risen by 10%. More strikingly, after six months they were still 7% up. Conversely, in the control they were now 9% *down,* suggesting that the original uplift had been a mere promotional spike; it was only FAST marketing that had paved the way for repeat purchasing. Since this product had been previously tried by around 95% of the population, it belied the suggestion that FAST marketing worked simply by inducing initial trial.

By such methods, we garnered plenty of empirical evidence that refuted all efforts to explain FAST marketing as a variant of orthodox theory. For example, it was said more than once that the activity produced results merely in consequence of exposing consumers to 'integrated' activity (i.e. both advertising and product trial); yet, when late delivery of a Reckitt-Benckiser product obliged us in one region to delay the sample distribution by just one week, the sales uplift dramatically fell *by half,* emphasising the importance in the new model of marrying up trial with a mental template still fresh in memory. Equally, increasing the product sampling density from 30% of the population to 40% did not lift the sales increment of a Kraft Foods product by a third but *threefold.* This demolished the theory that FAST marketing worked on the sales promotional basis of predictable conversion levels; the effects were more like emergent behaviour, such as happens when a small addition of heat causes milk to boil over.

Likewise, a Beiersdorf toiletry range, in which a number of different strategies were tried out for their effect on sales shortly after launch, yielded a rank order of FAST marketing, advertising plus sampling, and advertising only, with increments in the first four weeks of ca 690%, 320% and 260% respectively – a variance that bore little correlation with the amount of activity involved.

The longer FAST effect

The belief of us FAST marketing practitioners at the time was that its effects were large and enduring because we had actually created a lasting bond, or new belief if you like, in the purchaser's head. In this connection, something that proved truly interesting over the years was what we learned about FAST marketing's value in kick-starting commercially successful marketing campaigns. Thanks to a week of FAST marketing, one old and neglected household brand grew to five times its former size, falling back to around three times bigger six months later. After a single burst of orthodox TV advertising, however, it then resumed its peak and stayed there for eight weeks afterwards. This must have been a highly effective ad, one might think; yet, in a comparable control region, the *same* ad at the *same* weight put on only 15%, and decayed almost to nothing. How can one account for that? The answer is that it's another case of preaching to the converted. If suddenly the world is full not of people that don't give a fig about you and your brand, but recent converts who are quietly passionate about your product, they will *listen.* And if you give them reasons why the perhaps non-rational choice they've made is good, they will *believe.*

By transforming the mindset of populations, one can create a fertile seed-bed for traditional advertising messages that should transform payback. Psychological inertia can be likened to city walls, a bane when you're on the outside but, once you're in, something to be thankful for. When a consumer has had a eureka effect with your product or service, it is very much easier to sustain his or her habitual purchasing (as opposed to the tenuous concept of 'loyalty') with gentle reminders of the original experience that caused them to adopt, and weaving in information that helps cement the relationship. The kind of message called for by such sustenance tactics is necessarily far less aggressive than that depended on by orthodox marketers to create conversions. What's needed is something we called a 'bunch of flowers' strategy: not a hard sell, or indeed any kind of sell, but a gentle reminder and reinforcement of why they 'fell in love' in the first place. It's all that's necessary to gain that ongoing leverage that forms the substrate of demand-led growth.

As well as the selfish business angle, there is a cultural dimension to all this. Just contemplate the social benefit of such an approach on an industry-wide scale: no more voices of god, talking heads, side-by-side comparisons, testimonials and graphics of molecules, but instead an entertaining and comforting swathe of friendly reassurances. There would still be more than enough activity going on to keep the media in shoe leather, but without consumers continually reaching for the off-button. Could it happen? Certainly our evidence said so. Another household brand gave us a spectacular example of the principle at its most simple. It trebled in size and remained that way by courtesy of a sustained but low-key pulse campaign of orthodox advertising that started immediately afterwards. Intriguingly, it came from a company that is notorious around the world for its normally patronising old-school advertising; you'll have to guess which.

Such real-world activities were invariably designed to provide the client with a real commercial benefit at the same time as shedding light on the key principles involved. Though they made for impressive exhibits in their own right, we were always conscious that an aggregated picture would be a trump card over the industry-wide analyses that some pundits had attempted in advertising, with feeble results. (One such was Ephron and Pollak's finding that non-packaged goods advertisers on average recovered only 87% of their adspend after a year; for packaged goods brands, the figure was just 54%[6]). Roger had a good bash at it, but had to conclude that there was too much variability between measures to infer an overall score without taking liberties. He did however testify to three strong categories of growth that corresponded to brand maturity. New brands would typically double in size for the following eight weeks; mature brands would grow by 30-40% in the same period; and old brands with high market penetration might grow by around 10%. Such figures, though only a rule of thumb, make interesting reading alongside conventional marketing results.

Implicit in all of the above is of course one major assumption: that short-term sales effects matter. This needs addressing, because proponents of the orthodox model today tend to deny that they do. Analyses like Ephron and Pollak's are generally met with a shrug of the shoulders and the riposte that long-term effects are what really matter; short-term sales effects are for salesmen to muster. Now, long-term sales are indeed important; but you will struggle to find more evidence of general long-term payback from conventional advertising than you will in the short-term. There are naturally case studies that have genuinely paid back at length if not in the short term, but it is plainly not proven that campaigns that fail to pay back in the short term *generally* do so later. Longitudinal studies conducted by big consultancies on behalf of vested interests may actually be honest endeavours, but it is hard to be convinced by any calculations that depend on hopeful black-box assumptions. It is also misleading to pick out the successful brands and point to their heavy advertising spend if it is sales that create advertising rather than vice versa - a likelihood indicated by both the 'percentage of sales' model for advertising budget-setting and the fact that advertising falls during recessions but recovers afterwards. I prefer to trust the maxim of one client, the general manager of a large food company: 'If the sales effects aren't visible to begin with', she opined, 'they probably aren't bloody there'.

What seemed to us more likely was that a device that enabled customers to have an honestly primed experience of a product was substantially more likely to have them change their habitual behaviour - and therefore their attitudes - than any number of clumsy efforts to 'persuade' them, no matter how well hidden these efforts might be behind brand gloss. This is not to suggest that FAST marketing was a universal panacea. It depended on the activity being carried out precisely according to plan, and we discovered the hard way how easy it was to curtail the sales effects by, for example, failing to achieve sufficient television coverage, running inappropriate TV copy, or delaying the product sampling activity. It was the first of these that would ultimately lead us to pull the plug on our FAST marketing activities. The dramatic growth of digital technology was to scatter TV viewing across scores of different media, and leave media agencies complaining that they could no longer deliver the blitzkrieg TV campaigns we depended on. By that time, however, our thinking had moved a long way ahead. We had been fortunate to enjoy a ten-year window of opportunity, which now seems an eternity in today's breakneck media world. What we had observed was either larger or much larger behavioural effects, and a much higher rate of dependability. If ever FAST marketing didn't work, it was a surprise. When it was ordinary, it still beat the best of the rest. When it worked well, it was better than anything we could think of.

Several decades ago, advertising was likened to the wind on the sea: able to ruffle the surface, but no match for the strong currents beneath. Results like the ones we obtained showed what is possible when wind and tide are pulling in the same direction. If only all marketing campaigns worked like that. Such findings have potentially profound implications. Yet they proved barely more than the entrance hall to a new mode of thinking. FAST marketing had been a device for effecting a refined version of the Integrated Information Response Model in the marketplace. But the underpinning psychological principle was altogether broader and deeper, and had to be exploitable in more ways than one. Just as advertising is not the only means to set up an expectation, so too there are more ways to engineer an experience than product sampling alone. And then there was a much, much bigger question: just how far could we take this whole experience thing?

5

The Lesson of Experience

The Experience experience

The Potteries is an industrial region in the English Midlands from which are sprung some of the most famous makes of china in the world. It is also the birthplace of Richard Grisdale, whom I knew as an erudite Ayer copywriter in the same mould (if not the same office) as Salman Rushdie. I shall never forget the miserable look on his face when I called on him in his office one Monday morning. He had recently penned a poster campaign for Air France suggesting that the airline was the simple difference between a romantic trip to Paris and a dismal weekend in Stoke-on-Trent, the conurbation that forms the Potteries' heart. As soon as it was posted in that particular town, the local newspaper went ballistic, especially when the editor learned that Richard was one of the town's own sons. It mounted a campaign urging locals not only to boycott Air France but also to ostracise this traitor. Richard, always the mildest-mannered of men, looked at me balefully as I surveyed the front page pinned on his wall. 'It was only meant to be a joke', he said, 'but they've gone and pronounced a Potwa on me'.

Fortunately Richard survived his ordeal, and went on to have a distinctive bearing on the marketing lexicon. The occasion was a lunch on November 12th, 1993 at the Great Nepalese restaurant opposite London's Euston Station. Now at TBWA, I was keen to catch up with him; but I also had an ulterior motive. FAST marketing was proving a useful name for the tool we were using to exploit the basic principle of primed experiences. But what should we call the principle itself: the model that valued such experiences over persuasive communications? I had been using the term 'non-orthodox', but this was really just a statement of what it wasn't rather than anything positive. Knowing that Richard had been educated in the classics, I invited him along to ask him what Latin or Greek words might suggest an English adjective to encapsulate the credo. His recommendation, based on the Greek *empirikeion* (= 'experience'), was 'empirical'. On my way back to the office, I felt uncomfortable that the word was already in common usage in business with a quite distinct meaning. But Richard had also mentioned the Latin equivalent, *experientia*, which suggested to me something altogether unfamiliar to marketers: 'experiential'. Certainly I'd never encountered it before in a business context, and nor had anyone at TBWA. So 'experiential' it was.

The term was immediately adopted by the FAST marketing team in our published literature and new business presentations, the first to hear it probably being a former client of mine, Claire Watson, then at Haagen Dazs, who went on to act as Director-General of the Marketing Society. We incorporated it in our daily vocabulary in the formulation *experiential marketing* to discriminate our own activity from brand marketing; and it was enshrined in the term *experiential core.* This was a crucial device that we used to describe the facet(s) of a product most saliently identified by a trialist. Pinning this down was crucial because, in order to ensure accurate priming, we had to evoke it accurately in both the television advertising copy and in the visual and verbal communications incorporated in the product trialing activity. I well remember the occasion on which I formally unveiled the 'E' word in front of a large audience of marketers, the inaugural 'Creating Product Trial' conference in London on October 10th, 1994, which we organised along with Millward Brown and various representatives of the product sampling industry. Speaking immediately after Andy Farr, who again related the story of Project Janus, I remember expressing the grand ambition that our new philosophy should one day become the byword for behavioural change.

In the audience was the man whom I personally credit with inventing 'experiential marketing' in its present familiar guise: Barnett Fletcher, the aforementioned risk-taking product-sampler. I say that because, when I first met him, he had already performed three or four exercises for Nestlé involving intensive product-sampling at supermarkets, using uniformed staff and high-visibility display units. It was relatively simple fare compared with what we achieved subsequently, and certainly alongside the pyrotechnics that have latterly become commonplace; but it was essentially the same discipline. I daresay someone somewhere will lay claim to having performed similar exercises beforehand, but Barnett was the first in my knowledge to turn such activity into what one might call a product. Because his team at BFP ended up carrying out the face-to-face sampling activity for our earliest heavy-duty FAST marketing exercises, as well as large-scale projects for other clients, they gained a grounding that placed them way ahead of the field. It was no real surprise when we learned three years later that American ad agency McCann Erickson, part of the Interpublic Group (IPG) to which Lintas by then belonged, had done what agencies often do when they see a successful enterprise: they'd bought him out.

McCann's big idea was to create a global network of agencies selling activities rather like those offered by BFP. To this end, they acquired a New York-based event agency from Ayer after the 1996 Atlanta Olympics and merged it with their own 'presence-marketing' outfit that handled roadshows, exhibitions and the like. The expanded whole was relaunched as 'Momentum Experiential Marketing', BFP being added to lend some European weight. Naturally I was taken aback to find my distinctive nomenclature borrowed in this way. I was loath to take issue with his new bosses, however, BFP still being a key supplier; and in any case I had no legal leg to stand on, having only troubled to register the 'Experiential' trademark in Europe. But what followed made me appreciate the importance of nipping a thing in the bud. In the wake of the acquisition, a raft of former BFP employees jumped ship to set up their own competitive businesses in this lucrative new market, often using 'Experiential Marketing' in their company title. Firing off warning letters about trademark abuse to new arrivals, and indeed the trade magazines that adopted the term as another piece of jargon to prattle about, for a while became a regular occupation for me. I have to say I was astonished at how little protection a trademark actually gives, especially considering the expense and time involved in registering one. Be warned.

Brand theatre

What these proliferating enterprises did (and do) for a living needs some explaining, since even one or two of their proprietors will struggle to tell you what exactly experiential marketing is; indeed, I recall seven opinions being expressed in one short trade article alone[1]. I'm in no doubt: it is simply unmediated brand marketing. What do I mean by that? I mean that it does all the same things as brand marketing except that it is conducted face to face instead of via a communications medium. Some will dispute this definition on the basis that it makes no mention of trialing the product; but to that I reply that product sampling is not an intrinsic part of today's experiential marketing. Ideally it would be, but I defy you to do it when you are experientially marketing a bank or an airline or a parcel delivery service, except in the most symbolic way. Instead, today's experiential marketing is all about what I would call brand theatre, dramatising a brand outside of the home by means of more or less entertaining hyperbole. We are talking here about heavily branded interactive displays or entertainments sited at high-traffic locations such as shopping centres, tourist venues, fairs and the like. There are of course disagreements about the primary purpose of such events, but it seems that the commonly agreed definition nowadays is 'bringing brands to life'. In other words, where media advertising has traditionally been *the* means of communicating one's brand proposition, the argument is that face-to-face dramatisation is a more compelling way of getting the public to ingest it.

This genre has developed exponentially thanks to the ready availability of both high technology and cheap labour. One can easily see the appeal of this offering to your average twenty-something marketing manager, charged with creating brand differentiation and enticed by the exciting creativity applied to devising suitably eye-catching capers; not to mention the prospect of dealing with lots of other attractive twenty-somethings in the flesh. Needless to say, I was exposed to a lot of this activity myself in the industry, and had to be impressed by the sheer energy that was put into it. Two years after setting up the business, I created a separate division staffed by product-sampling specialists specifically to handle that side of our operations. It quickly became the biggest independent sampling company in the country, and we were often asked, because of the economies of scale we could offer, whether we would also handle conventional sampling and experiential campaigns. We seldom said no, if only out of politeness, but we never had much appetite for it. For one thing, we simply found it too hard work to justify the client's expenditure in terms of commercial benefit. The trouble was that, if I'd had difficulty making advertising budgets add up, I was completely stumped by a tool that cost not a few pounds or dollars per thousand people covered, but perhaps a pound per *person*.

I wasn't alone in this. In 2004 I was invited to the inaugural session of the Live Brand Experience Association (LBEA), an amalgamation of experiential agencies and location space-vendors. Amusingly, one of the speakers turned out to be the boss of the company that conducted the 'experiential' soft drinks launch I mentioned in chapter 4: the one we'd advised against. The case study she presented featured activity that was duly expensive-looking and no doubt professionally executed; but, when it came to results, we heard none, other than the stunning revelation that the activity had 'reached' well over three million consumers. Now, knowing as much as I do about the business, I found this more than a little hard to believe. It turned out that the figure had been concocted by adding to the small number who actually participated in the core activity (less than 5,000) a much bigger number consisting of those likely to have heard about it, and an even bigger one compromising the combined readership of all the newspapers that had carried reference to the activity in consequence of event publicity. Clearly the creativity had not stopped with the design of the activity itself.

We were asked more than once if we'd like to go into partnership or even acquire other experiential businesses; I never found it hard to say no. Aside from the issue of accountability, I could never see how to make money out of it, even before it became so fiercely competitive. I wasn't alone in that either. I was surprised on one occasion to be invited to an expensive lunch by the high-profile non-executive chairman of one of BFP's earliest rivals. What he wanted to ask me was how to make money out of experiential marketing. I felt rather a fraud, because I had to admit I really hadn't a clue. The LBEA obviously hadn't either. It was transparently set up with the aim of wresting marketing spend away from the advertising industry. Ironically, this shotgun was recently turned back on its wielders by the incoming IPA president, Rory Sutherland[2], who appealed to rival ad agencies to bury their differences for the sake of expanding their own slice of the pie, presumably at the expense of experiential marketers. To prove its own case, the LBEA needed evidence; but it presumably had none, for I received a request from one of its directors to let them use my FAST marketing case studies instead. Since this was dubious to the extent of being downright devious, I fobbed them off with some excuse or other, and was unsurprised to learn not long afterwards that the organisation had already folded. It was to prove a portent of a malaise that has now struck the whole industry, so badly oversupplied has it proved.

The new experiential orthodoxy

Despite this debacle, our own use of the term 'experiential' was plainly being systematically compromised by the new usage. As far as I was concerned, it was dealt two killer blows within four months of each other in the summer of 1999. The first came when a pair of American academic-consultancy types called Pine and Gilmore published a book called *The Experience Economy*[3], a full-length version of an article they had published two years earlier in the Harvard Business Review[4] that itself was inspired by a chapter in a 1970 work by the 'visionary' (or fanciful?) Alvin Toffler[5]. Their argument, after they'd cited dozens of eclectic instances of commercial activity that might conceivably be called 'experiential', was that businesses should literally resemble a theatre production. Unfortunately I only got as far as page 22 before I theatrically threw the book across the room, vexed by the assertion that the 'experience economy' must succeed the 'brand economy' as night follows day. Apart from there being no logical case to support the assumption, it was patently not a general trend. Even today, eleven years on, one can walk around an American shopping mall and see much more that is good old-fashioned retail than anything suggesting a new type of economy. But the book had a classic business-school air to it, and certainly got noticed.

The second hammer blow was *Experiential Marketing*[6], by another American academic-consultancy type, Bernd Schmitt. This book again cited dozens of examples of business activity deemed experiential by the author, who painstakingly organised them into several different categories of his own devising. To give him his due, I didn't use his book as a projectile, but was mildly tempted to on page 67 on account of his statement that there are five senses. The scientific view is that there are at least eleven - including balance and temperature - and arguably more than twenty, with at least five different types of taste alone. The idea that there are five in total was one of Aristotle's wild claims, as unscientific as the four elements, the seven colours of the rainbow and for all I know the four horsemen of the Apocalypse. Now, I'm aware that this may sound a little pedantic for most practical purposes, but it's reasonable to expect a book specifically about human experience to respect the basics, especially when such a solecism is liable to compound old ways of thinking about how the brain works; not to mention the reality that up-to-date knowledge could offer a big opportunity to an inventive designer. It was one thing when Pine and Gilmore used the same terminology, but if the author commands respect by billing himself as a professor, we're entitled to demand more precision.

The problem is that, a decade later, loose talk has become quite normal in a young and growing discipline, many of whose practitioners are inevitably more concerned with making a living than exploring the finer points of neuroscientific theory that underlie their exciting trade. Another 'truth' that's already becoming part of the industry dogma is the notion, commonly attributed to the inventor of semiotics, Saussure, that all human experience is fundamentally multi-sensory. The implication, experiential marketers will inform you, is that experiential marketing is invariably richer for targeting more than one sense. Now, I'm not so sure. Think about it. A scream in the dark; a taste of honey; the smell of gas; a picture of a newly born lamb; a touch of silk. By Aristotle's definition, all involve but one of the senses, but all are still undeniably experiences. All are no less emotionally affecting for being 'mono-sensory'. Indeed, you might hypothesise that by cluttering the mind with multiple inputs, you will sometimes diminish the power of such a stimulus (which is precisely the concern of the branch of psychology known as cognitive load theory). Where experiential marketing is concerned, there's no 'one size fits all' answer. Sometimes it helps to combine, but sometimes it doesn't. The stimulus that sparked Proust's mammoth *A la recherche du temps perdu*[7] was the taste of a simple madeleine cake; he'd no need of an accordion and a troupe of can-can dancers to embark on his literary odyssey.

Sensory experience is plainly a more complex matter than meets the eye. It was the subject of a whole branch of philosophy (called aesthetics), of a complete book by Kant, and even of a 19th-century movement. Neuroscience has barely scratched its surface, and it just can't be reduced to a sound bite. Consider for example the qualitative differences between the senses. We tend to think of them as panoramic windows of the world. In truth, they are largely limited to the evolutionarily valuable; which is why we lack bats' sonar and birds' magnetoception, and our powers of hearing, seeing and smelling are meagre beside those of dogs, hawks and sharks respectively. Human beings happen to be particularly visual creatures, with large areas of cortex devoted to drawing meaning from our visual environment - a handy fact for vendors of advertising space and airtime. Yet olfaction (smell), apart from being arguably the oldest sense we possess, is also unlike both vision and audition in that sensory input plugs straight into the limbic system, for which reason that emotional centre of the brain was once known as the rhinencephalon or 'nose brain'. So powerful is smell in evoking emotions that, in the visually obsessed world of marketing, one has to wonder just how big an opportunity the experiential industry is missing. Much the same can be said about that comparably extraordinary phenomenon called music - but that is a whole other story[8].

Given how much else the brain has to do, it is perhaps surprising how much of the human cortex is associated with 'cross-modal' activity, involving the processing of inputs from more than one source. This has everything to do with complexity. Cross-modal processes operate in ways that are both unconscious and counterintuitive. For example, experiencing a taste activates smell receptors at the back of the nose. Equally, when your eyes perceive a person being touched, there is activity in your somatosensory cortex, the region that deals with sensory inputs from, among others, your own sense of touch. The brain is densely interconnected via the association cortex, such that any sensory input to primary sensory cortices has the potential to connect up with other sensory areas. And the conscious mind does not faithfully report what the senses have told it. Its function is to construct existentially useful meaning out of the countless pressure waves, light particles and so on relayed to it as action potentials at every moment; this is the machinery that has evolved to help it. The only way to pick your way through all this as a marketer is not by laying down hard and fast rules derived from speculation. The answer is to suck it and see; in other words, to test ideas empirically in the real world for their observable effects.

You can understand why experiential pundits feel a need to reduce so much complexity to plausible catchphrases in order to justify their output. I'm not denying that a 'multi-sensory' experience can be both entertaining and informative; the fabulously expensive Guinness Storehouse in Dublin, for example, which lets you experience a journey through the brand, has attracted a large number of tourists, making it a workable brand advert. The problem with experiential marketing as a whole, however, is the rigid industry-wide conviction that the task involves creating a great sensory experience *regardless of the nature of the product experience itself*. What strikes me about most of the activities billed as multi-sensory is that any science that's gone into them appears both rudimentary and incidental to the product. Occasionally, it's actually false, and that can be the case even when the authors pose as sensory experts. A mailer distributed by one of the UK's most famous national enterprises contained three unscientific blunders - of which the ubiquitous 'five senses' was much the least egregious - on the first three pages of text, despite bearing the proud claim that it had been produced by the 'leading sensory consultancy'. I'm not alone in having concluded long ago that many experiential marketers haven't the foggiest idea how what they are peddling will affect customers' brains in a commercially useful way.

Experiential follies

What is enervating at a cultural level, however, is the way that the vocabulary of experiential thinking has come to be used witlessly - a ketchup-like seasoning on the creative output of every marketer and advertiser who has heard the new buzzword. The words 'experience' and 'senses' can now be heard as often in marketing communications as 'lashings' and 'piquant' are in pub menus, even to the extent that their use is now lampooned by satirists. Permutations on the formula 'Stimulate your senses' are as clichéd as the old 'As seen on TV'. But it is 'experience' that has grown particularly tired from overuse. It was not so bad when website designers spoke of improving the online experience, or utilities companies hoped to make their customers' billing experience less arduous. What has become quite laughable is the way that the word regularly has zero semantic value. Thus we quickly grew accustomed to the likes of 'Experience this quality' (Ford Focus), 'Experience intensity like never before' (Magnum ice-cream), and even 'Experience a new visual era' (Panasonic Viera). In another league is the tortured 'Experience the benefit'; but for sheer vacuity, none quite matches 'Experience the phenomenon', advertising a novel. All of these could of course be rendered more economically without any reference to experience ('It feels good', 'It tastes good', 'It looks good'), but this would of course fail to achieve the real purpose which, to be blunt, is to tick the marketing box called 'experiential'.

The reason why the practice is inane warrants spelling out. Experiences are for having, not for being idly talked about. Marketers who have learned the lesson that trial is Very Important apparently judge that, since advertising is indispensible but doesn't involve trial, mentioning the word 'experience' has to be a decent surrogate. They will presumably add that it may even encourage trial of the advertised product. Now, we've already seen that advertising alone seldom sells much product unless subsequent trial is actively facilitated. The corollary is that urging people via advertising to do things they wouldn't otherwise do tends to be counterproductive. Explicitly signalling the experience is tantamount to flagging up the fact that there's a manipulative marketing manager about. I witnessed a hilarious example of this in the mid-'nineties when P&G, having had their market share dented by a FAST market for Unilever's Organics brand, tried their own homemade version for Pantene. The product sample was fine; the problem was that, instead of evoking the true experience, the prior advertising warned customers to look out for the free sample they'd be receiving through the letterbox. They might almost have well have added an endline saying, 'Buy while stocks last'. There's enough empirical evidence around to warn against showing one's marketing hand, but the experiential revolution has been a launch pad for crassness on an impressive scale.

Naïvely telegraphing one's intentions is one thing; evoking bogus experiences is another. I probably must take some indirect blame for this. After years of making experientially accurate TV ads for FAST markets, we'd gathered some compelling evidence that, though intended only to prime a subsequent experience, they could also raise sales on their own more efficiently than conventional benefit-led ads. We assumed that this surprising finding had something to do with bypassing mental processing, and were not surprised when ex-adman Robert Heath belatedly published a monograph in 2001 advocating precisely such 'under-the-radar' advertising[9]. By that time, we'd long since been approached by an American TV director called Chuck Hallau who specialised in shooting experientially rich TV ads, and together begun marketing a new genre of TV advertisement that, for reasons that will soon become apparent, we called 'Heuristic TV'. The idea was that the creative treatment should be a precise metaphor for the product experience, and thus tantamount to a mental sampler. Now, we were by no means the first ever to make such soft-sell experientially accurate commercials (recall the stimulus for Project Janus in chapter 3), but ads of that type were then a rarity, yet have since become commonplace; think Marks & Spencer's now famous 'This is not just food' campaign.

Almost immediately, however, we could see a conceptual trapdoor in the ad industry's efforts; and I'm not referring to the practice of 'dramatising the negative' (i.e. evoking the problem the product would solve) that Gordon Brown had specifically warned against on the grounds that the problem was more likely to be remembered than the brand[10]. What I mean is the way that such ads were intended to rectify problems inherent in the product's performance. The thinking, in classic *Mad Men* fashion, ran, 'The product's not so great, so let's change its experiential image'. In other words, the experience became something new to fib about. One sublime example I remember was for Clairol Herbal Essences. This shampoo contains organic herbs, which led some witty creative team to an evocation of the experience as orgasmic. The advertising featured a young woman taking a shower and making Meg Ryan 'Yes! Yes! Yes!' noises suggestive of a product experience so enjoyable that it would surely make men redundant. The reality, however, was that the product turned out (at least in the author's reasonably well-informed opinion) to be strikingly standard. 'Experiential' as interpreted by the ad industry seldom implies experientially true to life.

Managing the experience

Though the two experiential books have to take some of the blame for fostering such inanities, what they did achieve more positively was the feat of putting 'experiential' under the managerial spotlight across the English-speaking world. I became poignantly aware of their effect when, at a new-millennium meeting of the Marketing Society, Claire Watson (the former Haagen Dazs marketer) announced the result of a poll of senior marketers inquiring what the biggest development of the next decade would be. The clear answer was 'experiential'. It would have been nice to imagine that our own evangelising had been a factor in it, but there was no doubt that it was these books that had lent the movement an 'expert' imprimatur. What would give it a further boost was the development of Customer Experience Management, the subject of Bernd Schmitt's next book five years later[11]. This new discipline was a natural progression from Customer Relationship Management, in short a software-based method of keeping track of a company's customer contacts. On the basis that exploitation of every existing customer is far more profitable than acquiring new ones, a focus on the experiential quality of those contacts made perfectly good sense.

What is noteworthy about the development of CEM is the way that it began to focus attention not on the devices used by marketers to draw attention to and, with luck, create interest in their wares, but on the nature of the product or service itself as experienced by the customer. This shift certainly chimed with our own thinking. When undertaking research to identify the experiential core of a product, we had naturally concentrated on providing an accurate description. However, it did not take much imagination to see that many products were not all they might be. This did not mean that there was an issue because they were either a little dull or generic; we had sparkling successes even with some very ordinary product experiences, provided that the priming provided was absolutely honest. What troubled the consumers we researched was when products didn't *add up.* For example, we encountered a frozen-food range that presented a very tangible organoleptic (i.e. sensory) experience that was not delivered anything like equally by all its variants, and a cleaning product which came in packaging that matched the brand advertising very well but barely touched base with the product experience. It always seemed to us that these things were rectifiable if one had the right philosophical approach, and CEM promised to endorse such an approach.

In practice, CEM has concerned itself much less with the packaged goods we worked with than with the sorts of organisations to whom customer retention is in effect a daily challenge: utilities, retail, financial, travel, and so on. Not having worked in the business, I can't pretend to have an insider's perspective, and can only offer impressions derived from lengthy exposure to its output. It seems to me that the personnel who populate CEM chiefly share the mindset of (and often have come from) the sales promotions industry. They depend heavily on questionnaires to garner information on satisfaction levels, and then create incentives for customers to spend extra or return more frequently, occasionally providing consultancy or coaching to identify growth opportunities or rectify shortcomings. The burgeoning CEM industry has been mirrored on the client side with a proliferation of new job titles containing the word 'experience'. Both were aided by the creation in 2003 of Net Promoter Score (NPS)[12], a numeric measure of the likelihood of customers recommending a particular product or service. NPS's own promoters argue that the net score is best improved by the increasingly modish policy of 'under-promise/over-deliver'. Finally we see here a system that attempts to bring together a model, a means of learning, a process, and metrics.

With its practical approach, CEM has to be counted on the right side in the war between substance and spin. Yet I have to admit to a serious reservation about CEM, NPS and all. Practitioners may use the information they glean perfectly well; but the information itself concerns me, as does any that is gathered by demanding people's impromptu opinions. Here's a personal example. I flew with my family from London to Phoenix, AZ. The children were upset because the in-flight electronic games weren't functioning. After the meal, my wife fell ill for the rest of the journey. Naturally I felt stressed. But the flight crew worked to cheer us up, the movies were a distraction, and we were told we'd be sped through immigration by a man with a wheelchair. While still in the air, I was given a form on which to rank my overall experience on a ten-point scale, and then the same regarding service, in-flight entertainment, etc. I asked myself: how could anyone possibly award a digital score to such an extremely fuzzy experience? It's a sample of one, but multiply out all those hard numbers and you get a very solid-looking average that tells you little of what really happened. I think of it every time that, after speaking to a call-centre representative, he asks me to rank his performance on an automated questionnaire. I wonder whether the business owners ever wonder about how dependable their scores really are. This is a big matter that we'll come back to in the next chapter.

The Heuristic take

While these developments were unfolding, we were undergoing our own little revolution that, almost by accident, would directly address this information problem. Strangely, it all started with a change of nomenclature prompted by Bernd Schmitt's book. If I'm honest, when I heard there was a new book out called *Experiential Marketing*, I was horrified. We'd spent nearly five years keeping ourselves to ourselves, and now it looked as though our thunder was being publicly stolen. It proved a vain expectation: the author clearly had no inkling of the journey we'd been on, and presented a view much closer to today's increasingly conventional interpretation of experiential. Nevertheless, it was time to speak up. By chance, sandwiched in between the appearance of *Experiential Marketing* and *The Experience Economy*, there came the publication of the one formal paper I ever wrote on FAST marketing for a broad audience. Published in *Admap* in May 1999 under the title, *When ads alone fail to boost sales*[13], it was a riposte to an academic paper published a year earlier by two US professors who'd picked up on Deighton and decreed that no one had yet drawn up a formal model of primed experience[14]. Of course, this gave everyone in the office a laugh of the 'yeah, right' variety, but it also prompted me to put down an academic marker before anyone else presumed to take the high ground. The new books persuaded me however that any remaining claim we had to the term 'experiential' was barely worth having, and it was then that we decided to throw in the towel and stop using it.

This did however leave something of a hole in our vocabulary. It was soon filled with a rather tidy substitute. A German newspaper ran a feature on FAST marketing[15] that made mention of its *'heureka'* effect. Investigating the 'h' that is absent from our English 'eureka' in the dictionary led to an interesting revelation. Most people know that Archimedes cried 'Eureka!' (or more exactly 'Heureka!') on discovering his famous Principle in the bath. What most people don't know is that it literally means, 'I have found it!' It now occurred to me, as it hadn't occurred to Richard Grisdale and me six years earlier, that there is a ready-made adjective in English encapsulating this very idea: *Heuristic*, meaning 'serving to find out' (OED). Now, as you already know, a 'heuristic' is a common term in psychology, meaning a decision-making rule of thumb. We decided to use it in a related sense, but one that was literally more correct than the psychological term - as an adjective to describe a business approach concerned entirely with the real world *as experienced* by customers. And one thing was for sure: nobody could lay claim to that term in the marketing world.

This sudden flurry of new developments after some years in which we'd been complacently earning a nice steady living prompted me to think hard and with some urgency about where we were and whither we were heading. This is the true beauty of competition. It is the best possible salve against complacency, and if necessity is the mother of invention, then urgency is the midwife. It seemed to me at this time that we really needed to up our game in terms of understanding our métier. If the two new books had provided me with no illumination concerning the mental processes of human experience in the commercial domain, then we needed to perform our own investigations. It wasn't easy. Where do you start, when the internet is still young, its search engines are slow and inefficient, and there's no Wikipedia to give you a head start? Believe me, if you don't know your way around, an academic library can be a pretty daunting place.

Not that I hadn't previously dipped my toe in the water. I had contacted Professor Stuart Sutherland, author of a splendid read called *Irrationality - the enemy within*[16] that as much as anything was a glass half-empty account of heuristics. He'd expressed an interest in getting involved in our work, but sadly died in 1998 before anything came of it. I'd sponsored a number of experiments on facets of sensory experience at the University of North London's consumer-psychology department, though nothing of a breakthrough nature. Dr David Lewis, who has since undertaken neuromarketing investigations for many an angle-seeking corporate client, had performed an analysis for us of alpha- and beta-waves of subjects while watching an ad; I wasn't surprised when he complained that advertisers were uninterested. Possibly the most practical measure I took was to pay the Institute of Food Research to undertake a thorough review of the relevant academic literature, which led to our acquiring a collection of papers that for the first time gave us a sense of knowing how far the world's academics had got; but also what they appeared not to know.

The penny dropped when I realised that, if the relevant answers were to be found anywhere, it was in our own archive. I don't mean to sound pretentious. I was perfectly aware that psychologists have studied perception in considerable depth, and that the philosophy of experience stretches back to the 17th and 18th-century Empiricists. However, I was also conscious of the shortcomings in perceptual theory, notably in respect of neurological explanations for observable phenomena. And as for Empiricism, John Locke's fanciful yet persistent idea that we are born with a mental 'blank slate' that is subsequently filled in by our experiences[17] seriously retarded understanding of the complex interplay between nature and nurture, and has now been astutely demolished by neuroscientist Steven Pinker[18]. The real point however was that our interest was in *commercial* experiences, and if we wanted a repository of case data that might shed new light, we had one sitting in our numerous filing cabinets.

A major source of this material was a research tool we had invented called Fastforward, that we used over a period of twelve years in markets from Austria to Australia. When we'd started up, Roger and I had had to think about how we would unearth the experiential core of whichever product we were planning to FAST market. This definition, of whichever elements of the experience of using or consuming that product were most salient, had to be rigorous. It would form not only the brief for advertising designed to capture the essence of the experience and therefore accurately prime it, but also direct the way in which the product to be sampled was to be introduced to large numbers of people. Included in this were the way the sampling equipment was designed, how the sampling staff looked and behaved, and what was said to recipients. When we talked to qualitative research companies, we got as little joy as I'd had from field marketing companies. It just wasn't what they did. They might accommodate our need, but only as part of their normal qualitative investigation, which was expensive, slow, and likely to provide brand-focused output. We wanted something quick, single-minded, and cheap. And so was born Fastforward.

This tool normally consisted of three or four group discussions conducted on one day in one location. Like all qualitative research, it was based on in-depth interviewing of relatively small samples of key target consumers (typically six to eight per session) for about ninety minutes. However, any resemblance to a focus group was superficial.

There was no general discussion of brands, needs, and claims; nor were subjects expected to judge a beauty contest of competing branded concepts. Instead, each session commenced with, or was immediately preceded by, actual trial of the product; and the entire enterprise consisted in a sequence of exercises designed to tease out what was going on in people's heads from different psychological perspectives. The protocol varied only if we also looked at an existing TV advertisement at the end of a session to ascertain how it differed from the experiential core that was unfolding. No more than this was required to arrive at a definition of the experiential core that the majority of human beings could agree upon. As they say, you don't need to read 'Hamlet' twice to know that Ophelia dies.

Heuristic profiling

Fastforward in practice proved surprisingly durable. Apart from being validated by third-party researchers, it turned out that, where exercises were undertaken on the same brand in different countries, results were remarkably consistent, which says something about the universality of human sensory perception despite cultural differences. The critical output was a single paragraph evoking the experiential core in such a way that any normal person trying the product would agree it matched up. We were helped in this process by the Forer Effect[19] whereby, as Deighton had recognised, we tend to seek confirmation; what was most important was to eliminate all possible bones of contention. The beauty of Fastforward was that it revealed not just the experiential core but a lot of other truths about the nature of how humans experience commercial products. The idea I had was to sponsor Roger to study all the Fastforward exercises we had conducted, some seventy in number, to see what they told us collectively. It was a mammoth task, involving reading some 3,500 pages of data. I hoped for a general picture of categories that experiential cores fell into. What came back was a lot more than I'd anticipated.

To cut to the chase, the key general finding was that experiences of packaged goods tended to fall into three categories: first, the functional: e.g. 'It really does clean beyond the surface'; second, the emotional or 'affective': e.g. 'I felt a better person for using it'; and third, the organoleptic: e.g. 'It is unexpectedly warming after the initial chill'. There was no prior certainty that a specific product would fall into a particular one of these categories. All Roger would venture was that household products tend towards the functional category, toiletries to the functional and/or emotional, and food and drink to the organoleptic; but this was by no means a fixed rule. It seemed reasonable to speculate that most consumer experiences would be embraced by this categorisation, though it was obviously a rule that would only be proved by exceptions. What we did meet within these broad categories was countless individual nuances, and the task of defining a whole experience systematically was clearly complex. Yet finding a way to manage these nuances for business purposes appeared a laudable ambition.

The trouble was that, so meagre had been the attention paid in the commercial realm to the nature of experience, it even lacked a taxonomic paradigm; in plain English, a theory of how experiences break into their component parts. This had made any analytical breakdown of a specific experience a long-hand affair. Armed with the Fastforward databank, however, we were able to address the issue, perhaps for the first time. What this meant was discerning the common threads among the component parts of our real-life product experiences. There were quite a few; but we were able at length to reduce them to four key elements, each of which we gave a single-syllable title for the sake of memorability. The first was 'Flash', relating to what is revelatory or surprising about an experience; the second 'Match', concerning congruence: the extent to which it fits with its context, including both one's existing attitudes and the real-world context; the third 'Charm', covering what is likeable or enjoyable; and the fourth Grasp, or what one makes of it cognitively. For any particular experience, each of these four elements could additionally be studied from the three perspectives (or 'facets') mentioned above - functional, affective, and organoleptic.

This twelve-part model, which could obviously be expressed very easily in diagrammatic form, really began as nothing more than a hypothesis. In other words, we had no pretensions to representing a watertight scientific account of the nature of experience. Instead, this *'Heuristic Profile'* or HP as it came to be known was a practical implement, intended to give an at-a-glance representation of an experience that we could readily analyse and critique. We have since found that we can use it rather like a doctor refers to an x-ray, holding it up and forming both a diagnosis and a course of action without having to plough through reams of text. It was also to prove a convenient means of communicating to third parties such as copywriters, designers or R&D scientists the nature of an experience we wanted to repair or replicate. Our hope always was that, with more extensive use over time, we should be able to refine the template. In reality, it has stood the test of time. We have changed nothing of its essence, and only improved the quality of the presentation of the data, to the extent of exploring 3D software.

As the basic analytic tool of Heuristic investigations, the HP has proved, if not indispensible, at least hugely convenient. One can start filling it in without ado, and keep refining it until it presents an experiential portrait that unmistakably matches the phenomenon it describes. In time, however, we would come to look at more complex matters than packaged goods alone, at which point a new and very challenging question assailed us: how do you secure the most dependable data with which to complete this thing? That will be the subject of the next chapter, bringing us onto the issue of how 21st-century businesses choose to inform themselves about the world around them; a vital matter, considering that consumer insight is at the heart of decision taking.

Any change?

Before we proceed, however, you're entitled to wonder how the marketing world was overtaken all of a sudden by this experiential new wave, after decades of dogged conservatism. The answer is desperately mundane. It's not that there was a penitent change of heart on philosophical grounds. It was all brought about by the same practical phenomenon that hobbled FAST marketing operations. A key result of the digital revolution is that human beings no longer have Hobson's choice over how they spend their evenings, but can spread their attention between scores of different channels; not to mention that whole new world of Web-surfing. As prey to intransigence as all human beings, marketers finally had to get out of their warm bath when Silicon Valley tipped it over. With the option of robotically putting two-thirds of their budgets into terrestrial TV advertising torn away, other options had to be contemplated; and the experiential movement was a visible and plausible candidate for their custom.

I'd be misleading you, however, if I made you think that experiential thinking is the only or even the dominant force in the new thinking. There are now so many new contenders for the marketer's attention (and budget) that it's hard to know where to start. For the sake of the argument, let me take social media, a topic that currently occupies a wondrous amount of talk time in marketing circles. I experienced this at first hand when speaking recently at the European Customer Experience World conference, where it came across as the dominant theme. I found the connection between experience and social media hard to grasp, until the penny dropped: there is none. Whatever value social media may offer marketers, *they have to seek custom*. Driving this is the hard-nosed reality that, for every medium, monetisation is essential if the franchise owners are to account for themselves to the markets. Hence a mythology is being woven around social media, replete with theory, case studies and passionate advocacy: a perfect microcosm of the mythology that grew up around the advertising industry. It's already clear that a lot of money will change hands before a balanced perspective evolves on social media's true value, and there's no guarantee that, like many a medium, social media won't turn out to be a solution looking for a problem. It spoke volumes when, on quitting a huge telecoms company, a friendly specialist in such matters wrote, 'I am on Facebook but don't use it much - never really understood what all this social media nonsense was about'. Of course, she may have been joking.

And that's just social media. I haven't mentioned advertising-funded programming or stealth marketing or crowdsourcing or geo-targeting or... whatever. So let me be frank. I have seen nothing that is not a permutation on a very old theme that would be recognisable even to Walter Dill Scott. As Deighton put it, the model is still 'adversarial'; in Keats's words, it still has 'palpable designs' on us. Still it is all about imparting information, plus or minus a rich brand gloss, with cost-per-hit the dominant criterion. What it all manifestly fails to do is tally with our new understanding of the functioning of the mind. Without that, the driving force of this new compact between marketing and media will continue to be the need to facilitate the former in order to make commercial sense of the latter. In place of unheeded u.s.p.'s and vacuous brand values in the media and on your doorstep, it promises a new generation of internet pages that take an eternity to load because of unwanted ad content, incessant unwarranted telesales calls from overseas call-centres, irrelevant suggestions of products you might like to buy on the basis of casual past searches, pop-ups that prevent you from proceeding with your urgent task, extended ad breaks and broadcaster messages in the middle of an exciting movie or sports broadcast, hidden devices that you know are tracking you all the way from the supermarket to your kitchen, and a myriad other saleable means of intruding upon you, the customer. It's a brave new world of jarring disruption. Until Rupert Murdoch or some other media maestro cracks that one, I'm sticking to my original answer: see above.

6
A Little Learning...

21st century, 1930's research

Imagine yourself as a 30-year-old account director in a big ad agency. One of your clients runs a tracking study on her biggest brand, which every month takes a read on such measures as brand awareness, attitudes, propensity to buy and purchasing among a large sample of people statistically representative of the population. She calls you late one afternoon to ask if the pre- and post-advertising awareness study you are currently planning could also include the key questions from her tracking study. The reason she gives is that her tracking research and your pre/post study are being conducted by two different major MR companies and, though the demographic profiles of the samples for the two exercises are identical, it would be prudent to authenticate 'your' numbers. You've only a moment to consider your reply; do you, like me, say, 'Yes, of course. I can't see any issue with that'? If yes, then, also like me, you're about to sin in haste and repent at leisure.

When our pre/post results came in, they looked fine. Trouble only brewed when I sat down to compare them with the latest tracking study results. It wasn't just that the scale of the numbers was a bit at variance. It was completely different across the board. Not only that: the pattern of the numbers also bore little relationship. At first I thought we must have the numbers for the wrong brand, but no such luck. I asked the planning director about it, but received neither clarification nor sympathy: 'That's quant for you', she said. '*You* agreed to it'. With much effort I fabricated some half-baked explanation that the client, after initial incredulity, graciously filed away for the sake of our professional relationship. So painful was the experience, however, that I've had a vivid somatic marker attached to the notion of 'market research' ever since.

My discomfort ultimately boiled down to one thing: foiled expectations. I'd always assumed, long before coming into business, that the numbers you see reproduced in print have scientific validity. When someone says, '57% of all we remember is visual', you don't automatically doubt it. There's no surprise in this, given the way that statistics tend to be treated by both journalists and businesspeople as hard facts. I use the present tense because, if anything, they've grown worse at it. Just recently I saw a headline reporting that consumer confidence levels have risen. On closer inspection, it turned out that the 'rise' was from 27% to 28% - a pair of numbers so close that, as any statistician will tell you, they allow for the possibility that confidence has really *dropped*. Of course, we're all aware of how the end-users of statistics routinely misrepresent them for selfish purposes, such as a quango's claim that a 20% claimed usage rate presents 'nearly a quarter'. What we're not so prepared for is the idea that the data themselves may be of fundamentally doubtful value, which becomes a real worry when they are likely to be influential in deciding what course to take.

In business today, MR is often all that stands between an informed decision and mere hunch. To understand how dependable a guide it is, however, you have to delve into its origins. For many centuries, all an enlightened trader could do was ask customers for their opinions or, more ambitiously, conduct a straw poll. Suddenly, in the 1930's, things turned more sophisticated. It began when New York adman George Gallup realised there was a more mathematical way to make predictions about the outcome of future elections, by asking the opinion of a large sample of people their voting intention. However, this would not be any sample, but one selected to represent demographically the population at large. He called it an opinion poll, and intended it as a more dependable way to predict which of candidate A or candidate B would win. Gallup got off to a flying start, correctly predicting the outcome of the 1936 presidential election. Luckily for him, its popularity was already secured by the time he got the 1948 contest spectacularly wrong. The opinion poll's potential for exploitation in the business sphere had also become obvious and, thanks to Gallup's efforts, a whole new industry was born: market research.

The idea as applied to business was the same - that a representative sample could tell you with quantifiable probability what you need to know in order to take more informed decisions. Aside from studying purchasing intentions, it catered for other knowledge wants, like product usage, reasons for purchase, brand awareness and attitudes, advertising recall and comprehension, and more. Of course, this MR machine delivered a vast amount of data, all based on the simple premise of asking people questions like: do you agree a lot, quite a lot, a little, not a lot, not at all? On the assumption that respondents are generally truthful, it came to be indispensible. Just as we've seen more recently in experiential marketing, organisations catering for different types of MR insight proliferated, and continue to do so to this day. Including retail audits, market analysis and the like, market research is now reckoned a $20-billion industry worldwide. To get an idea of its relative importance, consider that it accounts for around a third of Sir Martin Sorrell's £8-billion advertising empire.

MR did not long remain about numbers alone. Besides quantitative research, there was another movement, spawned in the 'fifties by Ernest Dichter, the 'father of motivational research' demonised in *The Hidden Persuaders*[1]. Coming from the Freudian tradition of psycho-analysis, he had a different focus: the qualitative. Much of his subject matter was the same, except that he used not an interviewer but a 'moderator' whose job was to stimulate discussion. The findings were not expressed numerically but as the moderator's interpretation, and the forum was not a street interview but a focus group that Dichter regarded as group therapy for brands. All sorts of clever devices were borrowed from psycho-analysis to stimulate discussion; it's him we have to thank for the notorious, 'if this car were an animal...' Though the techniques have evolved over the decades, they remain largely unchanged, for the reason that marketers feel lost without them, and few practitioners will change something that is still selling.

Trouble with words

The two movements, quant and qual, became symbiotic, the findings of the one often giving cause for undertaking the other. As I well recall, they give confidence of covering all the bases, providing both the intellectual challenge of concepts and the reassuring concreteness of numbers. Both are handy for getting respondents to express and explain a preference for stimuli placed in front of them. If they didn't exist, marketing would have to invent them, for modern marketing would be lost without its psychological apercus. There's just one snag. They suffer from the same problem as medicine did before the advent of x-rays and lab tests. They both depend to a large extent on *what the respondent tells you*. And there's the rub. It's not just a matter of whether respondents are honest, although deliberate sabotage by MR-weary interviewees is a growing issue. The real problem is more fundamental.

In order to participate, respondents have to express answers in *words,* and to do that they generally engage the *reasoning* parts of their brain. To marketers, this seems a good thing; after all, the marketing discipline is conducted in words, and its product, marketing, ought to be the product of reasoning; or so they assume. In reality, product choice often has little to do with reasoning, and nothing to do with speech. People tend to choose heuristically, following cues of which they're often unconscious. It was for his work in this field that Daniel Kahneman, the economist who demonstrated that choices in fact are often irrational[2], matched the utilitarian Gary Becker's Nobel Prize with one of his own in 2002. What is clear is that humans are good at post-rationalising; but asking them what they buy or plan to buy, and why, is notoriously unreliable. Consequently, MR-derived input to marketing activities is often no more reliable than the researcher's rational interpretation of subjects' rationalised response.

If what people say they will do (or have done) actually matched their behaviour, there'd be no issue. The trouble is that MR is notoriously hit and miss at making sound predictions. This may seem an arcane matter, but the essence of science is that it wants to know not just how things appear, but whether our beliefs about those appearances are solid enough to forecast what will happen in comparable circumstances in the future. Any scientist is obliged to make forecasts, known as hypotheses, that are expected to be borne out subsequently by reality. Such forecasts typically take the form of a statement like, 'If x, then y'. In the business world, this might translate as, 'If you broadcast advertisement x at a certain frequency, you should sell an additional y tonnes of chocolate'. Yet even matters as black and white as the outcomes of elections have demonstrated very publicly what an inexact practice MR is, and explain why market researchers are loath to make testable predictions. Without such dependability, there is inevitably a big onus on all-too fallible human judgement. This fact of life must have contributed substantially to the difficulty the various marketing disciplines have in providing general (as opposed to best-practice) proof of payback. The result is that much MR ends up serving at best as a fig-leaf; politically useful, admittedly, for any marketers wanting to justify their activities, but less good for their employers, depending as they do on accurate analysis.

Though most MR at least appears to be conducted honestly, one should also not assume that the industry is entirely immured against the abuse that's born of commercial pressures. I shall never forget how, in the mid-'nineties, the commercial director of a large drinks company asked us to work with his agency to create advertising that resonated with the product experience, as opposed to yet more eccentric ideas designed to grab headlines. The agency wrote two scripts, both so outlandishly wacky that they came across as the creative team's way of telling us to mind our own business. The client decided the best way out of this tricky situation was to let MR decide; the agency would arrange some focus groups, and I would attend. I sat through three painful hours of hearing the target audience guffaw at the ideas, only to have the agency planner announce afterwards, 'Fantastic! Not one winning idea, but two!' Worse, the moderator told me after the agency people had left that he'd simply been briefed to find out 'which idea was more edgy'. That's certainly not science, and it's not even clever client handling. It's tantamount to fraud, and the agency (once the hottest in town, now defunct) could have no complaints when it was sacked a few months later.

There are more subtle distractions from the pursuit of truth. Many an adman can testify to the sort of experience I had not so long ago, where a middle-manager objected to the possibility of new learning emerging from a Heuristic research project because it would 'create more work for us'. More than once we've heard a different objection from marketers: that the findings 'might contradict our MR'. But it is foolish to imagine that the gatekeepers who express such views are following the wishes of senior management. Professor Stuart Read of the IMD Business School in Lausanne published a study[3] identifying two entirely different behaviours in business. While *managers* tend to use market research as an indisputable touchstone, *entrepreneurs* are risk-taking empiricists who crave the new knowledge provided by real-world experimentation, presumably because, by challenging their own beliefs, they create the opportunity for advantage-seeking change. Just to prove that it's no mere hunch, Cambridge neuroscientists have subsequently demonstrated distinct neurological differences between the two types[4]. What we're talking here is separate species: *homo indocilis* and *homo inveniens*. The trouble is that it is the former that commissions research.

MR is the current marketing battlefield. Whatever its humble origins, it has evolved into the oracle of marketers, the ultimate and indisputable fount of knowledge upon which conclusions, plans and decisions are respectively made, drawn up and taken. Yet its ability to acquit itself dependably of such a tremendous responsibility is at least questionable. Though some MR companies make a big noise about change, they can only embrace it by repudiating their old model, which would inevitably divorce them from their bread-and-butter revenue. And there's the rub. So eye-watering are those revenues that there's a commercial imperative to resist challenges to the hegemony of old thinking. Happily for them, there's still a good market for their wares. Forty years after a handful of more perspicacious admen began to sense something rotten in the state of advertising strategy, old-school multinationals are still pressing for differentiating benefits. If you were running a big MR agency, you'd be stupid not to give them what they want, whatever you might privately believe.

A different perspective

That's not to say that all market researchers are happy with the status quo. In 2004, I attended a seminar of the Market Research Society at which the first speaker, a prominent figure in the industry, began by pronouncing portentously that 'the model is dead'. The rest of the day was a procession of speakers agreeing that something new was needed and a concerted effort by one or two of them to argue that the answer lay in 'brain science'. The discussion session at the end was like a funeral, except gloomier; and the best the chairperson could think of to draw the event to a positive close was the suggestion that every ad agency should acquire an fMRI brain scanner. He was no doubt unaware that few could afford the multi-million pound cost, let alone operate one. Worse, I could have told him that it would not be a prudent move for the MR industry. (One landmark fMRI experiment[5] had already demonstrated that what is subjectively reported as a preference may not be associated with the neuronal circuits by which conditioned behaviours are strongly determined. In plain English, what people say they *like better* is not the same as what they'll routinely *choose* - neurological evidence, at last, of the mismatch we'd found years earlier between claimed intentions and actual behaviour). It was as depressing an event as I can recall, not least because those present were conspicuously well intentioned and mostly very bright; one could only wish them well in their search.

One alternative approach that has gained purchase in recent years is the idea of investigating not what customers say but what they *do*. Supermarkets nowadays collect valuable data on customer purchases through their loyalty-card schemes. What such data do not reveal is how these purchases came about. Borrowed from anthropology, so-called 'ethnographic' research involves observing shoppers as they shop, often by filming them and analysing the footage later. Naturally it may also observe them doing other things, such as using a product. It can be quite sophisticated, even measuring vital signs such as heart rate and brainwaves. If, as Professor Ehrenberg demonstrated[6], it is a fact that we are creatures of habit, it follows logically that the most reliable guide to future behaviour is current behaviour, and observing current behaviour must prove more fruitful than asking hypothetical questions about it. This is not to say that there is no room for asking opinions in addition. On the contrary: contrasting subjects' stated intentions or beliefs with their actions often gives valuable clues to what is going on inside their heads. There are however two drawbacks to all such studies. First, they are not cheap; and second, they deliver a huge amount of data in the form of footage and readouts. Critically, all this material requires interpretation. Such interpretation may be the interpretation of an expert, but it is interpretation nonetheless. In consequence, it is not immune to theoretical biases or to commercial pressures on the researcher to draw usable conclusions.

Ethnographic research forms part of a new trend to embracing brain science within the market research department, now increasingly known as 'customer insight'. The 'nineties were the decade of the brain, and Antonio Damasio[7] single-handedly seems to have booted the marketing industry into the realisation that there's more to the human mind than cognition. In particular, the last five years has seen the emergence of neuromarketing, the use of formal brain-scanning and/or biometric equipment to answering the sort of issues normally addressed by questionnaire. A classic test might involve comparing activity in the brain while a person is watching two different TV ads and making inferences about attention, engagement and the like. Such technology is now being applied to an increasingly wide array of challenges: how well advertising performs in different media contexts; the relative strengths of different pack designs; the effect of trying products whilst seeing different packaging, hearing different sounds or smelling different smells; etc. The obvious drawback to comparative tests like these is that the sense of scientific certainty may create unjustifiably high confidence levels that encourage tunnel vision. It could be the case for example that, while the only way of deciding between A and B may be on the strength of a single neurological effect, the best commercial decision would in fact be to run *neither* Even so, a properly designed experiment may yield sufficiently more reliable feedback than conventional MR as to justify the higher cost.

Brain drain

This new focus on neuroscience should be nothing but a cause for celebration, you'd think. Instead, it has also become a shiny wrapper in which to conceal more traditional wares. Pictures of the brain are now ubiquitous in Powerpoint presentations that continue to spout the conventional wisdom. One marketing agency habitually places a 3D model of the brain on the table at new-business meetings; you can guess how relevant it is to what they're actually selling. An ad agency boss can regularly be heard pontificating in the media about the advertised brand that lurks in the synapses: a phenomenon as yet undetected by neuroscience, but that surely has to be in there somewhere. There are even consultants who've only ever picked up a Malcolm Gladwell paperback pitching themselves as experts in brain science; and I mean that quite literally. You can understand the selfish interests that make such developments inevitable, but it is no help to businesses if their marketers take the view that, by giving their outmoded model the imprimatur of neuroscientific machinery, they evade the need to challenge existing assumptions.

In many such marketers' minds, there is an easy confusion between the scientific method and use of scientific kit, rather as though a man in a white coat waving around a Bunsen burner constitutes scientific practice. Across the world, marketing agencies are allying themselves to tame scientists with the aim of exploiting this confusion. You have something to sell? Then do something unusual with it in connection with apparatus wielded by an academic, and you've got yourself a science-based press release. When you hear the inside stories of some of what goes on, you sense that it's not all what you would call neuroscience; the prefix 'pseudo' might be better suited. The trouble is that, when wheat gets mixed up with chaff, there's a likelihood of invoking general cynicism among third parties, notably journalists, who've seen the self-serving purposes to which such 'science' has been put.

One egregious case was Silverjet's investigation into stress levels at Heathrow airport. There was worse to this than the fact that the experiment was conducted among just four subjects, few enough to make any layman question its validity. The key finding reported by the media was that subjects wearing biometric vests had suffered stress levels exceeding those experienced during a mugging[8]. When the story was told on BBC Radio 4, interviewer Euan Davis publicly dismissed it as nonsense; after all, how could one possibly know? Silverjet is now history, but the bad taste lingers on. Equally, a book by one singularly conspicuous neuromarketer, calculated to excite interest in his sexy new version of hidden persuasion, succeeded in irking at least one reviewer[9] to such an extent that businesspeople can still be heard voicing the opinion that this 'brain science' has been overcooked.

The journalists do not always call it right. Take the brain-scans conducted at Baylor College in Houston which showed that Coca Cola lights up the part Pepsi cannot reach; specifically the medial prefrontal cortex, an area interestingly associated with decision-taking. The story was reported in the British press[10] as good news for advertisers and quickly parroted all over, though with scant justification. To start with, one has to wonder why Coke, the corporate symbol of America itself, was chosen for this test, and whether such a finding would hold for any other pair of brands one might think of. Second, the difference may be down entirely to greater previous experience of Coke, owing to its superior distribution. But, above all, one might conclude that this is in fact a disaster for advertisers everywhere, when a consistent heavy spender like Pepsi is unable to register. If one has to be as big as the world's most famous modern icon to get such a result - not to mention 120 years old - what's the point in even trying? This case is instructive because the story became public even though the scientist whose name was attached to it is one of the most respected in his field and, as I know at first hand, meticulous about ensuring that his science is not corrupted by shoddy commercialism.

The truth is that all the real scientists I now work with are equally punctilious, not to say fastidious, about the integrity of their scientific output. It a sad fact of life that not everyone sees things the same way. Human beings are the same self-interested survivalists that we evolved to be in the Pleistocene, and there will inevitably be some even in the academic community happy to subvert science to personal gain. If you don't believe me, then believe Professor Steve Jones the geneticist, who's up there in the Sir David Attenborough class for integrity. In 2008 he was to be heard on a BBC radio programme[11] concerning Trofim Denisovich Lysenko. In case you've not heard of him, Lysenko was Stalin's big scientific crony who single-handedly starved half the Ukraine to death with his crackpot theories of crop genetics. Listeners were entertained to an account of how he would approach the party with an idea for a scientific 'result' that would add to the fund of politically helpful 'results' he'd already provided; undertake an experiment to prove the 'result'; announce the 'result' before the fieldwork was completed; and have anyone who challenged the 'result' arrested. And Professor Jones's conclusion? After damning Lysenko as a fraud, he expressed the view that, with such a track record, the Russian would have no trouble in making a success of himself in contemporary British science.

Though you'd struggle to find a true Lysenko working in science today, the warning deserves respect – and not only in Britain. With ever more scientists happy to provide paying clients with access to their world, it's important that businesspeople should know what to look out for. Even where there's no actual dishonesty, science can tend to mislead if it ever becomes the handmaiden of ulterior motive. The lesson was brought home to me by a 2005 book called *The Advertised Mind*[12]. It described coherently how the brain works at a neural level, and demonstrated unequivocally why the functioning of the brain inevitably makes advertising powerful, particularly if it's the brand-focused, emotion-laden type beloved of account planning. The trouble was that the argument was a classic example of deduction, the evidence having been selected to prove the case for advertising, rather than building an impartial description from the bottom up. It was like an advert itself: there was nothing patently untrue in it, but it left much unsaid that might give a very different impression. You won't be surprised to learn that it was written by an employee of WPP. You can't blame a marketing communications group for promoting its commercial interests this way; it's just concerning when a senior colleague of the book's author takes to announcing publicly - as happened at a seminar I attended - that neuroscience only confirms what the ad industry already knew. He's not alone: I've heard the same statement from *three* other advertising mandarins. They're not lying. It's what they've been told, and they (probably) know no better.

The key to true science lies in isolating and discounting subjective interest, whether of the consumer or of the researcher. There is a very well tried and tested device for doing this, going by the unwieldy name of *hypothetico-deductive method*, more comfortably referred to as today's preferred 'scientific method'. It involves studying all available data, positing a hypothesis, and then designing experiments to test it (or, following Karl Popper's advice[13], to try and falsify it). Even if the result doesn't come out the way you'd like, which you have to accept uncomplainingly, you've learned something closer to the truth that you can then grapple with. In business, where the primary interest is (or should be) in what people do rather than what they say they do, such tests are best decided wherever possible by measures of subjects' behaviour in given situations. This makes possible learnings that are binary (yes/no) instead of fuzzy. It is a method that has been woefully neglected for ideological reasons in MR, still true to its roots in cognitive reaction against the Behaviourist movement that preceded it. What's more, experimental design takes great (and time-consuming) ingenuity; and the truth it exposes may not be palatable, either to the marketer, or to the marketer's suppliers, or to the marketer's boss. But it does deliver the demonstrable truth, and there's no better place to build a castle than on a solid foundation.

The true measure

Roger and I decided early on in the life of FAST marketing that a new model that aimed to identify experiences accurately, rather than invent branded differences, would demand an entirely different approach to finding out. What we ideally required was a device for peering inside people's heads to understand what is going on while they experience a product or service. This opened up for us a perennial problem facing psychologists: how can one tell exactly what, at any one time, a particular person is experiencing? After all, there is no way you can read their mind. Of course you can always ask, but the feedback received is contingent on more than the respondent's honesty. Not only is language itself structurally very limiting, in that one word can have many meanings whilst some sensations have no name at all; you also run into the problem of articulacy, which among the brightest of us loses something in the translation and among many seldom runs beyond the gamut of 'awesome' to 'awful'. There is also a social dimension to this: as any trained observer will testify, most people tend to hide their feelings until they know what the expected or acceptable response to a stimulus is. In a group situation, they can easily be led.

You may instead try to observe subjects as they explain themselves. Inadvertent gestures, smiles and body language can give strong clues, but they seldom if ever offer a full and accurate account. The signals detected can be entirely misleading, whether deliberately (crocodile tears, the salesman's smile) or not. Tools are already commercially available that endeavour to sort the real from the feigned, but these are still early days. And again there is the matter of interpretation, which can owe so much to the researcher's judgment that it becomes as much art as science. In the case of experiential enquiries, there is a further complication. Experiences are not at first sight amenable to objective description that all can agree upon. In philosopher David Hume's famous words, 'Beauty is no quality in things themselves. It exists merely in the mind which contemplates them; and each mind perceives a different beauty'[14]. Though his opinion is disputed by some aesthetes, it's unequivocally borne out by what neuroscience now knows of how the brain constructs its own subjective picture out of patterns of action potentials. The same might be said of any stimulus one's various senses can detect. The combinatorial possibilities across a population are enormous.

Now, very few businesses are equipped to market themselves, still less tailor their offering, on a one-to-one basis that takes every customer's sensory idiosyncrasies into account. What businesses demand is a dependable segmentation that tells them not only who is not worth troubling with but also what differentiated strategies and offerings are commercially worth (and capable of being) implemented among potential customers. Fortunately, it turns out in practice that there are by no means as many different *behaviours* in response to sensory stimuli as there are people. There may be dramatic variations in, say, response to the smell of a certain chemical; and we even know now that emotional response to a negative experience will differ between individuals according to a variation on a single gene[15]. But whatever the individuality of our mental apparatus, there is a remarkable degree of consistency in the way we act upon experiential phenomena, especially when you consider the range of possible responses. A red traffic light will elicit the same behavioural response from a colour-blind person as from anyone else. The same is to a large extent true even of matters of taste. While we may disagree heartily on some externals, in practice there are usually elements that the majority of any group can agree upon. Whereas an alien race might find having to listen to Chuck Berry music (as they will if ever Voyager 1 turns up) tantamount to a war crime, most earthlings can be depended upon to tap their feet.

The critical point here is that, though it is an easy mistake to assume (as do most experiential marketing pundits) that experience is all about the senses, our sensory inputs count for rather less than what our brain does with incoming material. It is misleading to describe the experience of climbing a mountain or servicing a car or making love in purely sensory terms, when the primary processing of sensory input may account for only a minority of brain activity. The early Empiricists' take on this state of affairs was that one can only gauge such phenomena by measuring their effect on individuals' *behaviour* - the basis of Behaviourism[16]. It is in fact behaviour that should ultimately be the primary concern of businesspeople, because a purchaser is worth any number of well-intentioned non-purchasers. Analysing how people actually behave, and *then* unearthing the mental activity that underlies that behaviour, is the key to being able to influence it systematically and affordably.

Moving on again

Fastforward had been our best shot at creating an alternative approach, and very practical it proved too; but we were always acutely aware of its limited scope. By the time we started to grapple with the issue in earnest, our ad industry connection was behind us. TBWA had undergone a succession of mergers in short order, the consequence of which was that almost the entire management team was replaced. (Certainly the advertising industry is no place for the faint-hearted). The new boss, a man renowned for single-mindedly pursuing his professional and personal goals, let it be known through an intermediary that he saw no space in his set-up for an enterprise that lay outside of his control, and indeed his understanding. By that time, my only real relationship with the agency was with the accounts department that divided the profits between us, all my friendly counsellors on the board having departed. Consequently I was willing and able to extract the entire business without ado, and to implement a plan that had been gestating for some while.

The catalyst for that plan turned out to be Barnett Fletcher, who was in the process of extricating himself from IPG with what he hoped would be a large payoff. (Unfortunately for him, IPG's finances at that time were proving a can of worms waiting to have its lid removed). Barnett had suggested the idea of filling a building with a number of marketing-services companies with complementary skills, who would work together as a quasi full-service agency whilst retaining their individual entrepreneurial impetus. Now, the idea tallied beautifully with my long-held belief that agencies represent bad value for money because they rack up vast overheads - through payroll and office rental - that have to be recouped from clients no matter how little work is done or however indifferent the quality. I also believed the problem to be compounded by the fact that few divisional heads enjoy any sense of ownership and therefore feel the incentive to make the kind of sacrifices peculiar to business owners. Barnett's idea suggested an arrangement less like a ship than a flotilla: a collection of bosses each with their own area of command, but all sailing in the same fleet and combining their forces as appropriate whenever the situation demanded.

We were conscious of one or two vaguely comparable ventures at the time, this being the year 1999, but nothing this single-mindedly experimental. Indeed, we even called it the 'Axe & Bottle Experiment' after the medieval tavern that had once stood on the site of the lovely old converted industrial building in which we housed it. The experiment ran for four years until the lease ran out. There were two reasons why we then formally concluded it. The first was that, though it worked very efficiently (with, for example, seven of the business units working simultaneously on a single piece of business and seldom a harsh word spoken) there was an issue over new-business acquisition in that the three biggest companies were expected to bear the brunt of its cost, which created a sense of unfairness. The second was that, by then, the whole marketing-services world had changed, and completely new horizons beckoned; horizons that I found myself unable to resist.

What I'm talking about is the appeal of life beyond packaged goods. When I'd started out in advertising, packaged goods had been the blue riband of business. How that had changed! The big supermarkets had squeezed manufacturers' margins so hard that the pips were crushed. With the money gone out of it, much of the best marketing talent had departed for pastures new, whether retail itself or sexy new industries like telecoms and the Web. The continual complaint of my own team was that they were seeing more and more foolish, short-lived decisions from more and more foolish, short-lived marketing managers. What added to the feeling was the substantive technical problem for our own business that I've already mentioned: the accelerating defection of viewers from the mainstream TV channels, which was making it ever harder to achieve the necessary levels of coverage within the short period that FAST marketing depended upon.

The turning-point occurred in the ironically experiential setting of a Chip 'n' Dale breakfast at a Disney hotel in Anaheim in March 2000. The newspaper headline I read over my ham and eggs told of the dramatic stock-market crash in the dot.com industry that had just about been keeping the terrestrial TV companies going. At the time, I felt a strange kind of relief on account of the extraordinary recklessness we'd been witnessing for some while; but I had no inkling of the consequences. Within a month of returning home, I was approached by both the large TV advertising sales houses, Granada and Carlton, asking if I could help out. The reason was obvious: for some years I'd been speaking on conference platforms about the power of television to drive FAST campaigns, and they were doubtless feeling a little desperate for a friend in need. I was happy to oblige, not least because I needed their business to thrive as much as my own. Apart from collaborating with them on sales initiatives both before and after the two merged in 2002, I also put to their board the idea of writing a book for them to explain how ad agencies - their clients - were letting the medium down with their defunct model, and using this as the springboard for a drive to inculcate new, more commercially advantageous thinking into the planning of TV commercials. In fairness, it would have taken some courage to agree.

Upstream thinking

A by-product of these discussions was a major breakthrough in my own thinking. The catalyst was Caroline Hunt, then the Commercial Director of Carlton, now CEO of a successful New York events company. It was while I was commiserating with her about their loss of dot.com revenues that she suddenly berated me, albeit in her typically wry manner, for being set in my ways and ignoring the 85% of advertising expenditure not accounted for by packaged goods. Despite iterating the routine objections, I knew she had scored a hit. Several other members of the Axe & Bottle Experiment had asked the same question, but having a number placed on the opportunity put a new perspective on it. Yet, if the thought was bound to be mother to the deed, the gestation would not be easy. After all, how do you create accelerated trial of durables, or retail stores, or airlines, or financial services, on a large enough scale to justify the cost of the activity? It was a conceptual conundrum I was to wrestle with for nearly three years until lateral thinking intervened. Luckily, however, I was to have valuable new help when the time came to make the change.

When I met him, Tim Routledge, an ex-WPP man, was head of the creative agency that Barnett introduced to the Axe and Bottle team. Tim is a unique individual who always reminds me of that Larsen cartoon of an Irish setter's expressions: whether joyful or depressed, it's always the same, and in his case an irrepressible grin. Though distantly related to the Routledge publishers, he actually comes from a family of film-makers, and made his way into consultancy via TV production. Apart from bringing both creative skills and experience in building networks, Tim had studied history and politics at university, and so was more interested than the average agency boss in the academic side of Heuristic thinking. From his start position of believing that what we were doing with FAST marketing was a salve to much of the nonsense we were witnessing about us, he learned Heuristic theory and practice over a period of four years in the best possible way, by taking our creative briefs and turning them into sharper evocations of the experiential core than most top ad agencies had managed.

Tim thus joined a small group applying their minds to the conundrum of taking Heuristic thinking beyond packaged goods. One big new idea eventually towered above all others, the notion that the product or service experience no longer had to be a given. This may sound trivial, but conceptually it was a vital advance. In any branch of marketing services, the understanding is that the thing you are given to promote is a fixed entity. Your task is to take it and, using all the artifice of marketing, make it appear as desirable as you're able. We had faced the same stricture. In dealing with packaged goods, life was simple: once we'd identified the experiential core that most people would inevitably recognise, there was little else to say. The same could never be said of, for example, a telephone company. There are far more touch-points between business and customer where the experiential core might vary. Common sense, a little psychology, and the evidence of seventy Fastforwards attested that consistency mattered. In fact, consistency must matter a great deal, judging from most people's frustrating personal experience of call-centres and the like. We didn't need just to identify the incongruities. We had to set them straight.

It was while we were mulling this over that CEM appeared on the scene and brought some method to the experiential thinking of Schmitt et al. Though its exponents did not appear to be doing anything risqué, the fact that they were being invited to scrutinise the 'customer experience' at all encouraged us that we might be permitted the same latitude. The whole concept of reshaping the product or service experience to fit with appropriate priming seemed radical, yet there was a reassuring echo to it. My mind was taken back fifteen years to my work at Ayer on Bassett's Liquorice Allsorts, and the relaunch that had proved unusually successful in sales terms. What was so different about that activity? Was it just the smart creative idea? Or was it the fact that we'd kicked off the project by extensively testing the product itself and, on discovering that the quality had diminished over the years in consequence of endless little cuts by marketing managers, persuaded the client to optimise it against the experiential core: the fact that, once you've eaten one, you have to finish off the whole bag?

Digging deeper

Consulting with the heads of different disciplines within the Axe & Bottle set-up reassured me that, by using a raft of sales promotional and field marketing devices, it should be possible to engineer a commercially viable equivalent of the product-sampling activity we performed as part of every FAST market. Paradoxically, the bigger challenge was a knowledge issue. How could we learn enough about the whole experience of a business not only to be able to isolate the experiential core, but also to identify those many points at which customer contact was likely to create dissonance with that core? In the Heuristic Profile, we had a useful tool for describing a complete experience authoritatively; but Fastforward, designed for capturing the essence of consumption of a single product, plainly had none of the versatility necessary to capture the complexity of any business in which personnel, environment, process, product and marketing are all potential spanners in the works.

What we needed was a new toolkit, incorporating a range of devices to explore different parts of an experience from various psychological perspectives. We started modestly, refining Fastforward so that its investigative techniques were specifically tailored to informing the different elements of the HP. This primarily consisted in creating four different exercises, corresponding to Flash, Match, Charm and Grasp, that were so much more like games than research that already we felt we were putting clear water between ourselves and the MR industry. The difference from focus groups was underscored when we turned our backs on the conventional number of subjects in a group (eight), which it seems had become the industry standard solely because it was the size of the army squad or section typically employed in post-War military research. It was obvious to us that a much more normal number for human beings to congregate in is four: think of a meal in a restaurant, or a car trip to the coast, or a game of cards. Indeed, evolutionary biologist Robin Dunbar has calculated that the typical social network of a human being compared with a chimpanzee's would predict an average conversation group of 3.7 participants; a figure corroborated empirically[17]. Add to that a more natural choice of venue than the automatic spoof living-room with two-way mirror - which has subsequently taken us to places as diverse as a Heathrow airport lounge and a Manchester nightclub - and you'll see how readily things were moved forward. The only wonder is that the MR industry has got away with groups the size of a rowing crew in a viewing facility for so long.

This revamped tool, which for slightly obvious reasons we renamed 'Condenser', was just the first of a toolkit that now contains no fewer than eleven others. As with any good toolkit, there is no need to use more than a selection for a particular task. It is simply a matter of picking out the right one, two or several required and keeping the others in reserve in case of emergencies. This task-based approach has the great advantage that costs are incurred only to the extent that particular tools are used - an exact analogy for the Axe & Bottle philosophy of 'charging by the yard'. The tools range from a handy online 'game' that seeks to quantify a business's particular strengths and weaknesses within each element of the HP by a process of pictorial association ('Correlator'), to heavy-duty devices for looking inside the brain ('Mentor') or the body ('Fusion') for physical evidence of mental activity. Rather than listing them all, however, a fuller account of just one other will give a flavour of how they were each conceived.

When making their classic album *The Dark Side of the Moon* in 1973, Pink Floyd decided to embellish various instrumental passages by overlaying snatches of recordings of people talking about such matters as violence, death and madness. Since sensitive issues like these will cause many of us to clam up in an interview situation, the band invited fellow occupants of the Abbey Road studios to sit before a microphone in a darkened studio booth where they could see only questions put to them on flashcards - questions that were simple to start with and gradually became more personal. The frankness of the responses they received spoke volumes about the constraining effect a human interrogator will normally exercise. We took this basic psychological principle and turned it to advantage in the form of a tool for probing into the emotional facets of business experiences. Subjects are placed in an immersive chamber in which all sensory factors (lighting, colour, fabrics, smell, ambient music) are tailored to evoke a particular mood state, for example 'relaxed attentiveness'. The subject is recorded and filmed as he talks his way through a questionnaire presented by a computer. In practice, he is likely to be perfectly relaxed after the first 'warm-up' question or two, and will soon be chatting away as though on the phone. Meanwhile, in an adjacent studio, the research team is looking on and undetectably adding in further questions in reaction to his earlier responses. It goes without saying that the output is often literally eye-opening.

Such new approaches serve to present intriguing new insights, in the same way that the invention of lenses did. As they have unfolded, it has proved possible to complete the HP in ever more intricate detail. This in turn has thrown a sharp light on the deficits of many existing experiences, and in turn the alterations that might improve them without much ado. It was almost inevitable that studying an HP, warts and all, would suggest the idea of creating a perfected HP to set alongside the actual one, so that current shortcomings could be identified and rectified. We call this aspirational HP a 'mountaintop view', and it represents the best place one can easily get to from where one is now. The important thing to bear in mind is that is not an *ideal* experience. Any talk of an ideal is pointless, as would be talk of climbing Everest when one is in the Appalachians. That is not to say, however, that when the nearest experiential peak has been attained, you cannot aspire to reach an even higher one further along the range. The first practical output of the process is a list of action points - often several dozen of them - that can be pinned to the wall as a managerial manifesto for improvement. Every one equates to another small step up the mountain.

That it is now possible to delve much deeper is due to the fact that new technologies are allowing hitherto unrealisable methods of scientific investigation to replace the less rigorous practices that traditionally have been used by businesses to fill their knowledge gap. This simple enough point actually represents an important philosophical breakthrough. Fifty years ago, science historian Charles Singer pointed out that, though we normally think of scientific innovation as the mother of new technologies, the process just as often happens in reverse[18]. Just as Galileo's telescope opened up the heavens to our gaze, it was when Robert Hooke acquired a primitive microscope that humanity suddenly learned of another world of minuscule creatures. The point is that new discoveries drive new ideas that yield new technologies, and so the chicken and egg go on and on. In this respect, we are at a critical juncture where business is concerned: the new technologies like the sort of biometric equipment mentioned earlier, capable of tracking heart rate, respiration and/or galvanic skin response in real time, are throwing up novel insights that embarrass the old ways of thinking. In response, while defenders of the old business faiths seek to shore up their model, a new generation is forging ahead, seeking new technologies to probe still further into the emerging realms of knowledge. For anyone who enjoys discovery, it is, as Walt Whitman is supposed to have said, a great age to be alive.

A neural network

The new toolkit being evidently more sophisticated than Fastforward, it didn't take long to realise that we'd need a lot more technical resource if we were to deploy it efficiently. This brought us into contact with academics with a sufficiently strong grasp of business to appreciate what we were trying to achieve. They in turn gave us access to dozens more neuroscientists and psychologists with varying perspectives on human experience, all of which vastly accelerated our understanding of the current academic take on decision-making. In parallel, we appreciated that there was no point in engineering revelations for clients if they could not be actioned. At the very least we would have to be capable of carrying all learnings seamlessly through to practice, should the client prefer not to undertake it all himself. Otherwise there was the risk of doing what market researchers the world over happily do: making recommendations for change but disappearing without imparting how they can be carried out. For this, we would need another large cadre of specialists; one able to implement our recommendations in the marketplace, whether that meant fixing the website, retraining the staff, or designing a new store.

Fortunately we had the perfect model already in the Axe & Bottle Experiment, which Tim embarked on enlarging massively to include not only a wealth of scientific talent but also more than forty disciplines that would come in useful for implementing the findings of our investigative process. To this we added a group of experienced project managers at the centre. In each case, the individuals or enterprises concerned would be able to continue to plough their own furrow, but be remunerated appropriately on any job in which we involved them. The new entity needed a new name, and we decided to call it the Newcomen Group. The Axe & Bottle office was in Newcomen Street near London Bridge, and seeing the sign every day had prompted me to look further into this neglected English inventor. It turned out that Thomas Newcomen had not only conceived the atmospheric steam-engine, specifically as a solution to the problem of removing floodwater from mines; he had used his blacksmith's skills to build one, and then sold a hundred at £1,000 each in the early eighteenth century. Not only did he thereby alleviate suffering by enabling homes to be heated and wealth generated; he also created the prototype of the principle of doing well by doing good. The group's name was intended as a tribute to the humanitarian ingenuity of this man who transformed the world.

When the lease was up on the building, several of the Axe & Bottle companies decided to continue together at another building just over the road. Tim and I, on the other hand, opted to make the leap. We were certain that the Newcomen concept's time had come, a conviction confirmed when one speaker at the annual conference of the American Association of Advertising Agencies in 2004 revealed startling proof that the American public was sick and tired of their output, even to the extent of being happy to pay more taxes if advertising would be curtailed[19]. We also felt that, with the climate-change issue coming to the fore at the very time that new technology was transforming communications, there was no justification for persisting with a central location. Instead we each had a technologically well equipped office built at home, mimicking Ralph Gregory's 'virtual office' concept. More than that, however, we settled down to running a true virtual *group* on the very lines predicted by Baroness Greenfield in her book *Tomorrow's People*[20]. No doubt there are others like it today, but it was sufficiently original back then to get our smiling faces onto the front page of the business section of the establishment newspaper of the day, the *Guardian*[21].

Since those early days, the Newcomen Group has put all its new tools to use in addressing commercial challenges. The beauty of knowing they exist is that they are proof that progress can be made quickly and expediently even in a field hidebound by conservatism. More practically, they indicate that Heuristic investigation is available to everyone. Try for yourself: start right now by drawing a circle, and dividing it into twelve sectors like a clock. Label the four quadrants Flash, Match, Charm and Grasp, and the three sectors within each quadrant Functional, Affective, and Organoleptic. Then spend fifteen minutes filling it in as best you can as a description of how you think your customers in general perceive your business when they encounter it. Use normal handwriting for small points, capitals for big ones, and underlined capitals for the really big ones. If you want to verify it or flesh it out further, get the opinions of colleagues, by asking them questions if necessary or, much better, by designing experimental tasks that will get to what you want to know without inviting them to post-rationalise. Once you've completed it, you will immediately see where the gaps are, which components deserve to be more prominent, and what simply doesn't hang together. Your business instincts will tell you how you can use that information to achieve the sorts of transformations you'll read about in the final chapter.

Meanwhile, how about those market researchers and their pursuit of something better? There was an ideal opportunity to ascertain how far they've got at London's prestigious annual 'Measuring Advertising Performance' conference in 2009. This showcase for the very latest thinking demonstrated unequivocally that the industry has taken giant strides - in presentation. No longer need respondents give survey answers on a scale of 1 to 5, or tick the appropriate box. Now they use a cartoon slider to indicate their degree of interest, or insert words into speech bubbles. And results are no longer displayed in tables, but represented as collages of adjectives where the strength of response is indicated by font size. There's nothing wrong with any of that - indeed, we've used versions of both those devices ourselves for years now. But there's a big, fat fly in the sweet-smelling ointment. They are still in the business of selling opinion polls, a concept even older than sportscaster Vin Scully's observation concerning drunks who use lampposts less for illumination than for support.

What really stuck out for me, however, was the appearance on the platform of one high-powered New York consultant. Starting with the premise that meeting expectations is all important, she promised to demonstrate how to measure the extent to which any brand matches up. Three or four slides in, I again had that sinking feeling that the two experiential books had induced a decade ago. I shouldn't have bothered. It turned out that her method involved (i) asking people to quantify an ideal experience in terms of its various components, and (ii) subtracting from those ideal scores their comparable ratings for the brand itself as they currently perceive it. In other words, it gave a beautifully specific set of numbers putting a number on the difference between a hypothetical construct and a reported perception, still without reference to the world of the real. If that's the best they can do, I couldn't help musing, they'd better not take off their thinking-caps just yet.

7

The Truth Drug

Subjective reality

It's a moment of truth. You once wrote a book[1] telling the world that the late Anna Anderson was in all probability Anastasia, youngest daughter of the Russian royal family murdered by the Bolsheviks in 1918. Her cause has been championed for decades by the son and granddaughter of the Tsar's personal physician, and you know her well enough to be sure they are right. There is no likelihood that this regal woman, who suffered such trauma that she had to spend time in a mental institution, could be anything but the real thing. Your conviction will recently have been confirmed by the discovery that the exhumed grave of the royal family was lacking the body of the son and one of the daughters. Now a mitochondrial DNA sample has been taken from Anna Anderson's corpse and compared with one from the Duke of Edinburgh, a blood relative of the Tsarina. You are about to be told the result of the test, and finally the world will know that you and Anna Anderson's many supporters were right, and she truly was the last of the Romanovs.

Except that it doesn't. Though the Duke of Edinburgh's sample is a clear match to the imperial family, Anna Anderson's is not. In fact, she turns out to have been one Franziska Schanzkowska, a Polish factory-worker. When you know that much, everything you've ever heard about her ought to fall into place: the fact that she originally claimed to be Anastasia's sister Tatiana, until it was pointed out that Tatiana was tall and had dark eyes; her claim to have been rescued by a revolutionary guard called 'Tchaikovsky'; her refusal to speak Russian... With the evidence there in black and white, all you can really do is throw in the towel and wonder what induced you all to persist in this farce. But no. What you actually do is insist there has been a mistake. You tell the TV crew that, if the woman was a Polish factory worker, you're the Pope[2]. And, if you're anything like other acolytes, you'll carry on believing it even after another grave is found whose remains are proved by DNA analysis to be the two missing Romanovs[3].

What's at work here is not an anomaly, but one of the most fundamental principles of the human mind, so fundamental that we've known about it for over two hundred years. Though Immanuel Kant is known as a Prussian philosopher, the branch of philosophy known as epistemology was the psychology of his day, and he was its greatest exponent. Kant was well aware of the dichotomy between rationalist and empiricist thinking, and set himself the task of reconciling the two. In his *Critique of Pure Reason*[4], he came up with an explanation that tallies uncannily well with modern psychological understanding. In short, he argued that reality as perceived by our senses is interpreted through a distorting lens of our own device. All that we experience is shaped by what we already know or believe. The consequence is that there is no objective truth in the heads of human beings. Instead, we create our own reality. This simple fact is fundamental to the theory and practice of persuasion, and is ignored at the marketer's peril. How it works in its particulars is the subject of this penultimate chapter.

Psychology's dismal history

I've a good reason for including a brief lesson in neuroscience towards the end of this business book. The trouble is that the brain is so complex - the most complex organic object we know of - that it been easy to get away with talking self-serving gibberish about it. Historically, this was down to plain ignorance. The Roman physician Galen, for example, thought the mind resided in the brain's empty spaces, the ventricles. Aristotle had the different but even more wrong idea that the brain simply sat atop the head cooling the blood. Sadly for all of us, the Church of Rome decided it was best for business to kill scientific debate by declaring Aristotle divine, so he couldn't be argued with for fifteen hundred years. It wasn't until William Harvey showed the heart is not the thinking organ but just a pump that ideas began to change. The interesting fact however is that, as soon as the barriers came down, the scientifically unsubstantiated hunches came flooding in. René Descartes[5] has a lot to answer for, particularly in the idea that mental life is somehow divorced from the physical - good old 'Cartesian dualism' - that's been responsible for any amount of misunderstanding. Next up was Locke's blank slate[6], the basis of leftist ideology, which still stalks the corridors of power despite being philosophically disproved in his lifetime and neuroscientifically demolished in ours[7].

The point about these two characters, however - the fathers of Rationalism and Empiricism respectively - is that they were at least striving to explain how the brain works. Ever since then, an awful lot of brain theory has borne out the axiom penned by Confucius: 'The superior man comprehends what is correct; the inferior man comprehends what will sell'. The big idea in the 19th century was phrenology, the doctrine that bumps on the skull are indicative of an individual's personality. We're all familiar with the cute china skulls with brain functions marked all over them - even if the mind boggles as to why, say, there's a region for destructiveness in the temporal lobe - and it could at least take credit for promoting the belief that the brain is not a single organ but a collection of many with diverse functions. Even the simplest experiment will however demonstrate that its predictive ability is no better than guesswork. More to the point, one has to ask why wholly unsubstantiated speculation like this prevailed for so long. The answer is obvious: money. It would be interesting to know how much of it changed hands on account of such recalcitrant hogwash.

Just about the time phrenology was first being dismissed as quackery, it was time for Sigmund Freud to make his entrance. Now, the great thing about the prototypical central-European psycho-analyst is that he did get the world thinking about mental life beyond the conscious. But that's where it ends. Aside from his frankly dodgy case work, I don't think anyone has ever located the ego or super-ego anywhere in the brain, let alone the id; so one up to the phrenologists. Even though, contrary to popular conception, Freud actually rejected the term 'subconscious', his coining of other spurious jargon ('sublimation', 'denial', 'repression') has left three generations with a doubtful conception of what constitutes scientifically verified psychological fact. And you have to confess that his followers made heaps of dollars out of it. They always put me in mind of the Tom Lehrer joke about a doctor who specialised in diseases of the rich.

Next in line was John Broadus Watson, the father of Behaviourism. The key tenet of his thinking was that the inner workings of the mind are irrelevant: what matters is our behavioural response to stimuli. Now, as you may have gathered, I have some time for this general principle, especially in practical matters like business. Marketing managers tend to obsess themselves with consumers' self-reports of opinions, attitudes and intentions, when what's really of interest to the company is whether or not people put their hand in their pocket. One can only speculate how marketing might have unfolded if he had not been in his dotage when the new advertising rulebook came to be written. But, let's be honest: Watson was not exactly averse to placing controversy above science. Tormenting a baby with a white rat, a hammer and a steel bar, as Watson did, probably wouldn't get ethical approval nowadays. His real legacy, however, is that, for fifty years, looking inside the brain was just about taboo, to the detriment of everyone who might wish to know *why* we make the behavioural decisions we do. With sublime irony, his later professional years were spent working very lucratively for JWT. I could go on in this vein: I haven't mentioned Rorschach tests or lobotomy or telepathy, all pretty lucrative bunkum and taken as serious science at some point, but bunkum nonetheless.

The rigid mind

Amid all the intellectual flotsam and jetsam, it's nevertheless possible to navigate a safe course through to contemporary scientific understanding of the human mind, starting with Kant's ground-breaking conclusion that we construct our own reality. Arrived at purely by a process of induction, his work received a lukewarm reception when it was first published. Nonetheless, the *Critique* had a critical implication, that knowledge - which we might define for the current purpose as our store of stable beliefs - is the product of an active and ongoing process of editing. Contrast this with the populist understanding of knowledge, even today, as a faithful catalogue of all we've learnt to be 'true'. Kant's view paved the way for a conception of the mind that is more at home in our Darwinian age: neither a disinterested calculator nor a passive receptacle of experience, but a machine for processing information in a way that optimises our individual fitness to procreate. Precisely such a view was espoused in the following century by William James, the philosopher who laid down ground-rules for the discipline of psychology. James argued that, while facts exist independently, what we each hold as *true* is that which serves our own existential purposes[8] - a theory that came to be known as Functionalism. It was finally in the twentieth century that systematic proof would start to emerge.

Jean Piaget, the pioneering Swiss psychologist, was first to shed some practical light, in consequence of a long period of meticulously managed observations of small children from which he inferred how the adult human mind unfolds[9]. He concluded that the mind is made up of any number of little groups of interconnected ideas he called *schemata* (a term coined by Kant) that we build gradually and painstakingly from our earliest days. A new-born baby arrives like a newly delivered computer. It has some pre-loaded software, courtesy of our genes, but otherwise it is basically on its own. What it is confronted with, every waking moment, is a torrent of meaningless stimuli striking its senses. What we know from rather ingeniously designed experiments is that, as babies, we are initially unable to make a distinction between ourselves and the rest of the world. Faces soon begin to mean something, but much else is a blur. Bit by bit, however, we start to build a picture; call it, if you will, a working model of the world that guides how we react to it.

How we make sense of this world is at first determined to a considerable extent by the particular nature of our brain's genetically derived pre-dispositions, which shape how we assimilate our experiences in a very personal way. We start building little structures out of pieces that seem to fit together - like mummy's breast, a happy feeling, and a sensation of dampness in the nether regions - linked to emotions peculiar to our own temperaments and circumstances. Then we begin connecting these together with other little groups of related ideas. Sometimes we will make wrong connections, and subsequent events will force us to break them down and build again. This is of course the process of learning, and it is the reason why play (including risky, sometimes dangerous play) is so important. Eventually we end up with a highly complex, interlocking description of the world that enables us to deal efficiently with most new stimuli it throws at us.

There are two important points to make about this way of building a schematic model of the world. First, no two such models are the same. Imagine asking a bunch of people each to build a huge model castle out of Lego. The end result for most will be recognisably a castle. But because we are all given rather different pieces as life goes on, there will inevitably be a fair amount of variation; and the very first pieces one is given will pretty well determine the entire later shape of the structure. Second, once these structures are in place, they're hard to change. This is not surprising, when one thinks about it. Building a schematic structure, and nursing it into a shape that just about holds together, demands a huge amount of cerebral effort. Changing one's mind every time one is presented with an idea that conflicts with existing schemata has potentially serious knock-on effects.

Although we may like to imagine that we carefully evaluate everything we see and hear, we actually have ingenious equipment that screens out everything we don't want to know about - things that conflict with our existing schemata - before they even spring into our consciousness. (Psychologist Daniel Goleman of *Emotional Intelligence* fame memorably pictured schemata as lions that guard the gateway to awareness[10]). What this means is that, perceptually speaking, we are purblind. We are simply incapable of taking in all that our senses throw at us and processing it objectively. Instead we squeeze it into pre-existing frameworks as though shoving overlarge blankets into inappropriately shaped pigeon holes. What won't fit is simply cast aside.

That is why, for all that we vaunt mankind's achievements, we as individuals are masters of prejudice, bias and judgementalism. It is these mental characteristics that make us as a species uniquely prey to the phenomena that plague our relations with others, from beliefs and partisanship to inertia and dogma. Now, this is not necessarily what we self-preening human beings want to hear. We like to consider ourselves smart, dispassionate, and open-minded. We also believe we are fundamentally rational. In practice, however, it's another matter. We habitually connect things together with cause-and-effect explanations when there's no real cause and effect. We post-rationalise like crazy (literally), as can easily be demonstrated experimentally in the laboratory. Split-brain patients, for example, will readily give reasons for their actions that are patently untrue; yet they actually believe that they *are* true[11]. It's easy to see why. Who can cope with knowing one's conscious self to be subject at all times to unconscious influences? But, like it or not, that's the way the evidence points.

An evolutionary compromise
To understand why we have such a problematic solution to the mind problem, you have to delve into an aspect of the brain that's only received serious study in the last decade or two: its evolution. The human brain was several hundred million years in the making, which helps explain why it's the most sophisticated natural mechanism we know of. But, crucially, Nature was unable to build an ideal human brain from scratch, and that is why our actual brain is in so many ways fallible. Irrationality is explained in part by the brain's structure. At every stage, evolution could only improve on what already existed. The consequence is that we arguably have not one brain, but several. Neuroscientist Paul D MacLean[12] suggested we have three in one. The first, the so-called 'reptilian' brain, handles autonomic processes such as breathing. The second, 'mammalian' brain deals with emotional response. The third, the most recent and human element, controls reasoning and planning. These 'sub-brains' respond to sensory stimuli in very different ways. Often they will steer and complement each other. At other times, they may be in conflict. Emotionally centred brain-parts may override the more rationally oriented. This in turn depends on factors like intelligence, tiredness, and how much one has had to drink. So the idea

that you can target a message to a 'brain' is already less simple than you might hope.

This idea of a 'triune' brain is no longer believed to be supported anatomically, but is a helpful pointer to the practical consequences of a brain consisting of numerous discrete parts that evolved at different times. The rest of the explanation lies in the brain's basic mechanics. Nature was obliged to work with whatever materials were to hand: specifically adapted cells, connectors, chemicals, and action potentials. All things considered, evolution did a remarkable job, especially considering the practical limitations placed upon it. Because our species lived amid scarcity for most of its history while evolving on the African savannah, Nature's solution to the brain problem had to be economical. Consequently, we have inherited a parsimonious means for processing information. The brain uses what is known as 'efficient coding'[13], meaning in practice that the mental activity we commit to as a rule is the least we can get away with. That way, we can continue to function even when critical chemicals like the sodium ions that neurons depend on to function are in short supply. It's like the secret radios constructed from bits and pieces by prisoners of war: not what you might design from scratch with no limits on components, but it's a marvel that they worked at all.

The bottom line is that we have a brain that might reasonably be called either energy-efficient or lazy: one that gets the job done with the least hassle. Picture it as a creature that likes to make up its mind and stick to it. It stores memories - its acquired 'truths' - solely to inform its future decisions. Imagine them as a great reference library at its disposal. Rereading any book would take too long to be useful, so it attaches sleeve notes to them as it acquires them. That way, it only has to look at the note it has made on the cover. Those notes are emotions: ready guides to how it should respond in any given circumstance. Instead of cogitating endlessly, it uses rules of thumb to get through life; for example, don't go down a dark alley if the shadows move. These are the rules of thumb known as heuristics. Some, like an automatic recoil from anything snake-like, are inherited. Others, such as a distaste for salesmen in bow-ties, may be acquired. When we say 'milk and no sugar, please' without thinking, it is experience that taught us. With our own sensory apparatus and experiences, we learn what works for *us*. And the system has proved its evolutionary worth. Brain-damage victims who have lost this facility cannot even decide which shirt to wear. Cognitive processing is inappropriate to most day-to-day tasks, being simply too demanding of physical resources, as well as time-consuming. In life-or-death situations, it can be fatally slow. Stop to consider a predator's intentions, and you may not live to pass on your genes.

The implications are crucial if you wish to influence human decision-taking. Most marketers, like most human beings, imagine that we normally see, then think, then act; remember AIDA? Marketing theorists over the decades have manifestly failed to take into account the truth that very little of what is communicated to us is even permitted to enter into consciousness, and much of what does is not actively considered. Their finely honed efforts continually founder on schemata like sailing ships on rocks. So how, in a world of conflicting subjective 'realities', does one avoid automatic rejection? There is no easy answer; but the best hope lies in *objective* reality. Two people are much more likely to share a fear of tigers than of ghosts. We are more likely to seek advice from a pharmacologist than from a witchdoctor. We will listen harder to someone offering advice on investments than one promising eternal afterlife. Why? Because the demonstrable truth in each case is more likely to work for *us*. Yet what we all learn about marketing communications is that they are seldom objectively real. They don't routinely lie; but they do routinely gild the truth. We learn to aim off for the chronic make-believe (hyperbole, spin, selective information) we are exposed to. We acquire another heuristic; one that says, 'If it's marketing, watch out'. That's why we don't believe all we're told, nor buy all we're sold. And why businesspeople should be obsessed with objective reality first and foremost.

Quick-and-easy decision-making

This brings us back to the central theme of this book. If Deighton demonstrated the value of advertising priming in shaping experiences, the FAST marketing era proved the principle on a very large canvas. Experiences are one thing; experiences that marry up with advertising-set expectations are in a different league. When you are priming experiences with behavioural change in mind, any old priming won't do. It is critical that the priming should match the true experience as accurately as possible. Though for a long time the FAST marketing team thought it was all about establishing a bond of trust, the full answer was residing one level further down. We realised at long last what we'd done. We'd discovered a new heuristic, that we now call the 'expectation-matching heuristic'. Of course, this was all very exciting at the time, but it only posed another question. Why on earth should the brain be concerned to have its expectations matched?

Fortunately, while we were busy thinking about the matter from a purely psychological point of view, some excellent research was being done in the neuroscientific domain that was to shed a big shining light. To understand it, you need to consider not the psychological organisation of the mind, but how the brain gets the job of living done down at the neural level with the limited resources available to it. It's clear from fMRI brain scans that we don't do sensible things that increase our chances of survival and procreation just because our prefrontal cortex rationally decrees it after due consideration. Rather, we've a more holistic system that flashes messages around the brain like a network of warning beacons, and often only allows us to post-rationalise after we've acted. We can easily observe what is happening inside the brain at a regional level, and even observe individual cells over time. But how are we to understand the basic mechanism whereby the brain decides what experiences are good for the whole of it, and which are to be avoided?

The critical discovery was first made by Professor Wolfram Schultz, now of Cambridge University, while studying the role of dopamine in Parkinson's disease[14]. While scanning the brains of apes to whom he administered a reward after they'd heard a warning tone, he found that cells responsible for the release of dopamine (known simply as dopamine neurons) would fire when the reward was delivered. Given dopamine's association with various addictive conditions, this much was nothing unusual. However, he found to his surprise that before long the dopamine reward would transfer to the moment of the warning tone itself, rather as with Pavlov's dogs. He also discovered that a failure then to deliver against the expectation would be punished with a dopamine *deficit*. In the case of an experience that *exceeded* expectation, however - in other words, when there was a pleasant surprise - the ape could expect a big shot of dopamine. In other words, it was not the experience itself that was creating the neurological reward, but the fact of whether or not the expectation was met. The role of dopamine in reward prediction has since been demonstrated in humans[15].

This idea, that we derive pleasure not from the chocolate drop itself but the fact of receiving it as anticipated, is an extraordinary one that takes some swallowing. The idea of misattribution of emotions is familiar to psychologists. You may already be familiar with the experiment in which men who walked over a rickety bridge were more likely to have masculine feelings towards their female interviewer than ones who crossed a steady one[16]. Professor David Zald of Vanderbilt University provided further evidence by means of an experiment in which subjects were brain-scanned while playing a card game[17]. It turned out that they got the biggest reward when they had an unlikely win; yet they also received a dopamine reward when they lost. The explanation was that these were cases where they were *expecting* to lose. This result perhaps explains at last the pleasure that long-suffering sports fans derive from following even a losing team.

Dopamine is a particularly interesting neurotransmitter. The fact that it appeared very early in evolutionary history points to its importance in many functions associated with survival, including attention, motivation, learning and movement. Its particularly significant role, however, lies in identifying natural rewards such as food or sex and encouraging the so-called approach behaviours whereby we take measures to improve our existential lot, which in the modern era embraces activities like shopping. Dopamine is chiefly produced in the mid-brain regions that connect directly with the decision-taking areas of the frontal cortex. It is involved with the process of unconsciously memorising the signs with which these rewards are associated, such as the packaging of a favourite drink. Dopamine is also considered the neurotransmitter with the most overt 'feel-good' associations. What's interesting in this respect is the effect of stress on dopamine release. Short-term stress, otherwise known as stimulation, causes the hormone cortisol to instigate the neuronal release of dopamine, which accounts for why a bungee jump is actually a pleasure. Conversely, the long-term stress of being trapped in a cable-car, for example, actually *suppresses* dopamine release, triggering a state of anhedonia - literally 'lack of pleasure'.

It's now known that the release of dopamine in the area of the mid-brain called the nucleus accumbens is increased by substances that trigger dependency in humans. Cocaine works by blocking the reuptake not only of dopamine but also of other neurotransmitters like noradrenaline and serotonin. In other words, it binds to the transporters that would normally remove these neurotransmitters from the synaptic cleft between one neuron and the next, leaving the excess neurotransmitters to stimulate repeated firing. The result is that neurons modified by exposure to cocaine create feelings of euphoria (dopamine), confidence (serotonin), and energy (nor-adrenalin). Needless to say, all this comes at a cost in terms of the subsequent crash[18], not to mention the long-term damage to the endogenous (i.e. natural) reward system, and adverse effects on the neuronal links to the orbitofrontal cortex that governs acceptable social behaviour. Yet the brain has no normal need of drugs, alcohol and tobacco to stimulate a happy state; dopamine can do it quite naturally and without the deleterious effects. Dopamine itself does not cross the blood-brain barrier, so it cannot usefully be taken by mouth; its precursor L-DOPA, though administered to victims of Parkinson's disease, brings some serious side-effects. Were it not for these bio-chemical facts, human society might be very different. So it is intriguing to contemplate the notion that businesses have it in their power to give harmless dopamine-derived pleasure on a population-wide scale, simply by living up to expectations.

Proof of the pudding

These were exciting discoveries that explained better how we form beliefs and behaviours. Positive surprises bring things to our attention and cause us to hold a hypothesis about them; in other words, to set a neural threshold. Subsequent exposures are then measured at the neural level on the basis of whether expectation is met. If yes, our emotional bond (our schematic sleeve note) is locked in. If no, the dopamine deficit creates a neural queasiness that warns us off. It's apparent that our brains can learn not by a process of persuasion, nor by the establishment of a feeling of affinity, but simply according to whether things turned out as expected. The dopamine reward system is like a satellite navigation system, warning us if we are straying from the true and safe path. It suggests a conception of the human brain not as an organic computer that translates sensory input into action, but instead a *predicting machine*: a tool that has evolved to make guesses at every instant about what's coming next, with a bio-electrical feedback system for validating good guesses and flagging up bad ones.

What may puzzle you is the big dopamine release we get when an event over-delivers against expectation, which at first sight appears to support the under-promise/over-deliver thesis. It's easily understood in terms of evolutionary psychology: a positive surprise serves to flag up something new that may add to our chances of survival. Clearly the research that went into the Heuristic Profile picked up its importance. But it does appear to conflict with the fact that, in our FAST marketing experience, ads that give accurate expectations plainly influence purchasing behaviour more than ones that over- or under-promise, as borne out experimentally by Marks and Kamins[19]. There's a simple explanation: you can have too much of a good thing[20]. A dopamine surfeit tends to engender a 'refractory period': an interval of involuntary withdrawal akin to that experienced by cocaine users. The biggest dopamine rush of all, orgasm, even promotes promiscuity, a phenomenon known as the Coolidge Effect[21]. Commercially, it looks like too much dopamine risks being counter-productive.

To check the theory, we decided to conduct a unique experiment that was to have eye-opening implications. We recruited nearly 500 participants to play a game in which they were invited to invest money over ten rounds with three anonymous traders. One trader routinely over-promised, another under-promised, and the third was true to his word; but the amounts delivered by each were always similar. Afterwards, asked which of the three they had opted to deal with most, participants asserted that their strong favourite was the under-promising/over-delivering trader. The amount of money taken told a completely different story. In reality, the under-promiser was by far the *least* patronised, and the *honest broker* by far the most. Indeed, the latter took all of 72% more than the supposedly favoured trader. Apart from demonstrating the truth of the principle that you can't believe what even sincere people tell you, this was a triumph for the notion that humans have evolved to seek out unconsciously others who are true to their word. Conversely, the 'under-promise, over-deliver' scenario, equating to the idea of a surprisingly good dopamine reward, appears not to resonate behaviourally. Clearly it's *matching* expectations that keeps our dopamine Satnav stable and happy.

This finding came as no surprise to us former FAST marketers, nor should it to anyone who believes that honesty is the best policy. Every behavioural economist can readily understand why the hyperbolic over-promiser did better than subjects imagined. Though our conscious mind is plainly averse to the braggart who's likely to let us down, the *anchoring effect*[22], whereby the initial amount mentioned drags towards it our subsequent perception of reality, would account for an unconscious propensity to go with the big talker. The asymmetrical nature of the results suggests however that this explanation alone cannot account for the poor showing of 'under-promise/over-deliver'. If you don't like the neuroscientific explanation that it is analogous to the way that the orgasmic release of dopamine prompts prolactin to suppress desire[23], you may prefer a simple psychological interpretation. The under- and over-promisers are equal liars, but the former is deemed the more untrustworthy because he additionally feigns beneficence. Parallels might be drawn with the greater disappointment we feel if a disgraced politician has previously promised to clean up politics.

At the end of the day, the fact that the brain works in this deeply mechanical way should not seem a surprise but inevitable. Think again of the basic mental building block, the neuron. If you had the task of constructing a brain with it, what would you do with a piece of kit that can only tell whether it's had enough charge or not? You'd devise a binary system, and quite likely one that operates on a 'did it?/didn't it?' basis[24] - a system that works moment by moment to make sure you're still on the right track. It all makes sense when you consider that our genes aren't interested in whether we're well informed. They just want us to be exposed to as few unpleasant surprises as possible. Professor David Huron of Ohio State University, who has made a particular study of expectation-matching in music, wrote: *'Since accurate predictions are of real benefit to an organism, it would be reasonable for psychological rewards and punishments to arise in response solely to the accuracy of the expectation... This response is considered so important in the extant literature on expectation that it is commonly referred to as the primary affect'*[25]. He argues that the reason for humans' universal love of music is that we receive a steady dopamine reward for correctly predicting rhythm, melody and cadence from instant to instant, and misattribute this pleasure to the music itself.

Congruence: the brain's mode of choice

What lies at the heart of all this is the concept of *congruence*: the fact of sitting effortlessly within context or, if you like, matching up to expectations. Congruence - or consistency or continuity or coherence - has a natural appeal to us as humans. Perhaps it is because it has a singular appeal to our brains, based on its evolutionary importance, in the same way as the sound of flowing water. This will seem counter-intuitive only to marketers trained to think of creativity in terms of shock, surprise, standout, disruption, and dissonance. Congruence implies simply going with the flow, causing least resistance. In retrospect, it's clear that congruence was what lay at the heart of FAST marketing's success, and its absence accounts for the broken dreams that lie at the ad industry's doorstep. If making predictions is central to the way the brain functions, it is inevitable that experiences that fail to cause potentiated neurons to fire will be marked down as better ignored. It's hard to believe that such a fundamental mechanic makes exceptions for WPP, or even P&G.

The more we learn about the dopamine reward system, the more it appears fundamental to the way we form our commercial behaviour. We don't rationally evaluate things and take a position: 'this toothpaste will solve my self-confidence problem'. We leave it to our brains to predict the outcome of an action or event such as brushing one's teeth, and to observe at the neural level whether its prediction matches perceptual reality. Dopamine does the rest. Clearly it's not a perfect way of proceeding; but it's got us this far. I'm not arguing that making and testing predictions is all the brain does, even in respect of marketing. People can buy into unrealisable dreams in areas like high-ticket skincare, continuing to purchase hope through expensive anti-oxidants despite the scientific evidence[26]. But if prediction-checking is so fundamental to decision-making and behaviour formation, it deserves far more attention from business people than it gets. Cast your mind back to what I've said about the brain: heterogeneous, frugal, and binary. All of that says that the communications approach to marketing that's been adopted all these years has been better for admen than for shareholders. Start considering the brain not as a calculator-with-feelings but a predicting machine, and you'll come up with a lot of different assumptions.

Most importantly, you have to stop thinking of marketing as the means of making your product sound bigger and better than it is in reality. A notorious example of such hyperbole was the slogan 'The Listening Bank', a claim that left the Midland Bank (later bought out by HSBC) open to derision when the press obtained evidence that it was anything but. It's like setting the bar in a high jump that you yourself then have to clear; the higher you set it, the more likely you are in reality to fail. Try test driving a Ford Focus after you've seen an advertisement likening it to a passionate kiss with a gorgeous girl, and then ask yourself how much less disappointing it would have been if the advertising hadn't exaggerated.

A matter of personal chemistry

Why this way of thinking about business is commercially valuable can be stated very briefly. It corresponds much more closely with the psychobiology of real human beings in real commercial situations. What sets our species apart is our massive success at social bonding, no small feat considering our natural primate belligerence. (It is notable that the cortical mass of all primates correlates with the average size of the social groups we inhabit, and the human cortex is much the biggest[27]). Despite the enormous evolutionary pressures to compete with each other, we gain a net survival benefit from co-operating. The branch of economics known as game theory has been endeavouring to understand the mechanics of this co-operation for six decades, commencing with the Nobel laureate John Nash of 'A Beautiful Mind' fame. Useful light has been shed by the game of Prisoners' Dilemma, study of which explores the relative benefits to individuals of co-operation and defection over many iterations[28]. Extraordinarily, we not only thrive collectively by shunning and punishing defectors; brain-scanning reveals that, when we and our opposite number in a transaction both co-operate, we actually obtain a stronger release of dopamine than when we defect on a would-be co-operator, despite any greater short-term gain we therefore relinquish[29]. Once started, co-operative relationships endure just as long as neither party lets the other down; but getting them started between mutually sceptical strangers is difficult. It seems that the expectation-matching heuristic serves as a perfect ice-breaker.

One-to-one co-operation is the theoretical substrate of any bonded relationship, whether mother-child, teacher-pupil, boss-employee, or vendor-customer. Like all psychological phenomena, such bonding has a neurological basis. A key part of it is oxytocin, an extraordinary neuropeptide that, even when simply sprayed into the nostrils, stimulates an increase in trust, generosity, and even ability to recognise faces. It is the hormone involved in falling in love, maternal affection for babies, and even social recognition. It may not be too fanciful to think of oxytocin as the dab of glue that bonds two into one. Oxytocin makes relationships resilient; without it, there really would be only individuals and no society, and certainly a less successful species. A lot of human bonding is accounted for by 'kin selection', the process whereby we unconsciously favour others in proportion to their genetic proximity to us. In today's shrinking and increasingly heterogeneous world, we are bound with mathematical inevitability to come across more and more strangers with whom we have no obvious genetic connection. This is where oxytocin comes in. Experimental evidence exists that it forges temporary bonds between strangers, such that they are able to do business together[30] - whether that be sharing a skin of water in the desert, or doing a deal on a used motor off Streatham High Road.

Now, what follows needs to come with a health warning, being at the fringes of neuroscientific knowledge and consequently speculative. It's clear that oxytocin release and the dopamine system are intimately connected within the mechanics of the brain. It has long since been demonstrated experimentally that dopamine acts as a stimulator and regulator of the release of oxytocin[31][32]; the critical interaction of both has subsequently been shown in the romantic bond formation of rodents[33] and, more recently, in human sexual behaviour[34]. My own tentative hypothesis is that oxytocin plays a fundamental role in conjunction with the dopamine reward system in establishing new commercial behaviours in humans. Putting it crudely, the dopamine system may work out whether a thing is matching up to expectations; if it is, the release of oxytocin may then establish a working social bond accordingly. This might explain for good why a surfeit of dopamine in the case of over-delivery against expectations appears not to correlate with observable behaviour. Certainly an experiment to test the hypothesis, if it has not been conducted already, would provide a breakthrough in our understanding of how satisfied expectations translate into loyal shopping behaviour.

Why does it matter? Because, for corporations wishing to do regular business with large bodies of strangers who are naturally inclined to distrust, effecting an oxytocin release by means of matched expectations is going to be invaluable. And it simply will not be achievable by dint of u.s.p.'s, benefits, claims and reasons why or other sophisticated claptrap. The only way to make it happen is to gain a realistic understanding of the current reality, evoke it accurately, and continue to provide proofs of it over time. That demands ridding oneself of the conceit that, if the reality isn't what it ought to be, one must set about changing perceptions of it, the preoccupation of lazy marketers for decades now. The challenge is to walk the talk and talk the walk, and the way to attain that hallowed modus operandi is by cultivating an ethos of honesty throughout the organisation. All it requires is a managerial commitment; once in place, it should look after itself. It's a truism that liars always have much more on their plate.

There is a lot more to this than a crude humanistic feel-good factor. A pair of experiments conducted by Professor Guido Hertel[35] have demonstrated that our choices are strongly determined by our mood state. When we are happy and/or secure, we tend to accept things on trust. Conversely, an uncomfortable feeling obliges us to engage rationality instead of just waving the matter through. In consequence of just thinking about it, we become more likely to react against the other party. Put another way, conscious processing is likely to incline the subject *against* a positive decision, whereas going with the flow constitutes what one might call a no-brainer. Directly counter to the views of generations of advertising theorists, rational processing appears to be very bad news. It's the positive *feelings* we have towards the vendor - feelings to do with trust, generosity, and reciprocity - that enable us to take the plunge without mental ado.

Another psychologist experimenting in the field of neuroeconomics, David DeSteno of Northeastern University in Boston, maintains that business relationships are predicated on the sort of 'moral sentiments' espoused by Adam Smith, that enable the partners to display empathy and hence forge long-term emotional bonds[36]. The key implication of all this is that there's much going on beyond our conscious ken that influences the commercial decisions we make more than we can ever realise. Just to emphasise what a critical issue this is for business-people everywhere: analysing levels of trust within different societies around the world has revealed a positive correlation with national economic performance[37]. To put it simply, business gets done most efficiently when the partners are not consumed by the fear of being shafted. So there in a nutshell is the key to business success. Concern yourself less with what the other guy thinks of what you're selling, and lots more with how he feels about *you*.

One final piece of evidence. Robert H Frank of Cornell University, one of the world's leading behavioural economists, co-devised an experiment to ascertain to what extent the transactions we make are determined by our initial perception of our trading partner[38]. Subjects were brain-scanned while dealing with three different traders, each of whom started with a defined personality: good, bad, and neutral. All three in reality behaved the same; yet subjects continued throughout to prefer to deal with the one with the good reputation. It transpired that, in the cases of the good and the bad trader, the subjects' caudate, the brain part associated with reacting to positive or negative feedback, ceased to activate normally as it did in the neutral case, suggesting what you might call 'mind made up'. In other words, the incoming evidence was *overridden* by prejudice about the trading partner. It may not be rational, but it's how real brains get by in the real world. The researchers concluded that subjects might be getting a reward simply from the fact of putting money into the pocket of a business partner they perceived as morally good. It's a feeling you may have had when (irrationally) leaving a generous tip for a good waiter, even though you may never encounter him again. It should speak volumes about the best way to persuade your customer to buy from you.

8
Practice Made Perfect

The case for caution

Aside from medics, scientists are not generally keen on 'case studies', and with good cause. They are an invitation to misrepresent. If you are trying to prove (or disprove) that 'if x, then y', you either need a killer experiment, or an aggregation of many examples to demonstrate statistically that the rule is valid generally. You can't just pick out the instances that seemed to work and say, 'Hey, presto!' The latter was the principle on which Sigmund Freud operated, not only selecting patients that suited his theories but even liberally re-inventing his data to fit. It's no wonder that he fell out with Jung, or that his legacy, psycho-analysis, has since been lampooned by the likes of Eysenck, Popper and even Wittgenstein. Of course, modern-day practitioners will tell you they've moved on his theory a lot, but you still won't see a lot of evidence rigorous enough to meet scientific standards.

The same, sad to say, is true of much marketing. The IPA Advertising Effectiveness Awards, for example, are a microcosm of how the advertising and marketing industries sell themselves, picking out the good bits and ignoring the bulk. When 'The Spectator' published a letter from me arguing against public service advertising, I received an angry email from a senior ad industry person informing me that she was publishing a book featuring forty IPA case studies 'proving' the case for advertising. (She called the IPA database the 'gold standard around the world'). I didn't have the heart to ask how many cases had therefore been left out. Being so conscious of the dangers of selective evidence, it pains me to present some 'case studies' here. That I feel permitted to do so is for one reason only. The stories I'll recite are not intended to prove any scientific rules, but to demonstrate how the new kinds of 'finding-out' techniques covered in the last chapter, allied to a Heuristic approach to developing businesses, have already been put to use in the real world. Although I shall mention some of the beneficial effects of such activity, I'd invite you to remember throughout that they are only individual cases. My hope is merely that, if these few can spark interest in this new way of doing things, they will give rise to broader usage of the techniques that will in time allow for convincing statistical proof, or otherwise.

Let me start then at the beginning. In 2005, we found ourselves with an army of good people, a detailed process based on strong theory and prior evidence, and a whole new toolkit. The question was: who was going to take the plunge? That honour goes to Ben McGannan, the proprietor of Water for Work, a regional English company that basically does what it says on the bottle; it supplies water coolers and natural spring water from its own source. He didn't so much volunteer to be a guinea pig as insist. He'd built the business from scratch, made a lot of money, but wanted to go from good to great. The deal was that he'd let us do anything we wanted, within reason, though he expected to pay rather less than anyone subsequently! The sole business criterion he set was that our investigation must be entirely commercially focused, aiming to lay bare the means whereby the company's Heuristic potential could be exploited with immediate effect. What he did not want was a fat report and no clue as to the practical measures he needed to take.

Putting life into Water

Our start point was to get a really good handle not on the business challenge per se but the thoughts and feelings of staff, customers, potential customers and even competitors about the business - which in turn told us a lot more about the business challenge itself and how to address it. To do this, we used some straight interviewing to get the business facts but mostly a gamut of psychological devices to get around the usual tendency for people to say what is politically correct. The picture we built up was revealing, to say the least. It was apparent that the business had been very successful on account of a simple formula, the provision of a product that very seldom disappointed, always delivered with impeccable service. In a conventional sense, this had proved a strong differentiator in a market dominated by big corporations that to us didn't appear that bothered about service. However, most of the growth had gone out of the market, and the big cloud on the horizon was the pressure on the public sector to save money in the face of growing discontent among ratepayers. This meant that, in the big volume area, commoditisation was the name of the game.

To cut a long story short, our key finding was that the business lacked any sense of a bigger purpose. It had been established to fulfil a basic need; and that, in the minds of its customers and staff alike, was all it did. Consequently, since the relationship was skin deep, it was too easy for both customers and staff to go elsewhere. Now, the standard consultancy response to such a situation is to say, 'You need a mission? Then let's invent one'. It is precisely such fabrications that create the sort of disconnect between reality and marketing that customers can sense unconsciously. What is critical is the congruence residing at the heart of truth, honesty, trust, and therefore bonding. We had to look for something grounded in the current reality. So we delved carefully into what the company already had within it that was in the nature of a cause.

The key to it we found in the man himself. He is a natural enthusiast. Unlike many a proprietor who maintains a healthy distance from whatever it is he's selling, Ben McGannan had a passion for getting people hydrated. This was well before the word became fashionable. He was wont to preach drinking water as an essential 'life skill' that should be taught in schools, and had been pumping his own money for years into children's charities. It was interesting to note how he had unwittingly recruited staff in his own image, because throughout the organisation we found people who got just as worked up as he did on the subject of how all of us, not just children, are routinely dehydrated, and what that costs us in terms of our physical, mental, and financial performance. Since there was growing evidence in the media of chronic dehydration in the workplace, with major economic implications for the nation, it had the feel of a worthwhile cause.

Our recommendation was really quite simple. We told him to make a job of his hobbyhorse. In other words, we drew up a manifesto for hydrating the masses, and translated it into an overhaul of the company's modus operandi and the way it was communicated congruently to the public. This certainly did not mean throwing out the baby with the bathwater. What it did mean was propagating those existing values actively throughout the organisation and ensuring that they imbued every facet of its operations. We started with the basics. The existing company logo, intended to resemble ripples, looked very much like the bottom of a baked-bean tin. Imagine it on the side of a white van and you get the full picture of the company's slightly dull personality. The start point for us was the introduction of a graphic new corporate logo, designed simply to say iconically, 'We are Water, and we are about hydration'. It was also made clear in words that the business of hydration is equally relevant to the home, since we don't cease to be human when we leave the office.

The new identity appeared first on the company letterhead, then on the side of the factory, and after that on a new fleet of vehicles which suddenly transformed from white van to something you'd notice on the motorway. The head office was redecorated, complete with ubiquitous little reminders of the cause. There was a new website that embraced all the new values, incorporating music designed by a musicologist to create an appropriate mood state and composed and performed by our own version of Brian Eno. A recruitment drive was conducted to locate appropriate personality types with a proclivity to share the passion as positions became vacant. An extensive programme of coaching was undertaken to inculcate the vision, teach many of the key facts about hydration, and encourage staff to live and breathe the passion in their new, specially designed apparel. The new focus spilled over into more than a dozen staff-organised activity groups associated with health and wellbeing, a particular favourite being the daily hula-hoop session.

On the science side, the company brought in a Ph.D to compile a library of academic papers and editorial on water and hydration issues, the aim being to create a repository of knowledge that should be the first port of call for anyone wanting a scientific opinion on hydration issues from the commercial world. The company then employed another Ph.D to act as its full-time science officer and spokesman. This facilitated a programme of research, first into means of optimising hydration in the home amongst children - and yes, there really are better alternatives than the usual choice between tap water or Coke - and then concerning general attitudes towards hydration as a sub-set of health and wellbeing generally. Now, it was inevitable that, having come so far, Ben would want to be doing something truly ground-breaking in this area. The upshot was that the company funded a pioneering fMRI study into acute dehydration in young adults which yielded a striking result representing a genuine addition to medical knowledge[1].

It's hard to believe in retrospect that a regional company in the water business could have travelled so far, so fast. Of course, we all hear lots of case studies, and they always have a happy ending, don't they? What we're talking here, however, is not just a marketing relaunch that finishes with some approving market-research ratings. The proof of the pudding is in the eating. In the year following the start of this overhaul, the company enjoyed its best ever business performance. But it's what has happened since then that is even more extraordinary. In the course of 2007-8, the whole industry suffered a pummeling from a triple whammy. First came the credit crunch and, in its wake, its ugly big sister the economic crash. Then it was two years of atrocious summer weather, including the worst on record for rainfall in the critical months for the water industry. And finally it was the turn of the UK government and public sector, making a political cause out of sticking the boot into the bottled-water industry.

In this dire context, it was alarming to witness what happened to the industry at a time when unemployment was already reaching record levels. Everyone suffered. A lot of companies quite simply went out of business, or sold up. One journalist gleefully told Ben that the industry was finished. Ben, however, was able to soldier on regardless. More than that, he set about making an acquisition or two of his own. Counterparts in the industry association who had raised eyebrows at what he was doing, and even ridiculed it, were openly envious of his position. Some, far from criticising, flattered him in the sincerest way, by adopting a similar stance. He was elected vice-chairman of the industry association, made the keynote speech at the industry body's conference, and was nominated for a 'Director of the Year' award by the Institute of Directors. That he should thrive in such difficult circumstances, however, was down to more than just determination and charm.

The particular reason for this bucking of the trend was embodied in a 21st-century version of a speak-your-weight machine: the 'Water Wellpoint'. This high-tech device was the fruit of Ben's realisation that dehydration is a threat to busy human beings because it's so hard to discern. Together we put together a team to create an algorithm that would make it possible to calculate a person's 'hydration quota', the amount of extra water they need to drink to bring them up to a normal level. The algorithm is useless without a means of applying it easily and en masse; so Water entered into a joint venture with the makers of the machine to write a programme that would measure six vital signs, including blood pressure and body mass index, within five minutes. Ben created an entire new Water Wellpoint division that now provides health and wellbeing programmes for large corporations and public bodies, incorporating instant health-checks with advice and a good amount of palatable education about the virtues of weight loss, smoking cessation, exercise, and of course proper hydration. Needless to say, it's proving popular with institutions that are all too conscious of the crippling cost of sickness absence. And it's brought the company a fair amount of recognition in the national media.

Ben regularly rings late at night to tell you what a great day the cause has had, and routinely ends his emails with 'C'mon!'; not your regular CEO, I think you'll agree. And he makes no bones about why all this has come to pass. 'The way science unleashes your business potential, just by dealing in proven truths', he said, 'has been an absolute revelation'. The benefit that he's had from a Heuristic investigation is tangible: a regional SME that simply sold water in bottles has been transformed into one that is on the front foot, possesses knowledge and expertise to envy, and has complete buy-in to the vision among every last one of its staff. If you don't believe that, consider this statistic. The amount of annual sickness absence per employee reduced from 6.4 sick days per to 3.1 in just two years. Translated nationally, that alone would save UK business £6.5 billion a year. Show me a CSR programme that's achieved a result like that, and I'll show you a huge bill.

Honda: The Power of Heuristics

Of course, it was a huge stroke of luck to come across someone as open-minded and liberal as Ben early in the Newcomen Group's existence. It gave us the chance not only to try out several of the tools - which, bear in mind, had been by no means certain to work in practice - but also to apply the findings in a concerted way to a company-wide business challenge. This provided the confidence that the process we had developed could successfully be applied to big corporate issues. The first forward-thinking employee of an international corporation to take an interest was Ian Armstrong, a besuited, bespectacled, shaven-headed marketer from the north-east of England who could easily be taken at first sight for a trader in the city. The fact that he rides a huge motorbike and climbs mountains for charity should tell you there's more to him. I'd first met him when he was a young marketer working on Tango, the soft-drinks brand that had once taken on the might of Coca-Cola Schweppes Beverages armed only with a singularly visible (and, to begin with, experientially accurate) advertising property. Ian gave the brand a new lease of life by insisting that his new agency reverted to the famous 'You know when you've been Tango'd' idea. He subsequently was poached by Honda, with whom he developed the famous 'The Power of Dreams' campaign. It's rare that managers succeed in two places, let alone with two such iconic ad campaigns. No wonder he was introduced to a conference of advertising account planners as a 'folk hero'.

While we were putting some of our Water learnings into practice, Ian gave us a task to perform as a trial run of our capabilities. He wisely set us a low-risk challenge to begin with, an investigation of the Heuristic properties of one of Honda's more sporty models. We started the process with a tool called Identifier that used a cunningly phrased questionnaire to relax company managers into talking openly about the car and their aspirations for it. We then used a series of toolkit exercises to create a Heuristic Profile of the vehicle that we could contrast with these aspirations. In classical hypothetico-deductive manner, we used phase one to put us in a position to posit a hypothesis that we then set out to demolish in phase two. All we managed to do, in fact, was to improve it. Perhaps the highlight of the project was the immersive chamber we put subjects through immediately after driving the car at speed, half of them for the first time, and became party to their adrenaline-soaked feelings. What we learned was that, contrary to current belief, the vehicle was experientially rather like Lauren Bacall: beautiful, potentially dangerous, but entirely dependable. Specifically, the inquiry exposed what was sacrosanct about this unique experience that made it addictive to its aficionados, a group of whom we went to meet at one of their regular gatherings to get a reality check. It left us in a position to tell the Honda marketers not only how best to promote the car, but also what the design team could and shouldn't change when the time came to revamp it.

Reassured that these new tools actually worked, Ian next decided to let us loose in a more public arena, the dealer network. Specifically, he introduced us to the management team of an independently owned group of Honda dealerships in the east of England. Our brief was to do what we could to ameliorate the business from the customer's perspective. What we didn't know was that the group's founder was planning to retire shortly and wanted us to help get the business in the best possible shape prior to negotiating a sale. We performed a number of exercises over a period of a month to build a Heuristic Profile that was again informed as much by staff insights as by customer investigation. Aside from a vision of what the business was ultimately capable of becoming, it yielded a list of over sixty action points that required addressing in order to optimise the smooth flow of the experience, starting with the chaotic parking lot that generally had people entering the building feeling frazzled. Aware that knowledge is worthless without action, the team set about addressing them immediately, and had already tackled two-thirds when I returned a month later. I could tell they'd been hard at it as soon as I pulled into the car park, which was now a model of convenience. I wasn't surprised when the outgoing MD later made a point of telling me the new owners had been impressed by the fact of their having undertaken the work, something that one trusts was reflected in the purchase price.

What this exercise also threw up, however, was a conundrum that affected not just this group but potentially the whole network and, who knows, maybe the motor trade around the entire globe. Honda has a strong advertising campaign whose intelligent, offbeat style is well known to owners. Though Honda's salesroom staff did not overtly embody the 'Power of Dreams' idea communicated by the advertising, the well-trained, friendly and knowledgeable persona we encountered everywhere was passably congruent with it. Rather less so was the sales environment itself. All customers viewed car showrooms, right across the motor trade, in much the same way: as featureless chambers whose cathedral-like calm was intimidating. We learned that the historical reason for it was that showrooms are deliberately kept a simple blank canvas so that the vehicles will shine against the backdrop. What this commonsense assumption meant, however, was that the environment appeared to exert an adverse influence on customers' emotional response to the sales process; and, in a supposedly experiential age, the motor trade was missing out on one its best opportunities to present a satisfying experience, let alone to match expectations. This looked a major problem-cum-opportunity, and Ian was understandably keen to understand it better, particularly in a competitive context.

His curiosity was to lead to a more ambitious, exacting and ultimately revelatory experiment than we ever could have imagined before that time: Project Brunel. The idea was simple enough. We would follow a number of individuals who wished to buy a car as they went through the actual process, scrutinising their thoughts and feelings at every moment along the way. The participants would visit not only Honda dealerships but any that sold models of interest to them. What complicated matters was that we knew we must not take their word for anything, but needed to contrast their expressed opinions with whatever non-verbal measures we could garner. In part this involved having them wear a biometric vest so that we could track heart rate, respiration, and other useful metrics. But that was only the beginning. In addition to wiring them up for sound, we also filmed them at most points in the process, so that we could read their facial expressions and body language. At Honda dealerships, this even included a hidden camera in the salesman's tie. This comprehensive catalogue meant we were able to create a full record whereby we could marry up the data at every point with actual events. By also observing a strict protocol, with fixed interviewing points at various stages and a purchasing process as standardised as the subjects' personal dictates would allow, we were able to gather data in such a way that comparisons could easily be made and patterns identified.

Naturally it turned out a mammoth undertaking. The personnel involved consisted of a chief project scientist, five physiologists, three AV technicians, two IT technicians, three researchers, four data analysts, two recruiters, two confederates, one project manager, two project assistants, thirteen subjects, three drivers, three chaperones and, not least, three salesmen. The fieldwork took fourteen weeks, with activity conducted on five days in every seven. Forty store visits were monitored, seventy-six interviews conducted, and over one hundred hours of live-time multi-source data collected, all of it needing to be teased apart and then rewoven into a coherent narrative. As so often in scientific inquiries, what we learned at the end of all this endeavour was that the hypothesis held water; but there was much more to it than we had appreciated.

One of the most startling revelations was the number of occasions on which subjects who'd intended either certainly or probably to buy were thrown off course by the salesman's language, behaviour or negotiating tactics; yet the salesman would be quite unaware of the fact, putting down the failure to a lack of interest on the customer's part or some other plausible pretext. (The word 'pretext' is chosen carefully: salesmen would credit customers with an intentionality that, to be honest, was often lacking from their behaviour). Some of the subjects' true reasons for not purchasing were painfully simple, such as a failure to be acknowledged on entry that would compound their initial anxiety enough to persuade the more nervous simply to leave. More complex were situations where female customers brought along a male companion to provide advice, only to find the salesman then ignoring them in favour of the companion, a source of considerable irritation. These 'tripping points' as we named them occurred so consistently that we were able to describe nearly three dozen, of which thirty could be addressed simply by drawing them to the sales personnel's attention, something that can now be done systematically in the form of a one-day training course.

The experimental design allowed us to gather a large body of evidence that such issues are endemic in the car industry. Part of the issue, we inferred, concerned the salespeople themselves, and specifically the personality types normally attracted to a career in the motor trade.

Mostly male, logical and focused, they are not generally recruited for their ability to empathise with others who see the world differently. I hasten to add that we did see some splendid examples of more experienced salesmen who had learned to look for telltale clues and made a point of establishing an appropriate rapport with the customer, but these were the exception that proved the rule. When we mapped out the consumer journey from initial interest to actual purchase from a psychological point of view, it was often striking that, at every stage, the salesperson's interpretation was out of kilter with the reality of the customer's mental process. For example, what the salesperson imagined was a matter of calm negotiation was, for the customer, a moment of intense anxiety. That many salespeople get this wrong has nothing to do with a lack of intelligence on their part; it says much more about the conventional wisdom that has taken root in a culture dominated by alpha males.

Where this mismatch of minds became most apparent was when customers who knew more or less what they were after and aimed to get it sorted quickly, in sharp contrast to those who talked in advance about looking forward to the process of mulling over which car to buy. What we observed was that the former would become agitated when things cropped up that interrupted their flow, whereas the latter were turned off if the salesperson hurried along the process with insufficient diversion. It struck us that this phenomenon tallied interestingly with the study of 'metamotivational states'; specifically, the condition of being in either a telic (goal-oriented) frame of mind, or a paratelic one where we are out to enjoy ourselves. Although we all tend to lean one way or another in our approach to life, we may each vary considerably according to whether we're out to buy a box of screws or a new suit[2]. Experimental research in shopping centres has shown that the very stimulus that saves a person in a paratelic state from getting bored will drive a telic subject to distraction[3]. What this suggested was that treating all customers the same way, as most motor-trade practice demands, will immediately alienate around half the custom. Being able to sort them readily, and then taking each through a tailored experience, is a fascinating and commercially promising challenge on which we have already embarked. Interestingly, it was only possible because our constant exposure to the world of science alerted us to a long line of academic evidence in this particular sphere dating back to 1972[4]; in any orthodox business culture, it is doubtful that the key to competitive advantage would even have been spotted.

Obviously there were other such findings of such commercial worth to Honda that they cannot yet be discussed publicly. The beauty of having undertaken such a rigorous study, however, was that virtually everything we uncovered not only rang true but also was hard to dispute. This second point needs emphasising, because what is good for the organisation is not necessarily good for every individual within it, and change often founders at the door of the first manager to say no. None of us knew what to expect the first time we presented the findings to a panel of Ian's fellow managers. They listened intently, in nerve-stretching silence, and then asked some tough questions. The moment of truth was a portentous pronouncement by one who'd still said not a word: 'I've always said the industry's had it wrong for ninety years', he said. 'Now no one can dispute it'. From that moment, we knew the only battle would concern how best to monetise the knowledge.

The first step, naturally enough, was to communicate the learnings to sales personnel across the network and show them how to take advantage. It was in the course of talking to showroom principals about this programme that we renewed our contact with the new managing director of the dealerships where we'd started our Honda explorations. At the nadir of the recession and with the Honda's UK factory on a three-month shut-down, he shared with us the news that business had never been better, his group's market share in the first quarter of January 2009 having climbed to *more than double* Honda's national average. Now, there's no way we'd take any of the credit away from him and his team; but it's interesting that the one place where the new thinking had first been put into action should stand out so conspicuously.

Heuristics in mid-air

Not that Heuristic thinking demands good times to get a look-in. The airline industry has had a frightful time of it, what with sky-high fuel prices and environmentalist pressures. On top of all that, the Open Skies agreement has thrown open the North Atlantic routes to all comers, placing huge pressure on the incumbents. One of these, Virgin Atlantic, wanted to know how they could cut costs in their Upper Class operation without affecting quality. This was even harder than it might sound, seeing that there were a lot of fixed ideas about what was and wasn't dispensable; a delicate matter in instances where the particular feature under consideration may literally have been introduced by the chairman's wife. We undertook an open-minded two-stage inquiry where, in the first instance, we performed a Condenser exercise, actually in an airport lounge, to help form hypotheses. These were then tested on a transatlantic journey on which we wired subjects for sound and had them comment on their feelings at various moments from the time they left home in the complimentary limo to their arrival at the other end. What we also did was covertly observe them the whole time as they encountered a number of stimuli we placed in their way.

The data we collected enabled us to compose a Heuristic Profile of the experience that told plenty about its appeal. The idea at the heart of it was a sense of being cocooned, shielded at every stage from the vicissitudes of long-distance travel. It was a feeling that new travelers relished, and regular travelers thought worth paying a premium for. It was also, incidentally, not to be found referred to explicitly in any of the company's marketing. Consequently, any thought that had previously been given to what was and was not integral to the experience had focused on consistency with the sexy brand rather than true psychological experience. It meant that we were able to point out not only the many ways in which the experience could be built upon with congruent additions and refinements, but particularly which elements of the existing experience were Heuristically redundant or even at odds with it. Armed with this knowledge, the company was put in a position to make economies amounting to £10 million (then $20 million) per annum. These changes were made without any decline in customer satisfaction levels and, crucially, the percentage of seats sold, or 'load factor', remained constant. It gave us a lot of pleasure when the results for the first full year came in. While British Airways had collapsed deep into the red, Virgin Atlantic had doubled its profits year on year. CEO Steve Ridgway specifically mentioned in his report a rise in premium-fare traffic, contrasting starkly with the arch competitor's 13% drop.

How and how not to sell

A very different challenge faced Carphone Warehouse, the biggest independent mobile-phone retailer in Europe. They were enjoying almost more custom than they could deal with, but wanted to know how they could capitalise on customer interest most efficiently. They were in for a surprise. Using a comparable methodology to Honda's Project Brunel, we took customers through a complete purchasing process, including their prior online search which we monitored keystroke by keystroke.

We were able to compare customers' expectations graphically with what happened when they walked through the door of a number of competing mobile-phone retailers. Interestingly, expectations were more than matched; but that was in this instance no good thing. The prospect of visiting a mobile-phone store filled most of them with trepidation. What they feared above all was 'the pounce', their word for the moment when the salesperson would latch onto them even before they had got their bearings. What made it worse was that, unlike in, say, a department store, there was nowhere to hide. In practice, the experience was even more grueling than anticipated, so well trained were the sales personnel in cutting to the chase. One subject's commentary summed it up: 'It's incredible in there, a sales machine'; and then, asked if he'd therefore been impressed, 'No! It's diabolical!'

The irony was that the requirement to buy a phone is essentially an enjoyable one for most, a new piece of kit of our very own that we can choose to match our needs with some precision and then further tailor to be a particularly personal accoutrement. Nor was there much wrong with most of the actual retail operations, which offered ample choice, a convenient (if rather utilitarian) environment, and generally presentable, well informed personnel. The problem arose entirely in the way in which staff had been trained to deal with customers. It contrasted vividly with subjects' experience in the control condition, in which they set about obtaining a new mortgage. This purchase was altogether less interesting, though far more daunting in that such large amounts of money were involved that any mistake was unconscionable. It appeared however that financial personnel were well groomed in putting customers at their ease, with the result that the latter actually came out with less of a sense of being pressurised. Carphone Warehouse subsequently undertook a nationwide programme of retraining to impress upon its own sales force the necessity of balancing anxiety to make the sale with a need to respect customers' personal space - a real opportunity for competitive advantage. The possibility of refinements to the store environment that might enhance a sense of comfort represents a further opportunity.

New approaches

An adjacent field - telecoms manufacturing - provided us with an early chance to apply Heuristic thinking to the acceleration of new product development. Samsung asked us a simple question: what should the next generation of phones for women look like? The challenge was intriguing, embracing as it did a number of cultural as well as technical challenges. What lent it added piquancy was a tight time-frame: twelve weeks from beginning to end, which needed to incorporate our acquiring a general understanding of principles, development of hypotheses, initial screening, and lastly quantitative testing. It is hard to imagine that the project would have been possible without a prior philosophy, process and tools. We used an inquisitive Ph.D to perform a worldwide sweep of existing ideas and technologies, Condenser exercises and technical interviews to garner new opportunities, immersive chambers and ostensibly informal gatherings to refine them into product ideas, and finally an online tool called Numerator to determine which would work in practice.

The extraordinary output of this investigation was a collection of fourteen ideas, thirteen of which were deemed by the client team strong and original enough to put into the final assessment. The result was astonishing. Where one might be glad to be left with one or two winners, there were actually *seven* that fell in the top box of customer appeal. Not for the first or last time, however, life was not simple. The marketing director also asked us to enter a number of other ideas that had currency among international management. All bombed rather badly. It was left to us to communicate this news, the said marketing director having left the company on the day of the debrief to join a rival. Not unsurprisingly, this did not go down conspicuously well with the party that had espoused the unsuccessful ideas. We had the consolation that at least two of the Heuristically developed ideas went straight into research and development, and the sponsor of the work expressed the view that it was the best research project she'd worked on. A year or two later, one couldn't help noticing that most of the ideas we'd developed were finding their way onto the market, under one brand name or another.

The perfect security blanket

A very different problem was presented by the global insurance group, Aviva. The management had decided on a comprehensive relaunch built on a differentiated benefit, all to do with recognising its customers as individuals. It was mapped out by the research agency with a thoroughness that would have brought joy to Jack Trout's heart. The company management was however very conscious of the need to ensure that the organisation delivered against this promise, itself an encouraging sign. We were asked to undertake a thorough investigation to ascertain how well the business was already performing in this respect, and what could be better. Aviva proved commendably open to rigorous inquiry, allowing us even to undertake an experiment where a sizeable number of customers were wired up whilst actually renewing their insurance or reacting to a recording of a claim they had made. Apart from casting considerable doubt on the industry-wide assumption that insurance is all about the cost of the premium, our investigations showed that, rather like with car sales, business could easily be lost because of a lack of congruence in the process. But there was more to it than that.

I recounted earlier the 'Honest Broker' experiment that demonstrated how we strangely irrational beings have evolved to do things our conscious brains are not even aware of, let alone able to account for. The final experiment we conducted for Aviva demonstrated vividly how empathetic human contact decisively influences the smooth running of a sales process. Another five hundred participants were invited to play a game in which they were to purchase insurance on behalf of an elderly relative who was concerned only that making a claim should not prove difficult. They were exposed to four 'insurers' with whom they could do business. Subjects answered the questions of each and were in turn offered a price. What they did not know is that the four insurers had been programmed to represent four different business processes. Two processes were congruent in the sense of flowing effortlessly according to expectations; the others were not. Of each pair, one was empathetic and one was not.

After completing the exercise, subjects almost universally reported that they had chosen according to price. The statistics told a different story. The congruent-and-empathetic process took *more than double* the amount of business that would be anticipated if price were indeed the key factor; contrariwise, both processes lacking in congruence won under a third of the deals expected. It's more evidence of the power of the unconscious mind, shaped by a long age of evolution, to select for us the relationship-based behaviour that is good for us in the long run, and not purely utilitarian. The findings challenged some fundamental corporate assumptions about how insurance transactions should be conducted, naturally prompting considerable internal debate, which owed much to the project sponsors' efforts to disseminate the output widely and encourage adoption of the new thinking across its various departmental functions. That is not to say, however, that their invitation has been universally taken up at the time of writing, a fact perhaps not unconnected with having to fight off a takeover bid.

Looking back over these projects, it's not hard to discern a common thread. Just think about them. A service company that is perfectly congruent in all its manifestations; a car manufacturer that does not deter you by unwittingly upsetting your expectations; an airline whose many product features add up to a coherent whole; a retailer that does not discomfort you by allowing its own agenda to interrupt your own; a mobile phone that works the way you intuitively expect it to, instead of demanding that you adapt to it; a financial company that turns a difficult transaction into a breeze. Until now, any inquiring journalist would have inferred that they were simply doing what's professional. What you can now see, armed with what you've learned of the most fundamental workings of the human brain, is that they have something else in common. They are all going with the neural flow, creating literally happy customers by setting expectations that they can live up to with ease; that is, by ignoring the old-school business manuals and just doing *what feels right*.

Having protested earlier about the practice of selecting case studies that support one's thesis and ignoring the rest, I am conscious of the risk of being hoist by my own petard. So let me testify now that, had I been attempting to *disprove* the case for Heuristic investigation and development, I would here be very short on material. In fact, I can recall only one case where a project ultimately proved fruitless. We undertook a psychobiological investigation into Al Gore's film *An Inconvenient Truth,* measuring response throughout and contrasting it with reaction to a ten-minute multi-modal experience we'd designed. The latter, which was intended to assist the sponsoring client in raising awareness of climate change among corporate staff, proved demonstrably more engaging; yet, for reasons best described as political, he was unable to gain the requisite directorial backing for his plans to put the findings to use. It was a disappointing pre-echo of the failed Copenhagen Summit. It just goes to show that any evidence can be dismissed by corporate types who can't see how it helps them. Nonetheless, we still have a nice memento in the form of the client's response to the initial report we sent him: 'Excellent. If you were here right now, I'd hug you'.

What this variety of early tasks taught us was the sheer versatility of Heuristic inquiry, to such an extent that we now kick ourselves for not making the transition from packaged goods much sooner. Having established a track record, we no longer have to persuade potential clients of its benefits; on the contrary, we are asked with satisfying frequency whether it might unravel a particular thorny problem. Without wishing to sound blasé, I can tell you that, when people ask what limits there are to Heuristic inquiry, we tend to say that it is only of use where human experience is involved. In other words, where business is concerned, its scope is practically unbounded. Consequently, the challenges grow ever broader. It is a pleasing sign that the notion of using superior comprehension to create coherence between experiential touch-points is catching on. Each of the examples above is a big advance on simply creating difference for surprise's sake. But it's only a start. Our aim has to be a commercial culture where communication-driven expectations and actual experience form a sufficiently congruent whole that the brains of consumers feel like they're bathing in honey; or dopamine. If that were ever to become the norm, the commercial world would look and feel entirely different. In principle, it's all perfectly achievable from where we stand. So what is there to hold us back?

Epilogue

Plus ça change...

During the editing of this book, a story broke that the Norfolk Broads, that lovely old magnet to tranquillity-seeking boatsmen, were to be marketed as 'Britain's Magical Waterland'[1]. The brainchild of a self-designated 'brand strategy guru', the idea immediately came in for a welter of derision. The charge levelled against it by the media was that it was the sort of top-drawer marketing bullshit that could have sprung from the pen of a TV comedy writer. What struck me as rather pitiful was the thought of all the kids who'd be dragged up the A11 under the illusion that they were in for a Disney-style Experience, only to find themselves whiling away the week on a windswept barge. Such dopamine-deficit misery is a crime when it would be so easy to make visitors neurochemically happy with their stay. The story says an awful lot about marketing's kneejerk recourse to hyperbole; not to mention gurus whose wisdom is rooted less in science than in brand dogma. But it does shed new light on the belief of that pithiest of Nobel laureates, Richard Feynman, that science is simply the belief that experts don't know a lot[2].

As ever, the practical difficulty is that, as Keynes observed, it's much better for one's reputation to suffer conventional failure than to enjoy unconventional success[3]. One problem faced by innovators is that it's not easy to get experts to revise their opinions even when you put innovation on a plate for them. A few years ago, I addressed an audience of scientists under the aegis of the Society for Chemical Industry's 'Consumer & Sensory Research Group'. I received an email afterwards from one of the delegates saying, 'I must admit my immediate reaction to your talk was one of surprise and I suppose frustration that something so fundamental is being hailed as new'. In a pedantic sense, she had a point. The psychological (though not the neuroscientific) precepts upon which Heuristic theory is based are not just well established, but actually date back at least to the middle of the last century. They are familiar to any psychology graduate, which is what the delegate was. The important point however is that, though these ideas that have taken root in the academic world, they have largely remained strangers to business. Orthodox marketing appears unable even to contemplate that body of learning. So dismissing this new application of scientific knowledge as 'been there, done that' is not unlike rubbishing Velcro because Nature came up with the idea first.

If change blindness is one thing, active resistance is another. Thanks to the schemata of self-interested experts, our species is cussedly averse to change. In the nineteenth century, a physician called Dr Ignaz Semmelweiss wondered why one of the two obstetrics wards in the Viennese hospital where he was an assistant endured such high mortality (one in three) that mothers-to-be literally prayed not to be admitted there. The death rate on the ward was in fact ten times higher than on the other ward, a fact which scientific theory of the day ascribed to 'universal patterns of fluctuation'. Dr Semmelweiss brilliantly deduced a connection with the fact that all deliveries on the notorious first ward were conducted by surgeons who'd just returned from performing operations and were covered in gore. Suspecting a causal relationship, he prevailed upon the surgeons to clean up before they were admitted. To everyone's astonishment, the death rate plummeted to an even lower level than the second, safer ward.

If only life could remain so simple. The surgeons were resentful of this upstart's interference, particularly because the bloodstains on their hands were regarded as a badge of honour. They soon had young Dr Semmelweiss forced out into obscurity, and his new protocol over-turned. The mortality rate reverted to its former level, and worse. It took Louis Pasteur, several decades and countless maternal deaths later, to set the scientific community straight, when he revealed to the world the existence of the invisible creatures we now know as microbes. Not that this came as any consolation to Dr Semmelweiss: by that time, he had been beaten to death in a lunatic asylum. Nor can we take the consolation that this was a battle won for all time. According to the Royal College of Physicians, the third biggest killer after heart disease and cancer in modern Britain is the medical profession itself, one factor being the proliferation in hospitals of the MRSA superbug in consequence of, guess what, poor hygiene standards among staff. And medicine is one of contemporary society's more scientific pursuits.

Thomas Kuhn's classic work *The Structure of Scientific Revolutions*[4] made the point that even communities of scientists can become so wed to a common set of assumptions that they will consider no alternative until a mooted disparity with reality becomes unacceptably large. Such in-built conservatism is not necessarily a bad thing: it serves as a salve against fashion, and ensures that the body of evidence needs to be sufficiently robust to justify a change of paradigm. If that is true of scientists, it's understandable if scepticism prevails among experts of all kinds, including marketers. My experience of FAST marketing revealed a lot about the response a genuinely new business idea can expect. Some marketing managers welcomed the new approach with open arms. But most had one of three responses: to dismiss it as irrelevant; to claim they were already doing it; or to construe it in line with what they already knew. The trouble for business owners is that one cannot prevent managers' survival instincts from overriding whatever natural inquisitiveness they possess, even when it's to the detriment of the organisations they work for. But the trouble runs deeper.

Les Binet is a senior ad industry theorist employed by DDB, today's incarnation of the BMP agency that once took the advertising world by storm with a string of ground-breaking ads; ads that, in eschewing the rational u.s.p. in favour of emotional bond-building, might have been expected to change the landscape forever. Though they have left their mark, they may be proving an evolutionary sidetrack. A few months ago, I stood in the agency's reception admiring some of those ads, still proudly displayed. Minutes later, listening to Les, I was left in no doubt that the old BMP philosophy had not been jettisoned with its name. What was depressing however was to hear him bewail the threat posed today by the rationality-led thinking still demanded by the biggest-spending marketers. When you hear a BMP stalwart saying this in 2009, decades after that battle seemed to have been won, you can only laugh at the doggedness of marketing reactionaries who unrepentantly espouse the concept of *homo economicus.* Though one can only sympathise with a clever man with such a burden of conservatism to contend with, it is astonishing that today's salient bone of contention is whether or not to drag 1950s thinking into the 1980s. This is a modern-day angels-on-pinheads debate, one that forestalls any heretical discussion of the real issue: whether the world needs orthodox advertising models at all.

Les is co-author of *Marketing in the era of accountability*[5], in which *Advertising Works*[6] case studies were compared with the aim of identifying what factors drive advantageous effects among this crème de la crème. Ironically, perhaps the book's most prominent finding was that marketers are obsessed with attitudinal measures at the expense of *payback*. This was a crushing retort, from the horse's own mouth, to that angry IPA mandarin who, when I challenged the commercial efficacy of even Advertising Effectiveness Awards winners, demanded to know what my problem was (chapter 2). To be fair, his was only typical of the industry's energetic response to 'unhelpful' news. After Gordon Brown's retirement many years ago, I wrote a piece for *Marketing* echoing his views on advertising memorability[7], and was publicly descended upon by two BMP planners pointing out my stupidity and demanding to know - yes, you've guessed it - why I hadn't studied *Advertising Works*. Another angry critic then gave me a lesson in 'brain science' that in the light of modern evidence looks more like pseudoscience. It was a portent of things to come. At a conference, I cited a TV sales house's own figures as evidence of advertising ineffectiveness, whereupon an industry representative rose to inform the audience indignantly that I was 'quite wrong': the figures had subsequently been revised and now were very convincing. When I asked afterwards to see these new figures, however, it turned out that I not only was familiar with them; I'd even been formally consulted by her own colleagues about them, and had had to advise that the sunny assumptions on which they had been calculated were pie in the sky.

The problem, of course, is that when there's a multi-billion-pound industry at stake ($300 billion in the USA), the argument *must* not be lost, whatever the evidence says. Standards of proof one meets in the marketing industry would often be considered risible in science. In researching this book, I analysed two papers by experts whose work is regarded as seminal and has considerably influenced strategic thinking. In both, data had been patently manipulated to fit the argument; so patently that, if such deeds were exposed in the scientific domain, the experts' reputations would be irreparable. Worryingly, the whole industry appears to have overlooked the sleight of hand. That's not to say that the industry lacks whistle-blowers. In the early 1990s, at the industry's blue-riband 'Measuring Advertising Performance' conference, I heard John Philip Jones, a veteran ex-JWT marketing academic, bravely describe the track record of advertising efficacy as 'atrocious'. And, just two years ago, a pair of account-planning veterans won a Market Research Society award for a paper called *50 years using the wrong model of advertising*[8] - a perfect case of 'better late than never'. Yet the industry at large still ploughs the same old furrows. The reason they can, of course, is that so many of their clients read the same textbooks.

I'm not alone in feeling that the cosy conservatism of the ad industry is ideologically ingrained, from theory to practice. The conclusive finding of the 'Honest Broker' experiment described in Chapter 7 was submitted as a meticulously written formal paper to the World Advertising Research Center's *Journal of Advertising Research*. After a considerable delay, it was rejected on the grounds that, as the executive editor expressed it, the topic was inappropriate for the Journal's readership, a response that generated quite some hilarity in my office. I guessed it was not appropriate for the same reasons that members of the medical profession ought not to hear upsetting stuff about their hygiene habits. In case this sounds like sour grapes, I should add that we'd taken the precaution of getting the paper informally peer-reviewed in advance, by two neuroscientists, two businesspeople, and an economist. All five had declared the methodology and conclusions hard to dispute. The gist of the comments that accompanied their reviews was that the experiment was a breakthrough demonstration of a principle with tremendous potential for commercial application. What the findings imply is that MR that depends on what people tell you may, in the absence of corroboration, be worse than useless, and that faith in the power of rational decision-taking is misguided. For advertisers the world over, however, this appears not to be appropriate to read, especially in the wake of an economic crash.

The marketing industry was presented with a unique opportunity to set its house in order by this recent collapse of the houses-built-on-clay that were constructed by a generation of corporate dissimulators. Disappointingly, what response there has been thus far runs the line of least resistance. If consumerdom has lost faith, the thinking goes, we must put that faith back; we must get across the message that we can be *trusted*. For most pundits, trust is a new u.s.p. The name of the game is not 'plain honesty' but 'brand authenticity', which may sound like an oxymoron but wasn't conceived as one. Tell the punters that you can be trusted in this untrustworthy jungle, and you've got yourself some branded differentiation that's worth paying a premium for. It apparently doesn't occur to the protagonists to ponder whether a reputation for trustworthiness is actually merited, or whether telling people that you're trustworthy might not prove counterproductive. Rather, the mindset dictates that, if that's what the public want, then that's what you must say you offer. It's the remedy attributed to comedian George Burns: 'The secret of success is sincerity. Once you can fake that, you've got it made'. Naturally, he meant it as a joke.

Such sentiments as these may make you suspect that, like Vance Packard, I've developed an aversion to advertising per se. I don't think so. I still enjoy ads that make me laugh. I particularly relish the ones that cleverly evoke a true experience. And I take an interest in ads that impress with their creativity, even if only for cinematographic reasons.

So what's my problem, since the IPA's director-general asked? My problem is with an industry that touts outmoded thinking *because it can.* I don't know how many admen still believe in their model, and how many take the view that it doesn't matter as long as there are clients who do believe in it and will pay the bills. Obviously every company is entitled to allow its money to be wasted if it wishes. But it's not good for shareholder confidence if advertising is just a cost rather than a magic ingredient. Ineffective marketing of goods cannot be much good for the economy. And society suffers when we're subjected daily to a miasma of time-wasting garbage.

This becomes an even bigger issue for every tax- and rate-payer when the clients in question are national and local government, dispensing our money to communications experts whose claim to the title evades most of us on the outside. British social policy has depended disproportionately in recent years on 'public information'; yet sky-rocketing amounts of it seem to have solved very few of the problems at which they are directed. When the government thereby morphs into the biggest marketing spender in the land, it becomes a genuine social problem all by itself. In the run-up to the recent general election, the Conservative Party boldly identified antiquated thinking as the reason for such wastefulness. Its leaders had been influenced by a book called *Nudge*[9], co-authored by a former associate of Daniel Kahneman. Apart from colourfully explaining the basics of behavioural economics (BE), it suggested a few heuristically based solutions to certain American social issues. It was colourful enough, in fact, that it appeared on the party's official reading list. The new Prime Minister, himself a former director of Carlton, now has his own think-tank designed to bring such new thinking to bear on UK social issues.

A reason to be cheerful? Well, the new government did take no time to slash its public information budget. Yet one of its first acts was to launch a film blaming the state of the economy on its predecessor, as though such 'messaging' were likely to achieve anything other than to antagonise critics of government cuts even further. Equally, though the Chief Executive of the Central Office of Information, a dyed-in-the-wool adman called Mark Lund, has prudently expressed the need to demonstrate 'payback and return on marketing investment', he points to best-case examples of old-model thinking as exemplars, and has publicly opined that today's challenge is to deliver 'excellent communications' via the most cost-effective medium. (Since his first job was at Lintas, and his first mentor one John Bunyard, I cannot help but feel indirectly responsible; I can only plead that we knew no better at the time).

Nonetheless, the ailing ad industry, aware that not only the UK prime minister but also the US president considers BE a money-saving magic bullet, is alert to its commercial possibilities. What Messrs Binet and Lund have in common is membership of IPA president Rory Sutherland's new BE Think Tank, the expressed raison d'être of which is to restore ad agency influence in the client boardroom (and presumably cabinet office). The mere existence of such a body may surprise, amuse, or appal you. Having met all three men within the last year, I have to admit that, though each is a highly successful adman, I formed the judgement, rightly or wrongly, that their prior relationship with BE was not unlike that between Lintas's Jeffrey and account planning (see chapter one). Of course, we may be seeing the new generation that eschews redundant old practices; but I suspect that any interest they stir in the industry will be more on account of its parlous financial state that any philosophical conversion.

Though advertising and BE may seem poles apart, one of the co-authors of *Nudge* has already alerted Sutherland to the opportunity to sell advertising as a means, would you believe, of *priming* BE initiatives[10]. BE nevertheless is a problematic solution to behavioural challenges, being less a coherent system than a collection of psychological anomalies. In marketing, it will lend itself more to experiential gimmicks than anything else. The IPA team has prudently recruited the author of a contrasting approach to *Nudge*, based on a 'Reflexive Holistic Model' of behaviour change[11], that at least looks more saleable. Under whatever guise, however, BE in the hands of politicians, consultants and admen is an intimidating prospect when one considers that the benefit offered by BE to advertisers is insights into human frailty. The irony is that, if they do get results, Vance Packard's nightmare may become real, and the 'Mad Men' will finally have become true hidden persuaders. One can only hope it will prove as fruitless as most fads.

Whatever happens, these new boys on the block needn't necessarily expect an easy ride from journalists, even if the media do remain in thrall to their advertising paymasters. Paranoia is already in the air. Having been marketed so hard by neuromarketers, the application of 'brain science' to behavioural challenges is coming in for a lot of journalistic flak on the grounds that its protagonists are somehow devious. I encountered the phenomenon at first hand when I was interviewed by 'Wired' magazine[12]. Asked whether neuromarketers' mission to find the 'buy button' in the brain wasn't unethical, I could only answer, 'They'll be lucky'. The writer got it, but not the editor, who led his special edition with 'Exposed: How the new persuaders are hacking your mind... to control your desires'. It's easy to laugh it off as lazy space-filling; but most neuroscientists will tell you that it's plain ignorance. If you understand the limitations even of brain-scanning technology, let alone our existing knowledge of how to 'manipulate' behaviour, you know it's as naive as claiming that we can now cure all disease.

The same 'hidden persuaders' charge was even levelled at our Heuristic model, once, by a mind-made-up marketing manager; I had to answer with a smile, 'Well, yes, if you accept that it's dishonest to make an experience as enjoyably coherent as possible and then tell only the absolute truth about it, then it's guilty as charged'. I rather suspected that the manager concerned was more comfortable with some of the pernicious outcomes of conventional marketing one sees regularly in media headlines, like schoolgirls ostracised for wearing the wrong make-up, teenage boys morally blackmailed into paying £45 for a five-pound football shirt, and children encouraged to pester their way to life-shortening obesity. It is sublimely ironic when the most cogent defence one hears for sticking with outmoded theory is that it is unlikely to have any effect on people's behaviour - a poignant echo of the industry argument that cigarette advertising is not a social problem because it doesn't actually work. The alternative presented in this book, the idea that *honesty itself persuades*, can only really be considered the antidote to hidden persuaders.

At this juncture, with manufacturing in the doldrums, unsustainable levels of debt, and unemployment reaching horrendous heights, cosy intransigence in business is the last thing we need. The self-servers who've wrecked economy, society and potentially planet have had their turn. It's time for bond-building honest brokers to speak up. As a culture we need to pull together as never before, and that will only be possible with the sort of collaboration that's built on biochemically reinforced empathy, trust, altruism, and reciprocity. So why should marketing matter in this? Because it represents the very face of the corporation, setting the expectations that will be fruitfully met or fatally missed. Marketing stands to be pivotal in the presentation of businesses as entities that are true to their word and therefore worthy of the trust that justifies patronising them. But change has to come from the top: from company bosses obsessed with growth but with no patience for self-indulgence. The major challenge they face is to coax marketing practitioners into abandoning their old mindset, starting with the advertising strategy.

The need for honest science and scientific honesty in business has become so pressing that, when I was invited to speak at the UK's first neuromarketing conference, I decided to make it my theme. I had no inkling of what lay in store for me. I was aware that I would be speaking after a procession of hyper-intelligent neuroscientists to an audience of their peers and an admixture of marketers. I was also conscious that my message - which amounted to a warning never to set aside their scientific principles - could have distinct lead-balloon tendencies. I was to be surprised more than once. Arriving at the speakers dinner on the eve of the conference, I was immediately asked after my subject matter by an American neuroscientist who, when I told him, followed up with, 'So you're talking about snake-oil salesmen?' When I tried to explain that I didn't intend to be quite so populist, a second professor who'd been listening in commented, 'I shouldn't worry if I were you. Snake-oil is very much in vogue'.

My second surprise came when, after delivering my speech the next day as unflinchingly as I could manage, I received an enthusiastic response and subsequently a number of messages with a common theme: 'It needed to be said'. I take no great credit for this: sometimes it just takes one outsider to point out that the emperor's clothes are a bit on the transparent side. I ultimately came out of that conference with my confidence restored. Whatever abuses you hear about in the media, we have available to us in science a wealth of brainpower, ever-evolving technologies, and a new appetite for bringing leading-edge knowledge to bear on business challenges; and all of it was to the fore at that event. Best of all, though, was the spirit of integrity that was ready to stand up and be counted. This was not a simple human response, even though the human inclination to co-operate fairly with others for mutual benefit is psychologically deep-seated among all of us other than the sociopathic. It was above all a businesslike approach that said, 'After all the nonsense that's got us into this mess, we've got to deal in objectively demonstrable truths, or we're sunk'. And this was beginning to sound like more than a worthy ambition. Behind the words, one could sense the steely determination that's born of impatience.

The beauty of change

If you're an avid reader of business books, it will have struck you that you've nearly reached the end and still have not been asked to memorise twelve great secrets of success or some clever seven-letter acronym or even learn verbatim a twenty-word mantra to repeat every night before going to bed. Such staples of the genre are invariably insisted upon by canny publishers, but would sit badly, in my opinion, in a book that more than anything is an appeal to revolt against the culture of self-serving claptrap we live in. You see, such formulae do sell books, as well as the lecture tours and coaching courses that follow in the books' wake; but it's a reasonable bet that any book that promises to fix your business, your relationships and/or your life in forty-one easy steps will be more beneficial to its author than to you.

Nevertheless, I'm aware that you may now be thinking, 'Well, that's all very interesting, but what am I actually supposed to do about it?' One simple answer is, 'Nothing conscious'. Now that I have seeded the notion in your brain, rather like Leonardo DiCaprio's character Cobb in *Inception*, it should inevitably do its work, urging you to infuse systematic honesty into your business's self-presentation and proper science into its means of informing itself. If you find this implausible, consider Dale Carnegie's *How to win friends and influence people*[13], which in planting the idea that we can positively change the way we're perceived by presenting ourselves differently must have shaped literally millions of conversations in the intervening decades. If you want to turn it into an active process, all you need do, whenever you pick up the phone or put finger to keyboard, is ask yourself one question: will what I am saying inevitably be borne out by reality? If it is, you can be confident that you're more likely to cause someone to feel good about you, by courtesy of a tidy dopamine release, than you are to be branded a fibber.

Big theoretical ideas are nevertheless only as good as their ability to be communicated to others and turned into practice by real-world managers. The beauty of the Heuristic approach is that, once grasped, it is eminently usable. In the course of endless hours of theorising and testing, three key lessons have emerged that can be easily memorised, passed on, and turned into the sort of working practice that brings real returns. First, free yourself from the old ways of informing yourself. Market research has evolved to satisfy a 'fifties model of how the brain works, and still relies substantially on cognition. There are now smarter and more lateral questions and ways to answer them. Second, concentrate on shaping up the product or service experience as well as you affordably can before you even think about the marketing. By this, I don't particularly mean making it better. I mean making it more *congruent* in its various manifestations. And third, don't think of marketing as a way to big up your business. Traditional marketing's stock-in trade, hyperbole, may come back and bite you when customers experience the real thing. The better course is to make your marketing a truthful, even modest reflection of reality.

You may be thinking that, though a recipe for a splendidly coherent product or service, these rules present no opportunity for marketing to provide a tempting reason for non-users to try out your offering. There's a simple answer. Orthodox marketing falls down because it sets the bar too high, such that the experience itself is no match for it. It's an outcome even worse than not engaging in the first place. The answer is to train yourself to jump higher: optimise the business experience you wish to tell your customers about by making all elements fit together seamlessly within a single Heuristic concept; one that makes for a strong story. (Remember Water for Work's wellbeing experience?) Then you can set your marketing bar higher without any fear of over-claiming. To do all of this with confidence, you need to know exactly what customers make of your product or service, what would help them feel better about it, and what you have to do to bridge the gap. Traditional market research cannot tell you. But the necessary new techniques and technologies already exist. And the Heuristic solution they yield can make all the difference. So why spend your life perfecting your Western Roll, when you can install a foam-filled mat and win gold with a Fosbury Flop?

We're all entitled to dream from time to time. What might a world dominated by Heuristic thinking be like? One thing is for sure: in such a world, the differences will be not only commercial, but cultural. This will be a world rid of the stifling pollution foist upon us by old-school marketing. The public face of brands will differ as much from today's appearances as a present-day TV sponsor's bumper-credit differs from a Pears Soap poster on an Edwardian tram. Gone will be the endless miasma of glossily presented nothing that likes to imagine it can persuade the public, overtly or covertly, to change its behaviour. Gone will be the deluge of messages fruitlessly screaming for one's attention from every TV set, every computer monitor, every wall and every doormat. Gone will be the brands that beg for success by pleading mindlessly for custom, like the unfortunates inside London's Charing Cross station who intone 'Any spare change?' at every indifferent passer-by; or perhaps more like the ones in luminous jackets outside who unremittingly ask, 'Have you got a moment?'

It will simultaneously mean a commercial world composed of an accumulation of pleasurable experiences, rather than acceptable ones coated in glitter. Businesses will expand themselves organically, by making themselves loved for what they truly are and letting their aficionados spread the word. All one hears about them will be or feel like impartial news. Our relationship with them will be the same as the one we have today with our hairdresser, or favourite team, or the local pub: we mostly won't remember how we came to associate ourselves with them, because they never actually sold themselves to us; but we'll feel as comfortable with them as with a pair of old shoes. Most of all, we will quietly love those products and services we adopt because they didn't try too hard; because they didn't prostitute themselves; because they were true to their word. They will be more like the preferred authors or actors or musicians or comedians we choose to let into our lives. They will no longer be 'brands', the spawn of avaricious corporations happy to say whatever it will take to part us from our money. They will become part of the fabric of our existence in a thoroughly complementary way. This is no longer parasitism, but symbiosis.

The great thing about such a world is that, instead of trying to inveigle us into doing things we might not want to do, commercial enterprises will respect our personal differences in terms of what we like and what we are. The winner of the great competition that is business will be no longer the smoothest liar but the contender that outperforms the rest in living up to the expectations it sets. Adopting a product or service will become more like forming a lasting sexual relationship: the loud seducer in gaudy clothes will eventually be shunned in favour of the quietly amusing chap whom one's friend has brought along and who turns out so dependable that he's the obvious one to settle down with. Naturally this will demand hard and serious thinking, not just about how the product or service is presented, but also about the nature of the product or service itself. To continue the mating analogy, it will no longer suffice for the bore, the nag or the dullard to pen a self-flattering lonely-hearts ad in the hope of conning an unsuspecting victim. He will need instead to work hard at developing his skills, his attainments and his sense of humour if he wants to get out of his bed-sit.

Ultimately, this is a world where the keynote is doing better by making things better. In our present world, shaken to its foundations by a culture of unprincipled rapacity, such an approach is not only the smarter way of effectively drawing custom. It is also a recipe for an efficiently performing economy in which honesty, reciprocity and trust are essential components. When you think about it, this vision - where spin no longer has a place in facilitating commerce - is almost utopian; and the trouble with any utopia is that, once the thing's said, the possibility of its being realised seems to recede like highland mist. There are many steps on a long road before we might reach this new world. But I can see two reasons why we should fondly bear it in mind as we strive towards it. First, the makings of it are already with us; all we are learning about the workings of the brain, the ways that behaviour can be propagated through populations, and indeed the plain consumer cynicism directed at big business, point down the road to that new place. And second, when one ponders the conundrum that is commerce today, it's the obvious place to head for.

A few weeks ago I attended an evening seminar in the very London thoroughfare on which Lintas House stood. Afterwards, I decided to stroll along the deserted street to take another look at my business alma mater for the first time since I left. It was gone. It and its wide forecourt had disappeared under the brightly lit new office blocks of lawyers and accountants. Indeed, the famous old name of Lintas itself, now subsumed into some other agency 'brand', has been all but expunged from the western world. It's sadly ironic that a business that spent so much time and effort trying to turn its clients' products into enduring brands could not even keep its own alive; *sic transit gloria mundi*. But that's the way it is with u.s.p.'s, brand positionings and the other assorted fluff. Three decades after walking into that world of make-believe, I've learned one lesson above all others: that, whatever you wish to be true, the objective truth is the most obdurate thing there is, and it's a good definition of madness to persuade oneself otherwise. As science fiction writer Philip K Dick put it, reality is what sticks around even when you've ceased to believe it[14].

Professor Steve Jones made a similar point about why science is so interesting: at the end of the day, the truth will out[15]. Just look at what's been going on in the western economy, from Enron to economic crash; one by one, regimes and industries that were living a lie have had to come to terms with the uncompromising truth. There's only one true safeguard against bunkum, and that's the scientific method. And if that sounds at all daunting, it shouldn't. The real beauty of science is that it's so much more fun finding out the truth. You may find your hunches proved wrong from time to time. But if you can face up to that, you'll build your castle on rock, not on sand. Science proves me wrong on a regular basis; and yet I know a lot more now than I used to, and I'm still smiling. And that really is what I want to see from this new offspring of the marriage of science and business: the smile that comes of being honestly persuaded to do what's good for you.

References

1: Reason to Believe

1. Packard, V., 1957. *The Hidden Persuaders*. New York: David McKay.
2. Brown, J.A.C., 1963. *Techniques of Persuasion*. London: Penguin.
3. Sampson, H., 1874. *A History of Advertising from the Earliest Times.* London: Chatto & Windus.
4. Goldstein, D.G. & Gigerenzer, G., 1999. The Recognition Heuristic: How ignorance makes us smart. In G. Gigerenzer, P.M. Todd & the ABC Research Group ed. *Simple Heuristics That Make Us Smart.* New York: Oxford University Press. Ch. 2.
5. Scott, W.D., 1903. *The Theory of Advertising: A simple exposition of the principles of psychology in their relation to successful advertising.* Boston: Small, Maynard & Co.
6. Festinger, L., 1957. *A Theory of Cognitive Dissonance*. Stanford: Stanford University Press.
7. Van Veen, V., Krug, M.K., Schooler, J.W. & Carter, C.S., 2009. Neural Activity Predicts Attitude Change in Cognitive Dissonance. *Nature Neuroscience*, 12, pp.1469–1474.
8. Ehrenberg, A. & Goodhardt, G., 2000. New Brands: Near-Instant Loyalty. *Journal of Marketing Management*, Vol. 16, Issue 6, pp.607 – 617.
9. Maslow, A.H., 1943. A Theory of Human Motivation. *Psychological Review*, 50(4), pp.370-96.
10. Reeves, R., 1961. *Reality in Advertising*. New York: Alfred A Knopf.
11. Bentham, J., 1789. *An Introduction to the Principles of Morals and Legislation*. Ch 1. Oxford: Clarendon Press.
12. Kahneman, D. & Tversky, A., 1979. Prospect Theory: An analysis of decisions under risk. *Econometrica*, 47, pp.313–327.
13. Güth, W., Schmittberger R. & Schwarze B., 1982. An Experimental Analysis of Ultimatum Bargaining. *Journal of Economic Behavior and Organization,* 3 (4): 367–388.
14. Knetsch, J., 1989. The Endowment Effect and Evidence of Non-reversible Indifference Curves. *American Economic Review*, 79, pp.1277–1284.
15. Wilson, T.D., Lisle, D.J., Schooler, J.W., Hodges, S.D., Klaaren K.J. & LaFleur S.J., 1993. Introspecting about Reasons can Reduce Post-Choice Satisfaction. *Personality & Social Psychology Bulletin*, 19, pp.331-339.
16. Bargh, J.A. & Chartrand, T.L., 1999. The Unbearable Automaticity of Being. *American Psychologist*, 54, pp.462-479.
17. Bargh, J.A., Chen, M., & Burrows, L., 1996. Automaticity of Social Behavior: Direct effects of trait construct and stereotype priming on action. *Journal of Personality and Social Psychology*, 71, pp.230-244.
18. Williams L.E. & Bargh J.A., 2008. Experiencing Physical Warmth Promotes Interpersonal Warmth. *Science,* Vol. 322, no. 5901, pp.606-607.
19. LeDoux, J., Wilson D. & Gazzaniga M., 1977. A Divided Mind: Observations on the conscious properties of the separated hemispheres. *Annals of Neurology*, 2, pp.417-421.
20. Libet, B., Gleason, C., Wright, E. & Pearl, D., 1983. Time of Conscious Intention to Act in Relation to Onset of Cerebral Activity (Readiness-Potential): the unconscious initiation of a freely voluntary act. *Brain*, 106, pp.623-642.
21. Soon C.S., Brass M., Heinze H-J., & Haynes, J-D., 2008. Unconscious Determinants of Free Decisions in the Human Brain. *Nature Neuroscience,* 11, pp.543-545.
22. Simon, H. A., 1956. Rational choice and the structure of the environment. *Psychological Review*, 63, pp.129-138.

23. Schwartz, B., 2004. *The Paradox of Choice: Why less is more*. New York: HarperCollins.
24. Ormerod, P., 1998. *Butterfly Economics: A new general theory of economic and social behaviour*. New York: Pantheon Books.

2: Brand Faith
1. Ries A. & Trout, J., 1980. *Positioning: The Battle for Your Mind*. New York: McGraw-Hill.
2. Ehrenberg, A.S.C., 1988. *Repeat-Buying: Facts, Theory and Applications*. 2nd ed. London: Edward Arnold.
3. Various ed, 1980-2010. *Advertising Works*. London: Institute of Practitioners in Advertising.
4. Schudson, M., 1984. *Advertising, the Uneasy Persuasion: its dubious impact on American society*. New York: Basic Books.
5. WARC, 2009. 'Consumers not engaged with brands, says ARF's Rubinson'. *WARC News* [Internet] March 30. Available at: www.warc.com/News/Top News.asp?ID=24915&Origin=WARCNewsEmail (Accessed 31 July 2010).
6. Brown, J.A.C., op cit. Ch. 7.
7. Needham, Harper & Steers, 1985. *1985 NH&S Life Style Survey*. Chicago, IL.
8. Ehrenberg, A., Barnard, N., Kennedy, R. & Bloom, H., 2002. Brand Advertising as Creative Publicity. *Journal of Advertising Research,* 42, pp.7-18.
9. Levy, K., 2010. 'Online shopping research puts brand websites in shade'. *Brand Republic*, [Internet] August 9. Available at: http://www.brandrepublic.com/bulletin/brandrepublicnewsbulletin/article/1021100/online-shopping-research-puts-brand-websites-shade/ (Accessed 9 August 2010).

3: The Power to Prime
1. Hine, T., 1995. *The Total Package: The evolution and secret meanings of boxes, bottles, cans tubes and other persuasive containers*. New York: Little Brown.
2. Bar, M. & Neta M., 2008. The Proactive Brain: Using rudimentary information to make predictive judgments. *Journal of Consumer Behaviour*, 7(4-5), pp.319-330.
3. Millward Brown, 1991. *How Advertising Affects the Sales of Packaged Goods Brands: A working hypothesis for the 1990s*. Warwick: Millward Brown International.
4. Deighton, J. & Schindler, R.M., 1988. Can Advertising Influence Experience? *Psychology and Marketing*, Vol. 5, No. 2, pp.103-115.
5. Deighton, J., 1984. The Interaction of Advertising and Evidence. *Journal of Consumer Research*, Vol. 11, No. 3, pp.763-70.
6. Smith, R.E. & Swinyard W.R., 1982. Information Response Models: An integrated approach. *Journal of Marketing*, Vol. 46, pp.81-93.
7. Marks, L.J. & Kamins, M.A., 1988. The Use of Product Sampling and Advertising: effects of sequence of exposure and degree of advertising claim exaggeration on consumers' belief strength, belief confidence, and attitudes. *Journal of Marketing Research,* Vol. XXV, pp.266-81.
8. Krugman, H.E., 1965. The Impact of Television Advertising: Learning without involvement. *Public Opinion Quarterly*, 29 (Fall), pp.349-356.
9. Farr A. & Brown G., 1994. Persuasion or enhancement? An experiment. In Market Research Society *MRS Annual Conference*. Birmingham, 17 March 1994. Market Research Society: London.
10. Zajonc, R.B., 1980. Feelings and Thinking: Preferences need no inferences. *American Psychologist*, 35(2), pp.151–175.

11. Damasio, A.R., 1995. *Descartes' Error: Emotion, reason, and the human brain*. New York: Putnam Publishing.
12. James, W., 1890. *The Principles of Psychology*. Boston: Henry Holt.
13. Keats, J., 1819. Letter to George and Georgiana Keats, 14 February.
14. *Open Book*, 2004. [Radio programme] BBC, BBC Radio 4, 28 November 2004 16.00.

4: Fast to the Future

1. Benady, A., 1994. New route to ad effectiveness? *Marketing*, 31 March.
2. Axelrod, R., 1984. *The Evolution of Cooperation*. New York: Basic Books.
3. Mitchell, A., 1995. Blitzkrieg branding wins over the cynical shoppers. *The Times*, 30 August, p.28e.
4. Mitchell, A., 1995. A testing time for marketers. *Marketing Week*, 8 September, pp.26-27.
5. Ehrenberg A. & Barnard N., 1994. Justifying Advertising Budgets. *Admap*, January, pp.11-13.
6. Ephron E. & Pollak G., 2003. The Curse of the Leverhulmes. In ARF/ESOMAR *Worldwide Audience Measurement Conference*. Los Angeles, 18 June 2003. Available at: www.esomar.org/web/publication/paper.php?id=93 (Accessed 31 December 2009).

5: The Lesson of Experience

1. Chadwick, P., 2003. Learning from experience. *Event Magazine,* Nov./Dec., p.37.
2. Sutherland, R., 2009. Inaugural address of new IPA President. Available at: http://www.ipa.co.uk/DisplayContent.aspx?id=5659 (Accessed 31 July 2010).
3. Pine, B.J. & Gilmore, J.H., 1999. *The Experience Economy: Work is theatre and every business a stage*. Boston: Harvard Business School Press.
4. Pine, B.J. & Gilmore, J.H., 1997. The Four Faces of Mass Customization. *Harvard Business Review,* January-February, 75(1) pp.91-101.
5. Toffler, A., 1970. *Future Shock*. New York: Random House.
6. Schmitt, B.H., 1999. *Experiential Marketing: How to get customers to sense, feel, think, act, relate*. New York: The Free Press.
7. Proust, M., 1913. *Du côté de chez Swann*. Paris: Editions Grasset.
8. Hargreaves D.J. & North A.C., 1997. *The Social Psychology of Music*. Oxford: Oxford University Press.
9. Heath, R., 2001. *The Hidden Power of Advertising: How low involvement processing influences the way we choose brands*. Henley-on-Thames: Admap.
10. Millward Brown, op. cit.
11. Schmitt, B.H., 2003. *Customer Experience Management*. New York: The Free Press.
12. Reichheld, F.F., 2003. The One Number You Need to Grow. *Harvard Business Review*. December, 81(12), pp.46-54, 124.
13. Bunyard, J., 1999. If ads alone fail to boost sales. *Admap*, No. 395, pp.18-21.
14. Kempf D.S. & Smith R.E., 1998. Consumer Processing of Product Trial and the Influence of Prior Advertising: A structural modeling approach. *Journal of Marketing Research*, Vol. 35, No. 3, pp.325-338.
15. Knüwer, T., 1997. Fast Marketing - auf die Probe kommt es an. *Handelsblatt,* July 15, p.39.
16. Sutherland, S., 1992. *Irrationality - The Enemy Within*. London: Constable.
17. Locke, J., 1690. *An Essay Concerning Human Understanding*. London: Thomas Basset.
18. Pinker, S., 2002. *The Blank Slate: The Modern Denial of Human Nature*. New York: Viking Penguin.

19. Forer, B.R., 1949. The Fallacy of Personal Validation: A classroom demonstration of gullibility. *Journal of Abnormal and Social Psychology*, 44 (1), pp.118–123.

6: A Little Learning...
1. Packard, V., op. cit.
2. Kahneman, D., Slovic, P. & Tversky, A., 1982. *Judgment Under Uncertainty: heuristics and biases*. New York: Cambridge University Press.
3. Read, J.S., 2008. *How Expertise Shapes Decision Making: Entrepreneurs versus corporate managers*. [Internet] Lausanne: IMD. Available at: www.imd.ch/research/challenges/upload/TC068_08_How_expertise_shapes_decision_making.pdf (Accessed 31 July 2010).
4. Lawrence A., Clark L., Labuzetta, J.N., Sahakian B. & Vyakarnum S., 2008. The innovative brain. *Nature,* 456, pp.168-169.
5. Berns G.S., McClure S.M., Pagnoni G. & Montague P.R., 2001. Predictability Modulates Human Brain Response to Reward. *The Journal of Neuroscience*, April 15, 2001, 21(8), pp.2793-2798.
6. Ehrenberg, A.S.C., op. cit.
7. Damasio, A., op. cit.
8. Boynton G., 2007. Ways to avoid the horrors of lost luggage. *The Daily Telegraph*, 7 August.
9. Mitchell, A., 2008. Heads-up from marketing mind-reader. *FT.com*, [Internet] December 18. Available at: www.ft.com/cms/s/0/988b21d0-cca2-11dd-_acbd-00077b07658.html?nclick_check=1 (Accessed 31 July 2010)
10. Jha, A., 2004. Coke or Pepsi? It's all in the head. *The Guardian,* 29 July.
11. *In Our Time*, 2008. [Radio programme] BBC, BBC Radio 4, 5 Jun 2008 09.00.
12. du Plessis, E., 2005. *The Advertised Mind: Groundbreaking insights into how our brains respond to advertising.* London: Kogan Page.
13. Popper, K., 1934. *Logik der Forschung*. Vienna: Julius Springer.
14. Hume, D., 1757. *Four Dissertations.* London: Andrew Millar.
15. Caspi, A., Sugden K., Moffitt, T.E., Taylor, A., Craig, I.A., Harrington, H., McClay, J., Mill, J., Martin, J., Braithwaite, A. & Poulton R., 2003. Influence of Life Stress on Depression: Moderation by a polymorphism in the 5-HTT gene. *Science*, Vol. 301. no. 5631, pp.386-389.
16. Watson, J.B., 1930. *Behaviorism (Revised edition).* Chicago: University of Chicago Press.
17. Dunbar, R., 1992. Why gossip is good for you. *New Scientist,* 21 November.
18. Singer, C., 1959. *A Short History of Scientific Ideas to 1900.* Oxford: Oxford University Press.
19. Walker Smith, J., 2004. *Consumer Resistance to Marketing Reaches All-Time High: Marketing productivity plummets, according to Yankelovich study.* (Press release) [Internet]: Chapel Hill, NC: Yankelovich (April 15). Available at: www.commercialalert.org/Yankelovich.pdf (Accessed 31 July 2010).
20. Greenfield, S., 2003. *Tomorrow's People: How 21st century technology is changing the way we think and feel.* London: Penguin, Allen Lane.
21. Norris, S., 2005. The Virtue of Being Virtual. *The Guardian Business Sense*, 25 November, p1.

7: The Truth Drug
1. Kurth, P., 1983. *Anastasia: The riddle of Anna Anderson.* New York: Little Brown.

2. *Nova: Anastasia Dead or Alive,* 1995. [TV programme] Wgbh Boston, PBS, 10 October 1995 20.00.
3. Kurth, P., 2008. *Anna-Anastasia: Notes on 'Franziska Schanzkowska'.* [Internet]. Available at: www.peterkurth.com/anna-anastasia%20notes%20on%20 franziska%20 schanzkowska.htm (Accessed 31 July 2010).
4. Kant, I., 1781. *Kritik der reinen Vernunft.* Riga: Hartknoch.
5. Descartes, R., 1637. *Discours de la méthode pour bien conduire sa raison, et chercher la vérité dans les sciences.* Leyden: Ian Maire.
6. Locke, J., 1690. *An Essay Concerning Human Understanding.* London: Thomas Basset.
7. Pinker, S., op. cit.
8. James, W., 1909. *The Meaning of Truth.* New York: Longmans, Green.
9. Piaget, J. & Inhelder, B., 1962. *The Psychology Of The Child.* New York: Basic Books.
10. Goleman, D., 1985. *Vital Lies, Simple Truths.* London: Bloomsbury Publishing. Pt. 2.
11. Sperry, R.W., 1968. Hemisphere Deconnection and Unity in Conscious Awareness. *American Psychologist* 23, pp.723-733.
12. MacLean, P. D., 1990. *The Triune Brain in Evolution: Role in paleocerebral functions.* New York: Springer.
13. Barlow, H.B., 1961. Possible principles underlying the transformation of sensory messages. In W Rosenblith ed. *Sensory Communication.* Cambridge, MA: MIT Press, pp 217-234.
14. Schultz, W., Tremblay, L. & Hollerman J.R., 2000. Reward Processing in Primate Orbitofrontal Cortex and Basal Ganglia. *Cerebral Cortex,* Vol. 10, No. 3, pp. 272-283.
15. Berns, McClure, Pagnoni & Montagu, op. cit.
16. Dutton, D.G. & Aron A.P., 1974. Some Evidence for Heightened Sexual Attraction Under Conditions of High Anxiety. *Journal of Personality and Social Psychology,* Vol. 30, No. 4, pp.510-517.
17. Zald, D.H., Boileau I., El-Dearedy W., Gunn R., McGlone F., Dichter G.S. & Dagher A., 2004. Dopamine Transmission in the Human Striatum during Monetary Reward Tasks. *Journal of Neuroscience,* Vol. 24, No. 17, pp.4105-4112.
18. Markou, A. & Koob, G.F., 1991. Postcocaine anhedonia: An animal model of cocaine withdrawal. *Neuropsychopharmacology,* 4, 1, pp.17-26.
19. Marks & Kamins, op. cit.
20. Olds, J. & Milner, P., 1954. Positive reinforcement produced by electrical stimulation of septal area and other regions of rat brain. *Journal of Comparative & Physiological Psychology,* 47, pp.419-427.
21. Fiorino D.F., Coury A. & Phillips, A.G., 1997. Dynamic Changes in Nucleus Accumbens Dopamine Efflux During the Coolidge Effect in Male Rats. *Journal of Neuroscience,* Vol. 17, 12, pp.4849-4855.
22. Tversky, A. & Kahneman, D., 1974. Judgment under uncertainty: Heuristics and biases. *Science,* 185, pp.1124-1130.
23. Haake, P., Exton M.S., Haverkamp J., Kramer, M., Leygraf, N., Hartmann, U., Schedlowski, M. & Krueger, T.H.C., 2002. Absence of orgasm-induced prolactin secretion in a healthy multi-orgasmic male subject. *International Journal of Impotence Research,* Vol. 14, 2, pp.133-135.
24. Broca, I. & Carrillo J.D., 2007. Reason, Emotion & Information Processing in the Brain. *CEPR Discussion Papers,* No. 6535, [Internet]. Available at: http://ideas.repec.org/p/cpr/ceprdp/6535.html (Accessed 31 July 2010).
25. Huron, D., 2008. *Sweet Anticipation: Music and the psychology of expectation.* Cambridge, MA: The MIT Press.

26. Pérez, V., van Remmen, H., Bokov, A., Epstein, C., Vijg, J. & Richardson, A., 2009. The Overexpression of Major Antioxidant Enzymes Does Not Extend the Lifespan of Mice. *Aging Cell,* 8, pp.73–75.
27. Dunbar, R., 1996. *Grooming, Gossip and the Evolution of Language.* London: Faber & Faber.
28. Axelrod, R., op. cit.
29. Rilling, J.K., Sanfey, A.G., Aronson, J.A., Nystrom, L.E. & Cohen, J.D., 2004. Opposing BOLD Responses to Reciprocated and Unreciprocated Altruism in Putative Reward Pathways. *NeuroReport*, Volume 15, Issue 16, pp. 2539-2243.
30. Kosfeld, M., Heinrichs, M., Zak, P.J., Fischbacher, U. & Fehr, E., 2005. Oxytocin Increases Trust in Humans. *Nature,* 435, pp.673-676.
31. Chiodera, P., Gnudi, A., Rossi, G., Camellini, L., Caiazza, A., Marchesi, C., Bianconi, L., Volpi, R. & Coiro, V., 1989. Dopaminergic But Not Cholinergic Involvement in Regulation of Hypoglycemia-Induced Oxytocin Release in Man. *Psychoneuroendocrinology*, Vol. 14, Issue 3, pp.203-208.
32. Crowley, W.R., Parker, S.L., Armstrong, W.E., Wang, W. & Grosvenor, C.E., 1991. Excitatory and Inhibitory Dopaminergic Regulation of Oxytocin Secretion in the Lactating Rat: Evidence for respective mediation by D-1 & D-2 dopamine receptor subtypes. *Neuroendocrinology*, Vol. 53, 5, pp. 493-502.
33. Liu, Y. & Wang, Z.X., 2003. Nucleus accumbens oxytocin and dopamine interact to regulate pair bond formation in female prairie voles. *Neuroscience*, 121(3), pp.537-44.
34. Baskerville, T.A. & Douglas, A.J., 2008. Interactions Between Dopamine & Oxytocin in the Control of Sexual Behaviour. *Progress in Brain Research*, 170, pp.277-290.
35. Hertel, G., Neuhof, J., Theuer T. & Kerr N.L., 2000. Mood Effects on Co-operation in Small Groups: Does positive mood simply lead to more cooperation? *Cognition & Emotion*, Vol. 14, Issue 4, July 2000, pp.441–472.
36. Begley, S., 2009. It Pays To Be Nice: How emotions shape our economic decisions. *Newsweek,* 10 September.
37. Zack, P. & Knack S., 2001. Trust and growth. *Economic Journal*, 111, No. 470, pp. 295-321.
38. Delgado, M.R., Frank R.H. & Phelps E.A., 2005. Perceptions of moral character modulate the neural systems of reward during the trust game. *Nature Neuroscience*, 8, pp.1611–1618.

8: Practice Made Perfect

1. Kempton, M.J., Ettinger, U., Foster R., Williams S.C.R., Calvert G.A., Hampshire A., Zelaya F.O., O'Gorman R.L., McMorris T., Owen A.M. & Smith M.S., 2010. Dehydration Affects Brain Structure and Function in Healthy Adolescents. *Human Brain Mapping.* (Accepted for publication December 2009).
2. Apter, M.J., *1989. Reversal Theory: Motivation, emotion, and personality.* London: Routledge.
3. Guido, G., Capestro, M. & Peluso, A.M., 2007. Experimental Shopping Analysis of Consumer Stimulation & Motivational States in Shopping Experiences. *International Journal of Market Research,* Vol. 49, No. 3, pp.365-386.
4. Tauber, E.M., 1972. Why Do People Shop? *The Journal of Marketing*, Vol. 36, No. 4, pp.46-49.

Epilogue

1. Smith, O., 2010. Norfolk Broads rebranded as 'Britain's Magical Waterland'. *The Daily Telegraph*, 23 July.
2. Feynman, R.P., 1999. *The Pleasure of Finding Things Out: The best short works of Richard Feynman.* New York: Perseus Books, p.187.
3. Keynes, J.M., 1936. *General Theory of Employment, Interest and Money.* London: Macmillan.
4. Kuhn, T.S, 1962. *The Structure of Scientific Revolutions.* Chicago: University of Chicago Press.
5. Binet, L. & Field P., 2007. *Marketing in the Era of Accountability: Identifying the marketing practices and metrics that truly increase profitability*. London: World Advertising Research Center.
6. Various ed, op. cit.
7. Bunyard, J., 1994. The Mystery of the Forgettable and Unrecalled. *Marketing*, June 2, p.8.
8. Heath, R. & Feldwick, P., 2008. 50 Years Using the Wrong Model of Advertising. *International Journal of Market Research,* Vol. 50, No. 1, pp.29-59.
9. Thaler, R. & Sunstein, C., 2008. *Nudge: improving decisions about health, wealth, and happiness*. New Haven: Yale University Press.
10. Sutherland, R., 2010. Address to Thinkbox seminar *The Winning Formula: TV creativity & effectiveness on demand*, June 16. Available at: http://www.thinkboxlive.tv/2010/16june/ (Accessed 31 August 2010).
11. Grist, M., 2008. *Steer: Mastering our behaviour through instinct, environment and reason.* London: RSA Projects.
12. Carter, M., 2009. Pushing the brain's buy button. *Wired*, July, pp.106-107.
13. Carnegie, D., 1936. *How to Win Friends and Influence People.* New York: Simon & Schuster.
14. Dick, P.K., 1978. How to Build a Universe That Doesn't Fall Apart Two Days Later. In M. Hurst & P. Williams ed. *I Hope I Shall Arrive Soon.* New York: Doubleday.
15. *In Our Time*, op.cit.

Index

1001, 28
1936 presidential election, 106
1973-4 oil crisis, 31
1987 stock market crash, 44
1996 Atlanta Olympics, 87
2000 dot.com crash, 118
50 years using the wrong model of advertising, 165

AIDA, 23-24, 134
Abbey National, 48
Abbey Road, 122
A Beautiful Mind, 141
accountability, 44-45
account planning, 36-42, 45, 60, 114, 168
action potentials, 92, 116, 133
Adams, Douglas, 41
addiction, 135
Admap, 97
adoption, 23
adrenaline, 70, 151
Advertised Mind, The, 114
advertising, 20, 114, 166, 168
    agency, 19, 51, 62, 105, 110, 117, 119, 168
    breaks, 103
    brief, 25, 34, 36, 37, 60, 77, 78, 99, 109
    budget-setting, 83
    bunch of flowers strategy, 81
    experientially accurate, 60, 62, 63, 67, 97, 103, 142, 155
    hyperbole, 32, 33, 52, 58, 67, 145
    industry, 54, 56-57, 59, 114, 139, 165, 168
    ineffectiveness, 165
    meaning, 22
    memorability, 28, 165
    obtrusiveness, 172-173
    orthodox, 15, 21-22, 34, 55-56, 76, 119, 164
    payback, 44, 83, 164
    public service, 145
    recall, 28, 79, 106
    role, 56, 76
    Roman, 21-22
    strategy, 38, 39, 40, 110, 170
    subliminal, 20
    television, 27
    under-the-radar, 76, 79, 94
    unpopularity of, 70, 125
    Victorian, 21-23
    as weak force, 76
Advertising Effectiveness Awards, 41, 44, 145, 164

Advertising Research Foundation, 46
Advertising Standards Authority, 33
Advertising Works, 44, 46, 164, 165
aesthetics, 91, 115
affective, 49, 56, 80, 100-101, 125
affordance, 48
Air France, 85
airlines, 119, 155, 160
A la recherche du temps perdu, 91
alpha-waves, 98
altruism, 169
American Association of Advertising Agencies, 125
American business theory, 26
Anaheim, 118
Anastasia, 127
Anderson, Anna, 127
anhedonia, 136
Anne of Cleves, 32
anthropology, 25, 110
Appalachians, 123
apparel, 148
Apple, 48-49
Aqua Libra, 61
Archimedes Principle, 97
argumentation, 24
Aristotle, 90, 91, 128
Arla Foods, 75
Armstrong, Ian, 150-152, 155
articulacy, 115
atmospheric steam engine, 124
Attenborough, David, 113
attention, 22, 23, 25, 56, 111, 136, 137, 172
Attention-Comprehension-Understanding, 23
attitudes, 37, 39, 83, 101, 129, 164
authenticity, 31
automaticity, 30
Aviva, 158-160
Axe & Bottle Experiment, 118, 119, 121, 122, 124, 125
Axelrod, Robert, 75
Ayer Barker, 38, 39, 41, 50, 62, 63, 64, 85, 120

baby, 130
Bargh, John, 30
Barnett Fletcher Promotions, 70, 86, 87, 89
Bass Brewers, 75
Bassett's
    Jelly Babies, 41
    Liquorice Allsorts, 41, 120

185

Bassett's *(cont)*
   Wine Gums, 72
Beattie, Trevor, 41, 63, 75
beauty, 115
Becker, Gary, 25, 108
behaviour, 29, 116, 159
   approach, 136
   attitudes follow, 23, 77
   business, 109
   challenges, 168
   changing of, 57, 58, 66, 75, 76, 77, 80, 86, 134, 172
   customer, 16, 44, 58, 140, 142
   emergent, 80
   in experiment, 114
   expert, 31
   formation of, 137, 141
   habitual, 48, 83
   manipulation of, 20, 169
   mismatch with claimed preference, 110
   observation of, 110-111, 142
   propagation of, 174
   response to stimuli, 129-130
   of salesmen, 153
   sexual, 142
   shaping of, 66
   social, 137, 159
Behaviourism, 114, 116, 129
Beiersdorf, 81
belief, 35, 37, 58, 81, 108, 130, 132, 137
benefit, 23, 24, 25, 33, 40, 110, 142
Bentham, Jeremy, 25
Berry, Chuck, 116
Bertie Bassett, 41
beta-waves, 98
bias, 67, 111, 132
Binet, Les, 164, 168
biometric, 111, 112, 123, 152
blank slate, 99, 128
Boase Massimi Pollitt, 37, 38, 41, 164, 165
Bolsheviks, 127
bonding, 141, 147
Boston radio, 55
brain
   of apes, 135
   binary, 114, 139, 140
   as calculating machine, 25
   complexity of, 128
   conservative, 35
   Darwinian account of, 130
   decade of the, 111
   evolution of, 132
   frugal, 67, 133-134, 140
   function, 68, 129, 160, 174
   heterogeneous, 132-133, 140
   mid-, 136

   as predicting machine, 137, 140
   scanning, 23, 30, 110, 135, 141, 143, 169
   'science', 110, 111-112, 165, 168
   and sharp angles, 53
   split-, 30, 132
   and survival, 66
   triune, 133
brand, 42-52, 112, 173
   attitudes, 77, 105, 106
   authenticity, 166
   awareness, 79, 105, 106
   choice, 53
   creation, 13, 48, 50
   differentiation, 49, 88, 116, 166
   economy, 90
   future, 173
   gloss, 83, 103
   group therapy for, 107
   loyalty, 13, 23, 43, 49, 50, 81
   marketing, 43, 86, 87
   personality, 42
   preference, 43, 65
   theatre, 87-88
   values, 43, 50, 103
branding, 42
Bretton Woods, 26
British Airways, 46, 156
Brobat, 48
Broca's region, 17
Brown, Gordon, 52, 53-55, 60, 61, 64, 65, 73, 94, 165
Brown, JAC, 20
Burns, George, 166
business books, 15, 71, 171
business model, 71
Butterfly Economics, 31
buy button, 169

CSR, 150
Cadbury Schweppes, 41, 72
call-centres, 97, 103, 120
Camelot, 73
Can advertising influence experience?, 55
car dealerships, 151, 152, 155
Carlton Communications, 118, 167
Carnegie, Dale, 171
Carphone Warehouse, 156-157
Cartesian dualism, 128
case studies, 73, 89, 145, 148, 160, 164
caudate, 143
cause and effect, 31, 132
Central Office of Information, 167
change blindness, 163
chaos, 31
Charles Barker, 22, 38
Charm, 101, 121, 125

Cheskin, Louis, 53, 54, 55
Chiat Day, 37
Churchill, Winston, 73
Church of Rome, 128
Citigroup, 48
claim, 13, 23-25, 28, 33, 50, 55, 56, 58, 140, 142
Clairol Herbal Essences, 94
claptrap, 13, 142, 171, 174
client
    agency influence on, 21, 24
    entertainment, 19
    selection, 74
climate change, 125, 160
Clover, 69-70, 72
coaching, 96, 148, 171
Cobb, 171
Coca Cola, 50
    brain-scans, 113
    complaint about advertising, 33
Coca Cola Schweppes, 75, 150
cocaine, 136, 138
cognition, 66, 76, 79, 101, 111, 114, 133, 177
cognitive dissonance, 23
cognitive load theory, 91
Colonel Sanders, 73
colour, 122
common sense, 17, 21, 23
communications model, 23, 27
competition, 22, 33, 98, 146, 173
competitive advantage, 45, 154, 157
Condenser, 122, 156, 158
confidence, 106, 111, 136
confirmation, 35, 56, 100
Confucius, 128
congruence, 101, 139, 147, 152, 156, 159-160, 161, 172
conscious, 14, 30, 56, 58, 66, 131, 134, 138, 143
conservatism, 163, 164, 165
Conservative Party, 167
Consumer & Sensory Research Group, 162
Consumer Association, 30
conversation group, 121
Coolidge Effect, 138
co-operation, 141, 170
Copenhagen Summit, 160
copywriting, 23, 27
Correlator, 122
cortex, 30, 91
    association, 92
    frontal, 136
    medial prefrontal, 113
    orbitofrontal, 137
    prefrontal, 135
    size, 141
    somatosensory, 92
cortisol, 136

Creating Product Trial, 86
Crelm toothpaste, 25
Critique of Pure Reason, 128, 130
cross-modal, 91
crowdsourcing, 103
Customer Experience Management, 95-97, 120
customer insight, 107, 111
Customer Relationship Management, 95
customers, 13-17, 48, 56, 95-96, 103, 106, 116, 144, 146, 153, 154, 156, 160, 172
cynicism, 14, 32, 112, 174

DDB, 164
DNA, 58, 127
Dairy Crest, 69, 71, 72
Damasio, Antonio, 66-67, 111
Dark Side of the Moon, The, 122
Davis, Euan, 112
death, 122, 163
deceit, 31-34
decision-taking, 29, 33, 102, 124, 130, 140
    brain, 17
    brain areas, 113, 136
    influencing, 134
deduction, 54, 114
defection, 23, 141
Deighton, John, 55-57, 58, 67, 97, 100, 103, 134
denial, 129
depth interviews, 38
de Saussure, Ferdinand, 90
Descartes, René, 128
Descartes' Error, 66
desire, 23, 138
DeSteno, David, 143
Diageo, 72, 75, 79
DiCaprio, Leonardo, 171
Dichter, Ernest, 20, 107
Dick, Philip K, 174
differentiation, 32, 40, 49, 66, 110, 146, 158
digital revolution, 21, 102
Dill Scott, Walter, 23, 103
disbelief, 31
Disney, 118, 162
disruption, 104, 130
dissonance, 121, 139
distrust, 142
Dixons, 48
dogma, 90, 132, 162
doorstep swap, 28-29
dopamine, 14, 135-142, 161, 162, 171
    and oxytocin, 142
    reward system, 137, 139
Douglas, Tony, 34
dramatising the negative, 94

187

Dunbar, Robin, 121
durables, 30, 119

EEG, 30
economic crash, 15, 31, 149, 166, 169, 174
economics
    behavioural, 29, 138, 143, 167-168
    neo-classical, 15, 26, 29, 30-31
Edinburgh, Duke of, 127
efficient coding, 133
efficient markets, 31
Egg, 48
ego, 129
Ehrenberg, Andrew, 51, 76, 110
Elida Faberge, 75
Emerson, Ralph Waldo, 13
emotion, 39, 45, 66, 68, 114, 131, 133, 135
    positive, 56
emotional, 39, 56, 91, 100-101, 137, 143, 164
Emotional Intelligence, 131
empathy, 75, 143, 169
empirical, 15, 51, 61, 85, 92, 109
Empiricism, 17, 99, 116, 128
endogenous reward system, 136
energy, 136
enhancement, 54, 56, 57, 60, 62, 69, 72
Eno, Brian, 148
Enron, 174
entrepreneurs, 13, 32, 71, 73, 109, 117
Ephron, Erwin, 82
ethnographic, 110-111
euphoria, 136
eureka effect, 80, 81, 97
European Customer Experience World, 103
Everest, 123
evidence, 15, 51, 55, 59, 114, 127, 143, 160
Evolution of Co-operation, The, 75
expectation, 66
    matching, 76, 79, 134-139, 141, 142, 152, 157, 173
    setting, 15, 32, 67, 94, 134, 160, 169, 173
experience 55-57, 60, 67, 76, 90, 93, 95-96, 98
    congruence of, 120, 172
    evocation of, 59, 76, 80, 94, 100, 166
    incongruities in, 120
    multi-modal, 160
    priming of, 83, 97, 99, 134
    questionnaires, 96
    reshaping of, 120, 172
    satisfying, 152
    sensory, 91-92, 98
    taxonomy, 101
Experience Economy, The, 89-90, 97
experiential, 86, 95, 97, 102
    books, 89-90
    core, 80, 86, 99, 100, 120

hyperbole, 94-95
marketing, 70, 86-89, 90-92, 106, 116, 168
research, 115-116
slogans, 93
universality, 100
Experiential Marketing, 90, 97
experimentation, 15, 109, 111
    bogus, 113
    choice, 30, 142-143
    dehydration, 148
    developmental, 130-131
    expectations, 137-138
    heuristic, 22, 29-30
    Honest Broker, 138, 159, 165
    marketing, 16, 111
    marketplace, 68
    misattribution, 135
    mood state, 142
    neuromarketing, 112
    oxytocin, 142
    preference, 110
    prejudice, 143
    priming, 30, 53, 55, 59-60
    psychological, 98
    shopping, 152-154
    split-brain, 30, 132
    transaction, 159-160
experts, 31, 111, 162, 163, 167
Eysenck, Hans, 145

FAST marketing, 72-77, 83-84, 85-86, 93-94, 97, 99, 115, 120, 121, 134, 137, 139
    case evidence for, 77-83, 89
    false explanations of, 80-81
    long-term effects of, 82-83
    obstacles to, 83, 102, 118, 164
    short-term effects of, 82-83
    technique, 76
fMRI, 23, 30, 110, 135, 148
fabrics, 122
Facebook, 103
face recognition, 141
face-to-face, 47, 69, 86, 88
Fairy Liquid, 39
falsification, 114
Farr, Andy, 61, 86
fashion, 50, 54
Fastforward, 99-101, 117, 120-121, 124
Fast Marketing company, 75
feelings, 136, 143
Festinger, Leon, 23, 77
Feynman, Richard, 162
Fiat, 46
financial, 96, 119
five senses, 90, 92
Flash, 101, 121, 125

flashcards, 122
Fletcher, Barnett, 70, 86, 117, 119
Focused Advertising/Sampling Technique, 72
focus groups, 38, 43, 50, 99, 107, 109
    size, 121
Ford, 50
Ford Focus, 93, 140
Forer Effect, 100
Fosbury Flop, 172
Fox's Crinkle Crunch, 61
Frank, Robert H, 143
frauduline, 25
free will, 29
Freudian, 20, 107
Freud, Sigmund, 129, 145
Frijj, 71
functional, 100-101, 125
Functionalism, 130
Fusion, 122

Galen, 128
Galileo, 122, 123
Gallup, George, 106
Gallup poll, 47, 106
galvanic skin response, 123
game theory, 141
generosity, 141, 143
genetics, 17, 113, 116, 131, 139, 141
geo-targeting, 103
Gigerenzer, Gerd, 22, 47
Gillette, 53
Gilmore, James, 89, 90
Gladwell, Malcolm, 112
God, 42, 51
Goleman, Daniel, 131
Google, 42
Gore, Al, 160
government, 149, 167
Granada, 118
Grasp, 101, 121, 125
Great Nepalese, 85
Greenfield, Susan, 125
Gregory, Ralph, 125
Grey Advertising, 35, 37, 64
Grisdale, Richard, 85, 98
Guardian, The, 125
Guinness Storehouse, 92

HSBC, 140
Haagen Dazs, 86, 95
habit, 43, 77, 81, 110
Hallau, Chuck, 94
Hamlet, 100
Harvard Business Review, 89
Harvey, William, 128
head office, 148

health and wellbeing, 148, 149
heart rate, 110, 123, 152
Heath, Robert, 94
Heathrow airport, 112, 121
hedonic states, 154
Heinz Salad Cream, 48
Henry VIII, 32
Hertel, Guido, 142
Heuristic, 98, 102, 109, 120, 125, 150, 155, 160-161, 162, 169, 172
Heuristic Profile, 101-102, 121, 122, 123, 125, 137
    categories, 101
    examples, 151, 156
    facets, 101
heuristics, 67, 98, 108, 133, 134, 167
    anchoring effect, 138
    expectation-matching, 134, 141
    recognition, 22
Heuristic TV ads, 94
Heuristic toolkit, 121-122, 124, 146, 151
Hidden Persuaders, The, 20, 53, 107
hierarchy of needs, 24
high jump, 140, 172
History of Advertising, 21
Hitchhiker's Guide to the Galaxy, The, 41
Holbein, Hans, 32
homo economicus, 25, 164
Honda, 150-155, 156
honest broker, 175
honesty, 115, 138, 142, 147, 169, 170, 171, 174
Hooke, Robert, 123
hormone, 136, 141
housewives, 27, 28
How advertising affects the sales of packaged goods brands, 53-54
How to win friends & influence people, 171
Hume, David, 115
Hunt, Caroline, 119
Huron, David, 139
hydration, 147-149
hyperbole, 31, 32, 57, 88, 134, 140, 162, 172
hypothesis, 16, 55, 61, 108, 114, 137, 153, 156
hypothetico-deductive method, 114, 151

id, 129
Identifier, 151
immediate challenge, 54
immersive chamber, 122, 151, 158
impulse, 23
Inception, 171
Inconvenient Truth, An, 160
induction, 130
inertia, 43, 47, 81, 132
information, 25, 30, 33, 81, 96, 103, 130, 133
    selective, 134

189

Institute for Behavioural Studies, 20
Institute of Directors, 149
Institute of Food Research, 98
Institute of Practitioners in Advertising, 41, 45, 89, 145, 164, 167, 168
insurance, 158-159
Integrated Information Response Model, 56, 84
integrity, 113, 170
intention to purchase, 59, 60
interest, 23, 126, 153, 154, 156
interest-status, 54, 79
internet, 51, 57, 98, 103
Interpublic Group, 86, 117
irrationality, 22, 25, 29, 108, 132, 143, 159
Irrationality - the enemy within, 98

J. Walter Thompson, 37, 38, 50, 64, 130, 165
James, William, 67, 130
jingle, 28
Jobs, Steve, 48
Jones, John Philip, 165
Jones, Steve, 113, 174
Jordan, Michael, 48
Journal of Advertising Research, 165
journalism, 20, 47, 50, 105, 112-113, 168
Judgement and Decision Making, 67
judgementalism, 132
Jung, Carl, 145

Kahneman, Daniel, 29, 108, 167
Kamins, Michael, 56, 57, 58, 65, 79, 138
Kant, Immanuel, 91, 127-128, 130
Keats, John, 68, 103
Kellogg, 42, 78
Kennedy, John, 70
Kennomeat, 48
Keynes, John M, 26, 162
King, Stephen, 37, 46
King's Cross, 63
kin selection, 141
Kraft Foods, 41, 65, 73, 78, 80
Krugman, Herb, 58
Kuhn, Thomas, 163

L-DOPA, 137
language, 115, 153
learning, 131, 136
leftism, 128
Lego, 131
Lehrer, Tom, 129
letterhead, 148
Levi's, 46
Lewis, David, 98
lighting, 122
limbic system, 68, 91
Lintas, 19-21, 27, 32, 37, 38, 39, 86, 167, 168, 174

Listening Bank, The, 140
Live Brand Experience Association, 88-89
load factor, 156
lobotomy, 130
Locke, John, 99, 128
logo, 41, 42, 48, 147
London, 22, 35, 63, 67, 85, 86, 96, 174
London Bridge, 124
L'Oreal, 65
loyalty-card, 110
Lucozade, 40
Lund, Mark, 167, 168
luxury goods, 50
Lysenko, Trofim Denisovich, 113

MRSA, 163
MacLean, Paul D, 132
Madison Avenue, 39, 64
madeleine cake, 91
Mad Men, 19, 94, 168
madness, 122, 174
magnetoception, 91
Magnum, 93
marketing, 172
    academic, 51, 165
    as corporate face, 169
    crassness, 94
    hyperbole, 140
    ineffectiveness, 167
    intrusiveness, 47
    manager, 29, 32, 33, 72, 88, 93, 109, 118, 120, 129, 164, 169
    orthodox, 76 162, 172
    pollution, 172
    presence-, 87
    stealth-, 103
Marketing, 73, 165
Marketing in the era of accountability, 164
Marketing Society, 86, 95
Marketing Week, 70
marketplace testing, 77
market research, 13, 23, 27, 42, 57, 64, 66, 68, 79, 105-110, 124, 171, 172
Market Research Society, 61, 65, 110, 165
Marks, Lawrence, 56, 57, 58, 65, 79, 138
Marks & Spencer, 94
Mars Confectionery, 42
Maslow, Abraham, 24
Match, 101, 121, 125
McCain, 77
McCann Erickson, 86
McDonald's, 50
McGannan, Ben, 146, 147, 149-150
meaning, 91, 92
Measuring Advertising Performance, 126, 165
media fragmentation, 83, 102, 118

media planning, 59
memory, 25, 27, 67, 133
mendacity, 31
Mentor, 122
messaging, 167
microbes, 163
Midland Bank, 48, 140
Millward Brown, 53, 54, 60, 62, 64, 65, 66, 68, 86
misattribution, 135, 139
mission, 147
Mitchell, Alan, 75
mobile-phone stores, 156-157
Momentum Experiential Marketing, 87
Monty Python's Flying Circus, 25
mood state, 122, 148
moral sentiments, 143
motivation, 136
Motor Show, 48
mountaintop view, 123
mousetrap, 13-14, 49, 71
movement, 136
multi-sensory, 90-92
Murdoch, Rupert, 104
music, 55, 91, 116, 139, 148
    ambient, 122
My First Toothbrush, 63

NW Ayer, 38, 57, 87
Nash, John, 141
nature versus nurture, 99
Needlers Sensations, 61
needs, 13, 24, 25, 100, 157
Nestlé, 80, 86
Net Promoter Score, 96
neuroeconomics, 143
neuromarketing, 111, 168, 170
neuron, 58, 110, 133, 135, 137, 139
neuropeptide, 141
neuroscience, 14, 15, 91, 111, 114, 128, 135, 169
    abuse of, 112
neurotransmitter, 136
Newcomen Group, 124-125, 150
Newcomen, Thomas, 124
New Labour, 63
next day recall, 27
Nietzsche, Friedrich, 51
Nobel Prize, 25, 58, 108, 141, 162
non-verbal, 152
noradrenalin, 136
Norfolk Broads, 162
Norwich Union, 48
nostrils, 141
nucleus accumbens, 136
Nudge, 167, 168
Numerator, 158

Oatso Simple, 33
obstetrics, 163
Ogilvy & Mather, 64
Oil of Olay, 47
olfaction, 91
Omnicom, 63, 64, 70
Opal Fruits, 47
Ophelia, 100
Organics, 93
organoleptic, 95, 100-101, 125
orgasm, 94, 138
Ormerod, Paul, 31
oxytocin, 141, 142

packaged goods, 78, 82, 100, 120
packaging, 53, 96, 111, 136
Packard, Vance, 20, 45, 53, 166, 168
Panasonic Viera, 93
Pantene, 33, 93
Paradox of Choice, 30
paranoia, 20, 168
parasitism, 173
paratelic, 154
Paris, 85
Parkinson's disease, 135, 137
partisanship, 132
Pasteur, Louis, 163
pathetic fallacy, 42
Pavlov's dogs, 135
payback, 108, 167
Pears Soap, 22, 172
peer review, 166
Pepsi, 113
Pepys, Samuel, 17
perception, 37, 67, 99, 126, 138, 136, 142, 143
Perot, Ross, 73
perseverance, 73
Persil, 39, 49
persuasion, 20, 23-25, 29, 83, 85, 128, 137, 172
Persuasion or Enhancement?, 61
Phoenix, AZ, 96
phrenology, 129
Piaget, Jean, 130-132
Pine, Joseph, 89, 90
Pinker, Steven, 99
Pink Floyd, 122
pitfalls, 71, 72-73
Plato, 51
plausibility, 24
play, 131
Pleistocene, 113
poll
    opinion, 95, 106, 126
    straw, 106
Pollak, Gerry, 82
Popper, Karl, 114, 145

positioning, 40, 60, 174
post-rationalisation, 29, 108, 125, 132, 135
Posturepedic, 34
Pot Noodle, 33
Potteries, 85
pounce, 157
Power of Dreams, The, 150, 152
prediction, 17, 106, 108, 129, 139-140
preference, 22, 49, 53, 107, 143
prejudice, 132
press release, 112
pre-testing, 78
price, 40, 47, 159
    premium, 44, 156, 166
    promotion, 71, 72-73
priming, 30, 53-57, 66, 78, 85, 97, 134, 168
Prisoners' Dilemma, 141
Procter & Gamble, 27, 93, 140
    advertising, 27, 35, 39, 42
    brands, 27
    complaint against, 33
    research and development, 27
product, 13, 22, 31, 33, 46, 47, 49, 50, 56, 81, 94
    coherence, 95-96
    equivalence, 15
    focus, 95
    me-too, 48
    optimisation, 120
    perception, 60, 79
    sampling, 64, 69, 84, 86, 121
    trial, 56-57, 59, 100, 111
    usage, 106
Project Brunel, 152-155, 156
Project Janus, 60-62, 86, 94
Project Mnemosyne, 65, 67, 68
projective techniques, 39
promise, 25, 27, 33, 34, 65, 159
proof, 25, 73, 108, 130, 146, 165
proposition, 24, 25, 39, 40, 42, 88
Prospect Theory, 29
Proust, Marcel, 91
pseudoscience, 112, 165
psycho-analysis, 107, 129, 145
psychobiology, 140, 160
psychology, 37, 66, 98, 128, 130, 162
    cognitive, 24
    evolutionary, 137
    Freudian, 39
    humanistic, 24
    social, 30
publicity, 13, 22, 27
public information, 167
purchase intention, 65, 106
purchasing, 25, 39, 43, 65-66, 81, 105, 110, 137

Quaker, 33

quale, 53, 79

Radcliffe, Paula, 33
rational, 24-26, 30, 66, 132, 143, 164, 166
Rational Choice Theory, 25
Rationalism, 128
Read, Stuart, 109
reality, 31, 67, 128, 130, 147
    gap, 50, 172
    objective, 134, 174
reasoning, 107-108, 132
reason why, 25, 33, 34, 142
recession, 19, 83, 155
reciprocity, 75, 143, 169, 174
Reckitt-Benckiser, 80
Reeves, Rosser, 24, 37, 41
Reflexive Holistic Model, 168
refractory period, 138
repertoire, 43
repression, 129
research
    abuse of, 106, 108-109
    moderator, 43, 107
    motivational, 107
    qualitative, 39, 99
    quantitative, 107
respiration, 123, 152
retail, 90, 96, 118, 119, 156, 160
reward, 135-137
rhinencephalon, 91
Ridgway, Steve, 156
Ries, Al, 40, 46
Ritchie, Alasdair, 63, 73, 75
Romanovs, 127
Rorschach tests, 130
Routledge, Tim, 119-120, 124, 125
Royal College of Physicians, 163
rule of thumb, 67, 98, 133
Rushdie, Salman, 41, 85
Ryanair, 46
Ryan, Meg, 94

Saatchi & Saatchi, 62
St Michael, 46
sales, 28, 32, 71
    long-term, 71, 78, 82-83
salesman, 152-155
sample, 61, 68, 105, 106
Sampson, Henry, 21, 22
Samsung, 157-158
satisficing, 30
Schanzkowska, Franziska, 127
schemata, 130-132, 134, 137, 163
Schindler, Robert, 55, 57, 58
Schmitt, Bernd, 90, 95, 97, 120
Schudson, Michael, 45

Schultz, Wolfram, 135
Schwartz, Barry, 30
science
    abuse of, 113, 170
    in business, 171
scientific innovation, 123
scientific method, 16, 17, 68, 112, 114, 174
Scully, Vin, 126
Sealy, 34
search, 42, 103, 156
Seat, 46
Semmelweiss, Ignaz, 163
sensory, 77, 90-91, 115-117, 122, 133
    perception, 53, 100, 131
    response, 115-116
    stimulus, 116, 132
serotonin, 136
service, 96, 146
shopping, 27, 43, 90, 110, 136, 142
showroom, 49, 152, 155
sickness absence, 149, 150
signals, 115
Silicon Valley, 102
Silverjet, 112
sincerity, 166
Singer, Charles, 123
Skol, 48
Slartibartfast, 41
slogan, 28-29, 140
smell, 91, 92, 111, 116, 122
Smith, Adam, 143
Smith, Phil, 73
Smith, Robert, 56, 57, 58
snake oil, 170
social bonding, 140
social issues, 167
social media, 102-103
society, 137, 141, 163, 167, 169
Society for Chemical Industry, 162
sociopathy, 170
somatic marker, 67, 105
Sorrell, Martin, 64-65, 107
Spectator, The, 145
speech, 108
spin, 14, 15, 31, 32, 96, 134, 174
split-transmission test, 79
staff, 19, 124, 146, 151, 157, 160, 163
Stalin, 113
standout, 13, 47, 139
statistics, 105-106
stimulation, 136
Stoke-on-Trent, 85
stress, 112, 136
Structure of Scientific Revolutions, The, 163
subconscious, 38, 39, 129
subjectivity, 110, 114, 116, 134

subliminal priming, 30
sublimation, 129
Sunlight Soap, 22
super-ego, 129
supermarkets, 27, 31, 43, 86, 103, 110, 118
    own label, 46, 71
surprise, 135, 137, 139
survey, 36, 39, 47, 126
Sutherland, John, 68
Sutherland, Rory, 89, 168
Sutherland, Stuart, 98
Swinyard, William, 56, 57, 58
symbiosis, 173
synapse, 18, 112
synaptic cleft, 136

TBWA, 63-64, 70, 73, 85, 86, 117
talking head, 82
Tango, 150
taste, 90, 91, 92, 116
Techniques of Persuasion, 20
technology, 125
Ted Bates, 24
telecoms, 103, 118, 157
telepathy, 130
telesales, 103
television, 31, 118
    terrestrial, 102, 118
telic, 154
Tesco, 48
testimonial, 82
'that's why', 31
therapy, 24
Times, The, 22
Titford, Roger, 50, 51, 54, 58, 59, 63, 82, 99, 100, 115
Toffler, Alvin, 89
Tomorrow's People, 125
tracking study, 105
trademark, 72, 75, 87
training, 124, 153, 157
travel, 96, 156
Trebor Bassett, 72
tripping points, 153
Trout, Jack, 40, 158
trust
    in author, 17
    as basis of relationship, 32, 143, 169
    bond of, 75, 134, 147
    and economic performance, 143, 174
    mutual, 14-15
    and oxytocin, 142
    as u.s.p., 166
truth, 31-32, 43, 115, 128, 133, 134, 147
Tversky, Amos, 29
two women in a kitchen, 28

Ultimatum Game, 29
unconscious, 13, 14-15, 30, 108, 132, 138, 141, 159
under-promise/over-deliver, 96, 137-138
Unilever, 21, 27, 28, 39, 77, 78, 93
uniqueness, 24, 29, 31
unique selling proposition, 24-28, 31-32, 35, 37, 39, 60, 103, 142, 164, 174
University of North London, 98
utilitarianism, 25
utilities, 93, 96
utility, 25, 54
utopia, 174

Velcro, 163
ventricles, 128
Vienna, 163
viewing facility, 121
Vimto, 33
violence, 122
Virgin Atlantic, 155-156
virtual office, 125
voice of God, 27, 82
Voyager 1, 116

WPP, 51, 64, 114, 119, 140
water coolers, 146
Water for Work, 146-150, 172
Water Wellpoint, 149
Watson, Claire, 86, 95
Watson, James, 58
Watson, John Broadus, 129-130
Web, 102, 118
Webster, John, 37
wellbeing, 172
Western Roll, 172
When ads alone fail to sell, 97
Which?, 30-31
Whitman, Walt, 123
Wikipedia, 98
Wired, 168
Wisdom Reflex, 61
Wittgenstein, Ludwig, 145
Woolworth, 28
World Advertising Research Center, 165

Young & Rubicam, 64

Zajonc, Robert, 66
Zald, David, 136
Zilli, Signor, 75

Copyright and Trademarks

The quotations on pages 53, 57, 58, 70, and 143 are reproduced with the kind permission of the author or primary author.

The following registered trademarks are used without the permission of the owner, and such usage is not authorised by, associated with or sponsored by the said trademark owner: '1001' (WD-40 Company Ltd.); 'Aqua Libra' (Orchid Drinks Ltd.); 'Bassett's Jelly Babies', 'Bassett's Liquorice Allsorts' and 'Bassett's Wine Gums' (Trebor Bassett Ltd.); 'Brobat' (Jeyes Group Ltd.); 'Clover' and 'Frijj' (Dairy Crest Ltd.); 'Coca Cola' and 'Coke' (The Coca Cola Company); 'Disney' (Disney Enterprises, Inc.); 'Egg' (Egg Banking plc); 'Ariel', 'Bold', 'Crest', 'Daz', 'Dreft', 'Fairy Liquid', 'Clairol Herbal Essences', 'Oil of Olay', 'Oil of Olaz', 'Pantene', 'Tide' (The Procter & Gamble Company); 'Ford Focus' (Ford Motor Company); 'Fox's Crinkle Crunch' (Northern Foods Grocery Group Ltd.); 'Guinness Storehouse' (Diageo Great Britain Ltd.); 'Haagen Dazs' (General Mills Marketing, Inc.); 'Heinz Salad Cream' (H.J. Heinz Company Ltd.); 'Lego' (LEGO Juris A/S); 'Levi's' (Levi Strauss & Co.); 'Lucozade' (Glaxo Group Ltd.); 'Magnum' (Unilever Plc); 'Midland Bank' (HSBC Bank plc); 'Needlers Sensations' (Ashbury Chocolates Ltd); 'Norwich Union' (Aviva plc); 'Oatso Simple' (Quaker Oats Ltd.); 'Opal Fruits' (Wrigley Candy UK); 'Organics', 'Pears's Original Transparent Soap', 'Persil', 'Sunlight' (Unilever Plc); 'Pepsi' (Pepsico, Inc); 'Posturepedic' (Sealy Technology LLC); 'Pot Noodle' (Knorr-Nährmittel Aktiengesellschaft); 'St Michael' (Marks and Spencer Plc); 'Skol' (Carlsberg Breweries A/S); 'Tango', 'You know when you've been Tango'd' (Britvic Soft Drinks Limited); 'Velcro' (Velcro Industries B.V.); 'Viera' (Panasonic Corporation); 'Vimto' (Nichols plc); 'Virgin Atlantic' (Virgin Enterprises Ltd.); 'Wellpoint' (Wellpoint Group Ltd.); 'Wisdom' (Wisdom Toothbrushes Ltd.); 'Woolworth' (Littlewoods Ltd.)

Acknowledgements

Like acceptance speeches, book acknowledgements run the twin risks of going on for far too long and of leaving out someone important. I will sidestep both by condensing the addressees of this note into five cherished groups:

1. The academics, scientists and thinkers who lit the way for this new mode of thinking; you all get a mention somewhere within these covers.

2. The clients of Fast Marketing and the Newcomen Group. It took courage to attempt something different from the norm, and you deserve credit.

3. The employees and business associates of those two organisations who've treated their involvement as more than a job. You know who you are.

4. The small band of trusted advisors who told me frankly and, dare I say it, expertly how I could turn my initial effort into the book you see before you.

5. Last but not least, my family, who never stinted in their support and now know the real reason why I was shut away in my garret for those many hours.

To all of you, my sincere and humble thanks.

John Bunyard
London, August 2010.

About the Author

After studying Modern Languages at Oxford, John Bunyard became one of the 'hidden persuaders' in the advertising industry. Despite persisting for 15 years, he never really got it. Advertising's essentially deceitful approach seemed to him to be at odds with human nature: even if adept liars, we dislike being lied to. In 1992, he proposed an alternative model based on the principle of telling the absolute truth and, critically, getting people to verify it for themselves. The tool he used to do this on a large scale, called 'Fast marketing', was hugely successful and yielded reams of comparative evidence. This in turn brought him into contact with plenty of neuroscientific literature and expertise that bears out the importance of demonstrable honesty. In 2005 he co-founded the Newcomen Group of scientists and business professionals that aims to explore such ideas and propagate their use in business and public life. He lives in Kent, England, with his wife and two children.